I0100914

WHY RELIGIOUS FREEDOM MATTERS

WHY RELIGIOUS FREEDOM MATTERS

Human Rights and Human Flourishing

ALLEN D. HERTZKE

University of Notre Dame Press
Notre Dame, Indiana

Notre Dame, Indiana 46556
undpress.nd.edu

Published in the United States of America

Library of Congress Control Number: 2025948067

ISBN: 978-0-268-21106-6 (Hardback)
ISBN: 978-0-268-21109-7 (WebPDF)
ISBN: 978-0-268-21108-0 (Epub3)

GPSR Compliance Inquiries:
Lightning Source France, 1 Av. Johannes Gutenberg, 78310 Maurepas, France
compliance@lightningsource.fr | Phone: +33 1 30 49 23 42

To Barbara, ever and always . . .

CONTENTS

FIGURES

ACKNOWLEDGEMENTS

It is humbling to realize how much this book reflects the contributions of so many individuals and institutions. I am blessed.

My immersion in global networks of advocacy and scholarship on religious freedom began with research for my book, *Freeing God's Children: The Unlikely Alliance for Global Human Rights* (2004). A consultancy for the Pew Charitable Trusts in 2008 expanded that work to write a report on international religious freedom, which prompted an even larger project with the John Templeton Foundation. I am very grateful to the Templeton Foundation and the late Jack Templeton for tasking me with organizing a major conference in Istanbul in April of 2009, which brought together some of the leading scholars of international law and policy on religious rights. Out of that conference, I produced an edited volume, *The Future of Religious Freedom: Global Challenges* (New York: Oxford University Press, 2013), and a guidebook for potential grantmaking on religious freedom. I am pleased to say that I have drawn upon subsequent Templeton-funded research initiatives in this book. I am also grateful to Luis Lugo, former director of the Pew Forum on Religion and Public Life, for providing me with an institutional home in Washington, DC, and sponsoring my Pew research project on national religious lobbying and advocacy.

Due to my work in producing reports for the Templeton Foundation, I was invited to present a paper on the status of international religious freedom at the Vatican in the spring of 2011. I am deeply indebted to Mary Ann Glendon, then president of the Pontifical Academy of Social Sciences, who extended that invitation, which connected me to a cadre of international authorities. That presentation and paper provided the basic framework of my thinking on the crisis of religious persecution in the world today and why it mattered. Quite by surprise, a year later, I was appointed by Pope Benedict XVI to a ten-year term on the Pontifical Academy, which deepened my international connections and enabled me to present other research on religious agency, which found its way into this book. So many fruitful crosscurrents, so much luck, or better, grace.

The real impetus for this book, however, involved my participation in the initiatives of the Religious Freedom Research Project (RFRP) at Georgetown University's Berkley Center for Religion, Peace & World Affairs, from 2011 until 2016. During that time, I co-directed the Christianity and Freedom Project, under the auspices of the RFRP—with my colleague and friend, Timothy Shah—which included a gathering in Rome of scholars and compelling voices for the persecuted. Some of the scholarship in the two edited volumes with Cambridge University Press, resulting from that project, is integrated into this work.

More directly, I was a participant with a dozen leading scholars—from political science, sociology, economics, and history—to document empirically the contributions of religious freedom to democracy, human rights, economic growth, uplift for the poor, empowerment of women, and peace. As the reader will note, the fruits of that scholarship provide the structure for this book and a considerable amount of its documentation. Indeed, as research papers came into the RFRP, I began the process of synthesizing the pathbreaking contributions to what I discerned as a new understanding of human dynamics, which I introduce in Chapter 1. I am therefore deeply grateful to Thomas Farr, director of the RFRP from 2011 until 2018, whose leadership in the field continued as president of the independent Religious Freedom Institute (RFI) until his retirement in 2023. The RFI sponsored a pivotal research project on institutional religious freedom that I have incorporated into this volume.

I especially treasure my dear friends and colleagues in the RFRP who have been an enormous source of encouragement to me in this labor and whose scholarship is featured herein. Tim Shah and I go back over two decades, in a variety of settings, and it was a singular grace to collaborate with him on the Christianity and Freedom project, an experience I will always treasure. Rebecca Shah, Tim's wife and global collaborator, is an inspiring voice for women's empowerment. Her stunning research on religious agency and uplift of the poor features prominently in Chapter 4. I learned a lot from her. Daniel Philpott at Notre Dame is not only one of the most important authorities on global religion and politics but also a special friend and inspiration. We first connected in 2000 to co-author a piece on global religious freedom, titled "Defending the Faiths." So we have been brothers-in-arms on religious liberty for over 25 years. I consider myself blessed to have Brother Dan in my life.

A more recent scholar and friend, Nilay Saiya of Nanyang Technological University in Singapore, is the leading authority on the sources of religious violence in the world today and a landmark scholar on religion-state religions. We have shared drafts of each other's work and enjoyed conversations across many miles on Zoom. As the reader will note, he features heavily in Chapter 5, but his stunning research on the "paradox of privilege" informs the conclusion.

I am also pleased to acknowledge the pivotal support of my academic home, the University of Oklahoma's Political Science Department, along with the many supportive colleagues I have known over the years. The department backed this research and provided a source of wonderful undergraduate research assistants, whose assiduous investigations are represented throughout this volume. Over the years, those former students included Derek Bixler, Alissa Bretz, Philip Bretz, Mark Brockway, Austin Coffey, Alex Davis, Joey DeAngelis, Grayson Kuehl, Sarah Miles, Jackson Monroe, and Daniella Royer. Now an alumnus, Alissa Bretz helped with final manuscript revisions. I am also indebted to my former doctoral student, Lihui Zhang, who wrote her dissertation on the correlates of international religious freedom and provided excellent advice to me in grasping the more recondite aspects of quantitative analyses of global data on religion.

I am especially indebted to the late David Boren, president of the University of Oklahoma (OU) from 1994 to 2018. He took the initiative to fund my position as Faculty Fellow in Religious Freedom for OU's Institute for the American Constitutional Heritage. The Institute's former director, Professor Kyle Harper, in turn, provided leadership and collaboration in sponsoring a major conference on domestic religious freedom scholarship and in supporting research for this book. Kyle is a model scholar, teacher, and colleague, and he has been a great source of encouragement.

A special shout-out goes to Julie Reyes, a former undergraduate student of mine who went on to receive her doctorate in anthropology and enjoyed a distinguished academic career of teaching and research in that field. Through a fortuitous circumstance, we reconnected when she retired in Norman, at precisely the time I was in the last push to complete this book. More than a research assistant, Julie became a colleague and advisor, reading drafts and providing incisive feedback. Our brainstorming sessions sparked creative thinking and inspired me to push through when fatigue and age began to take their toll. She also provided key anthropological insights as I strove to incorporate ethnographic research on indigenous ways of life. I am indebted to you, Julie.

Also pivotal in aiding the push to complete the manuscript was a five-day retreat at St. Gregory's Abbey in Shawnee, Oklahoma. The monks extended their storied Benedictine hospitality, with great food and conversation, worshipful rhythms, and the perfect room to write. To the brothers of St. Gregory's, God bless you all!

There is one scholar, however, who deserves singular credit for helping make this project possible. He is my friend and colleague, Anthony Gill of the Political Science Department at the University of Washington. Tony and I began as collaborators. During our time on the RFRP at Georgetown, Tony and I began conversations about the idea of a grand synthesis of the cutting-edge research taking place on the value of religious freedom to the kind of world we seek. That conversation turned into plans for coauthoring this book together. That plan took shape as we met on each other's campus for extended sessions of whiteboard brainstorming and chapter outlining. We then began the process of divvying and drafting chapters, but before we were very deep in the project, Tony was faced with new professional responsibilities and reluctantly had to step back. Despite that, his input in the chapter on economics was pivotal, as the extended citations show. But more than this contribution, his spirit lives in the manuscript. I will always treasure our times together, in part because of Tony's wry sense of humor and down-home style. He can always make me laugh and think. Thank you, Tony! May our paths cross again.

I am, of course, profoundly grateful to the University of Notre Dame Press, its director, Stephen Wrinn, and acquisitions editor Rachel Kindler, for embracing this project. I was particularly impressed that Rachel moved with such alacrity in recruiting three outstanding readers—Daniel Philpott, Nilay Saiya, and Knox Thames—who were assiduous and thorough in their reviews of the original manuscript. Their astute recommendations made this a much stronger and more cogent book, for which I am enormously indebted. I am also deeply grateful for the entire professional staff at Notre Dame Press, especially for the superb work of Managing Editor Matthew Dowd, Wendy McMillen and the design and production team, and Steffi Marchman and the marketing team. I must also give a shout-out to freelancers Dabian Witherspoon, who meticulously copyedited the manuscript, and Alexa Selph, who produced the fine index for the book.

Most importantly, I humbly acknowledge all who inspired this project—the courageous champions of religious freedom of many lands who risked persecution, imprisonment, torture, and exile to defend the right to faith. To these heroes of conscience across the globe, I salute you.

Something about this deep immersion in the great quest for human flourishing led me to grasp the singular blessings of my family, who inspire and sustain me. I am grateful for my late parents, Luverne and Annie Hertzke, who live on through the love and spiritual foundation they instilled in me. I am also thankful for the supportive embrace of my far-flung extended family. You all know who you are. Finally, I am profoundly blessed by my immediate family—my special daughter, Sarah, who keeps me grounded, humble, and hip to social media; my firstborn, Patrick, and his lovely wife, Rachael; and my three grandsons: Liam, Finn, and Jack. I pray that the world you all inherit will move closer to the vision embodied in this book.

Of course, this book would not have happened without the love, collaboration, and discernment of my beloved spouse, Barbara Leonhard Norton. It has been the singular grace of my life that I married a person who always understood my calling better than I did and who often had more confidence in my capacity than I did. Barbara's support, patience, and sometimes astringent critiques consistently made this book better. I cannot imagine being the scholar or person I have become without our mystical partnership.

Deo gratias

CHAPTER ONE

RELIGIOUS FREEDOM MATTERS

Imagine a social force, a potent "X Factor," that underpins democracy, bolsters civil liberties, builds citizen loyalty, undermines religious fanaticism, reduces societal violence, improves women's status, fosters economic development, spurs uplift for the poor, and nurtures international peace.

Remarkable as it seems, new global research powerfully links *religious freedom* to all these social outcomes. Not by itself, of course. But compelling evidence points to religious freedom—rightly understood and generously protected—as pivotal to the kind of world we want to inhabit: *An X factor for flourishing societies.*

Such a claim may seem startling to some modern ears, especially given the religious fanaticism and sectarian strife afflicting the globe today. Why promote such a divisive impulse as religion? Moreover, in our fraught and polarized times, religious liberty itself has gotten a bad name in some progressive circles, depicted as a rightwing cause, an excuse for bigotry and discrimination, or a weapon in the culture war.[1] We also see distorted views about religious freedom on the right—from religious nationalists who falsely believe that imposing a dominant religious identity on diverse societies will preserve their spiritual heritage.[2]

Equally troubling, a chorus of intellectual critics attacks the very *idea* of religious freedom as a definable, coherent set of rights. Or they see it as a Western construct imposed on indigenous societies, a cover for imperialism, or a pretext for aggressive Christian proselytizing. This critique reflects some legitimate concerns about how the *promotion* of international religious freedom by nations can become enmeshed in power politics. But it also evokes a general post-modern skepticism about religious freedom as a universal ideal.[3] I address these criticisms more fully in the concluding chapter.

For those of us engaged in scholarship and advocacy on global religious freedom, such perceptions are anguishing. They often reflect a misunderstanding of what genuine religious freedom is and why it matters profoundly for the future most of us seek. Religious freedom especially matters *now*, given five interrelated global trends.

(1) RELIGIOUS FREEDOM MATTERS NOW BECAUSE RELIGION MATTERS AND INCREASINGLY SO

The global resurgence of religion, both demographically and in public impact, came as the great surprise of our age.[4] Contrary to the predictions of the West's leading minds from the nineteenth century onward, secularization peaked in 1970. Then, it began to retreat in most parts of the globe as religious communities began to push back at their marginalization by states in what Gilles Kepel termed *The Revenge of God*.[5] The very character of modernity, moreover, seems to be propelling the global resurgence of religion, as people seek anchors of faith amidst disorientating change.[6] As key beneficiaries of this trend, the great missionary faiths of Christianity and Islam are projected to increase their share of the world population to over 60 percent by 2050.[7] Although scholars continue to document the decline of religious practice in the West, or speak of Western secularization,[8] that appears to be the exception to general patterns around the globe.

To be sure, certain forces in the modern world—global capitalism, consumerism, technology, mass communication, and the digital revolution—seem to operate independently of transcendent visions. But these disruptive forces can, in turn, spark religious movements, whether in the form of violent religious tribalism or earnest efforts to build communitarian enclaves of vibrant faith.[9]

Not only have we seen a demographic expansion of religious affiliation, but religious movements now transcend national borders and marshal formidable resources to challenge states. This is, for good or ill, *God's*

Century.[10] Because religion influences public life and politics, many states attempt to repress or co-opt religious communities, producing the very thing they fear: religious strife and violence.

Today, nearly 85 percent of the world's population professes religious affiliation or belief.[11] Global demographic growth rates, moreover, indicate that the world's population will become even more religious in the future, dwarfing the nonreligious. This trend owes to the fact that fertility rates are extremely low for nonreligious or unaffiliated populations, while the religiously devout (of diverse religious traditions) tend to have larger families and often invite others into their ranks.[12] In a nutshell, religious couples have more babies than secular couples.

Drawing upon the best demographic sources available, Grim and Connor chart the changing religious and nonreligious shares of the global population. In 1970, the unaffiliated (or nonreligious)[13] share of the world's population stood at nearly a fifth (19 percent). This reflected, in large part, the height of communist (and atheist) power in the Soviet Union, Eastern Europe, China, North Korea, and Southeast Asia. In many cases, religious movements have filled the void left by the collapse of communism. So, despite the steep decline of religious affiliation in Western Europe since 1970, the unaffiliated share of global population had shrunk to 16 percent by 2010 and is projected to decline further, to 13 percent, by 2050.[14] Moreover, this latter figure hinges on very conservative estimates of the growth rates of religious affiliation in China, especially for Christianity. If projections by the leading expert on religion in China bear out, then the global percentage of the nonreligious will be even lower than 13 percent.[15]

Consequently, for an increasing majority of the global population, religion will powerfully anchor forms of identity, meaning, community, and purpose in the future. This is particularly fateful for poor women, the doubly marginalized. Given that women in developing societies often disproportionately belong to religious communities and adhere to faith commitments,[16] guaranteeing or expanding their religious freedom, as we will see in chapter 4, will be pivotal to their broader uplift.

Religion is here to stay. As Timothy Shah documents, research from anthropology to cognitive science suggests "that the capacity for religious belief is natural; that belief appears early and easily in the lives of individuals; that it appeared full-blown at the dawn of human civilization;

and that the suppression of religious belief, expression, and practice runs against the grain of human nature and experience."[17] Repression of what people experience as fundamental to their human dignity fuels division, destabilizes societies, spawns violence, and undermines economic uplift.

(2) RELIGIOUS FREEDOM MATTERS BECAUSE RELIGIOUS DIVERSITY IS EXPANDING

Sociologists of religion find that, at the deepest level, the natural condition of religion is pluralistic.[18] While societies and states once expected (and some still strive to impose) religious uniformity, that model is increasingly untenable in the global age. Sociologist Peter Berger, once a leading theorist of the secularization thesis, now says he was wrong in thinking that modernization and globalization would bring secularization; rather, they bring plurality. People of widely diverse religious beliefs and practices find themselves cheek by jowl with religious others. With travel, migrations, and now massive refugee flows, people encounter a dizzying religious pluralism, where "everyone is everywhere," as Berger puts it.[19] Religious freedom recognizes the natural human impulse to produce diverse religious expressions. The denial or repression of this natural diversity produces persecution, social hostility, violence, and instability. People in a diverse and fervently religious world must find a way of navigating their shared lives, and the guarantee of religious freedom and equality serves that purpose powerfully.

(3) RELIGIOUS FREEDOM MATTERS BECAUSE IT IS ENSHRINED AS A FUNDAMENTAL RIGHT IN INTERNATIONAL LAW

Article 18 of the *Universal Declaration of Human Rights*, adopted by the United Nations in 1948, reads as follows:

> Everyone has the right to freedom of thought, conscience, and religion. This right includes freedom to change his religion or belief, and freedom, either alone or in community with others and in

public or private, to manifest his religion or belief in teaching, practice, worship, and observance.[20]

Notice the emphasis on active agency in the definition, the capacity to "*manifest*" one's religion "in teaching, practice, worship, and observance." Also notice the relational aspect, that people must be free "in community with others" to manifest their faith or beliefs. The "Preface" of the *Universal Declaration* anchors all rights in the "inherent dignity" and "worth of the human person" and in the "equal and inalienable rights of all members of the human family" who are "endowed with reason and conscience." *Inherent Dignity, equal worth, reason, conscience, and community*—these traits of common humanity provide clues to why religious freedom is such a potent human right.

Similar language is found in covenants that implement the Declaration as binding on signatories. These include the *International Covenant on Civil and Political Rights,* the *Declaration on the Elimination of All Forms of Intolerance and Discrimination Based on Religion or Belief,* and the *European Convention for the Protection of Human Rights and Fundamental Freedoms.*[21]

This basis for religious freedom in international law, while widely violated, provides a standard by which to measure progress and as an inspiration for advocacy.

(4) RELIGIOUS FREEDOM MATTERS AS A NEAR-UNIVERSAL ASPIRATION

Contrary to the claim that religious freedom is a Western construct, the aspiration is found throughout ancient civilizations. Over two and a half millennia ago, as recorded in both Hebrew scriptures and Persian documentation, Cyrus the Great established a broad regime of religious tolerance, which included restoring freedom for Jewish exiles to return to their homeland. In ancient India, the Buddhist emperor Ashoka issued decrees that embody religious liberty, while the later Mughal emperor Akbar promoted broad respect for diverse religious communities.[22] From Sophocles' *Antigone* to the Maccabean revolt, the abuse of transcendent callings is grasped as a violation of human dignity and deeply disruptive to the social order. In diverse sacred texts, we learn that homage to the divine cannot be coerced, that, according to the Koran, "There is no compulsion in religion."[23]

In the contemporary world, religious freedom matters to people across the globe. In a Pew Global Attitudes Survey, over 90 percent of respondents in every region on earth indicated that it was important to them to live in a country where they can practice religion freely (only 2 percent saying it was not important at all).[24]

At the most basic level, all people want to be treated with respect and consideration. Variations of the golden rule—to treat others as we wish to be treated—are found in virtually every major religion and many philosophical traditions (such as Confucianism). This trait of common humanity—potentially recognizable by people of all faiths or no faith—can provide a justification for religious liberty understood as the freedom to live in accord with one's conscience or belief.[25]

(5) RELIGIOUS FREEDOM MATTERS BECAUSE IT IS MASSIVELY DENIED

In the early decades of the twenty-first century, we see a worldwide crisis of religious repression and persecution. Annual global measures by the Pew Research Center consistently find that more than eight out of ten of the world's people live amidst high restrictions on their religious practice, either by repressive government actions or hostile social agents.[26] Companion global data from the Religion and State Project documents an astonishing array of repressive government practices against religion, especially targeting religious and ethnic minorities who are uniquely vulnerable to marginalization.[27]

Both sources document a rise in restrictions on religion over the past couple of decades. Figure 1.1 depicts the dramatic increase in the number of countries where religious groups faced harassment by governments or restrictions on worship. When mob pressure is added to government actions, religious groups endured harassment in even more countries, as figure 1.2 illustrates. Figure 1.2 also shows that every religious group, because it is a minority somewhere, faces harassment in a growing number of places.[28] Separate analysis by Brian Grim shows that the growth of restrictions on religion outpaced population growth by a ratio of two to one: The global

Since 2007, the number of countries where governments have harassed religious groups or interfered in worship has increased

Number of countries and territories where there was __ in 2022

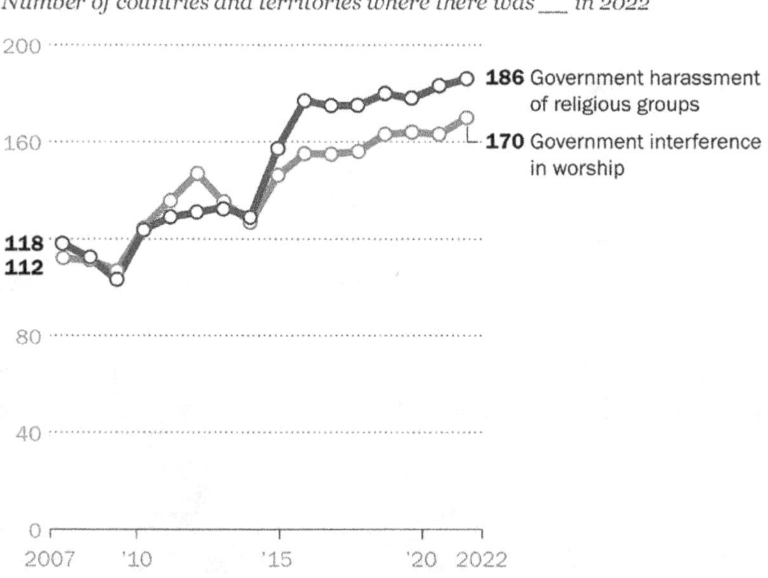

Note: The number of countries and territories studied increased in 2011, from 197 to 198, with the addition of South Sudan.
Source: Pew Research Center analysis of external data. Refer to the Methodology for details.
"Government Restrictions on Religion Stayed at Peak Levels Globally in 2022"

FIGURE 1.1. Increases in Government Restrictions of Religion Over the Past Fifteen Years, from the Pew Research Center.

population grew by 1 billion between 2007 and 2017, but the population living with high restrictions on religion grew by 2 billion.[29]

Diverse measures reinforce this bleak portrait. A systematic summary by the Association of Religion Data Archives found that "86 percent of the nations had at least one law restricting religious freedoms and 38 percent had four or more such laws."[30] Another summary of global data found that 86 percent of countries had documented cases of people

Religious groups were harassed by governments or social groups in 192 countries and territories in 2022

Number of countries and territories where religious groups were harassed, by year

	2007	'13	'14	'15	'16	'17	'18	'19	'20	'21	'22
Christians	107	102	108	128	144	143	145	153	155	160	166
Muslims	96	99	100	125	142	140	139	147	145	141	148
Jews	51	77	81	74	87	87	88	89	94	91	90
Other religions	33	38	43	50	57	50	56	68	62	64	68
Folk religions**	24	34	21	32	41	38	37	32	33	40	49
Hindus	21	9	14	18	23	23	19	21	21	24	26
Buddhists	10	12	10	7	17	19	24	25	21	28	25
Religiously unaffiliated	–	5	4	14	14	23	18	22	27	27	32
Any of above	**152**	**164**	**160**	**169**	**187**	**187**	**185**	**190**	**189**	**190**	**192**

* Includes Sikhs, members of ancient faiths such as Zoroastrianism, members of newer faiths such as Baha'i, and other religious groups.
** Includes, for example, followers of African traditional religions, Chinese folk religions, Native American religions and Australian Aboriginal religions.
Note: This measure looks at the number of countries in which groups were harassed, either by the government or by individuals/social groups. It does not assess the severity of the harassment. Numbers do not add to totals shown because multiple religious groups can be harassed in a country.
Source: Pew Research Center analysis of external data. Refer to the Methodology for details.
"Government Restrictions on Religion Stayed at Peak Levels Globally in 2022"

FIGURE 1.2. Increases in Harassment of Religious Groups over the Past Fifteen Years, from the Pew Research Center.

being physically abused or displaced from their homes because of "*religious persecution*."[31]

In other words, religious believers in many places suffer discrimination, intimidation, arrest, torture, and martyrdom. Religious communities face burdensome restrictions on their ability to build houses of worship or schools, see their property shuttered by authorities or destroyed by mob violence, and find themselves stigmatized in state media or by dominant societal groups. Religious freedom, indeed, is a "beleaguered human right,"[32] violated by a variety of nations, political systems, and societies.[33]

Rising restrictions on religious practices coincide with the general decline of freedom in the world. As documented by Freedom House, after three decades of solid progress, democratic freedom in the world reached a high point in 1998. It then stagnated and ominously began a long decline. By 2024, freedom in the world had declined for the nineteenth consecutive year.[34] As I will show, the rising repression of religion during that same period was a driver of this global decline of freedom, not just associated with it.

Today, religious liberty echoes with the cries of oppressed religious peoples around the world—of besieged Iranian Baha'is, Tibetan Buddhists, Middle Eastern Sufis and Ahmadis, Chinese Falun Gong practitioners, Chaldean Christians, North Korean believers, Shia Muslims in Saudi Arabia, and Sunni Muslims in Iran. Sometimes persecution rises to genocidal levels, as with Muslim Uyghurs in China, Muslim Rohingya in Burma, and Yazidis in the Nineveh Plains during the ISIS assault. Their simple plea: free to be.

The global votaries of religious freedom include human rights champions, pro-democracy activists, religious reformers, and political dissidents.

WHAT IS RELIGION?

In one sense, defining religion can be relatively straightforward, if we employ a common-sense understanding of it. Religion concerns beliefs and practices that connect humans to what they experience as a powerful spiritual reality beyond their physical existence. That supernatural power can be grasped as transcending the physical world, infused with it, or both. As a central aspect of human culture, religion encompasses fundamental spiritual understandings of the meaning and purpose of life, answers to ultimate questions, and sources of moral obligation.[35] Rooted in the social dimension of human life, religion commonly entails communal practices that manifest and reinforce the faith.

Recent scholarship deepens and elaborates on this definition by exploring the *dimensions* of religion that explain its enduring salience, justify its expression as a human right, and show why denial of its free exercise is so disruptive to human flourishing.

The first dimension concerns the possible universality of religion. Are humans naturally religious? "Do they possess a set of common characteristics transcending time, place, and culture that incline them towards religion?" The answer, "according to a growing body of research in the cognitive and evolutionary sciences of religion, appears to be yes."[36] This is the conclusion of a major initiative by Timothy Shah and Jack Friedman to bring together scholars from diverse fields to explore both the innateness of religion and the moral imperative of religious freedom. While not everyone is religious, obviously, religion springs naturally from human experience. Indeed, "there are certain emerging early cognitive biases that make it natural to believe in Gods and spirits, in an afterlife, and the divine creation of the universe."[37] If religion is thus natural, its denial violates a central aspect of human life.

Another dimension of religion is the quality of religious obligations and how people organize their lives around them. Timothy Shah's definition of religion captures this centrality of religious belief to human organization:

> Religion is the effort of individuals and communities to understand, to express, and to seek harmony with a transcendent reality of such importance that they feel compelled to organize their lives around their understanding of it, to be guided by it in their moral conduct, and to communicate their devotion to others.[38]

Here, again, we see why people attach such importance to this capacity.

Finally, a set of dimensions addresses the question of whether religion is a basic human good. In an extended essay justifying religious freedom as a human right, Daniel Philpott offers a definition of religion that emphasizes the quest of humans to align their lives with the divine, with a power beyond human creation. Not merely a set of ideas, religion entails purposive acts aimed at harmony or "right relation" with what Philpott calls a superhuman power. Philpott acknowledges that the term "superhuman" conjures images of superheroes in comics and movies, but he finds that it best captures the encompassing range of religious experiences and obligations. In theistic traditions, practitioners seek a right relation with a transcendent god or gods. In indigenous ways of life, people seek harmony with spirits inherent in the natural world that define the meaning of existence. In folk religions, people might venerate ancestors who exist in a "realm beyond the world where they take on abilities beyond those of humans in this world."[39] In each case, humans strive for right relation, or harmony, with a superhuman power as they experience it. This makes religious commitment central to human identity and dignity, an intrinsic good of exceeding value, and a dimension of human flourishing sought for its own sake.[40]

Philpott's elegant essay elaborates on the wide variety of religious practices, worship being the most central, by which humans seek right relation with the divine. This harmony is experienced as a good in itself, but religious practices aimed at that harmony also serve other human ends: "community, friendship, peace, happiness, comfort in suffering."[41] A central aspect of religious practices entails interiority, engaging "the will, the mind, and the heart," which is why people experience restrictions as such a violation of their human dignity.[42]

In sum, Philpott's definition of religion as human acts aimed at right relation with a superhuman power is both capacious enough to encompass the religious landscape but clearly bounded to omit other forms of human commitment, such as nationalism. Religion entails capacities, aims, and goods beyond prosaic existence, and thus is precious. For a fuller elaboration of the nature of spiritual aims and practices that define religion, see this endnote.[43]

Some definitions of religion expand their ambit to encompass an "ultimate concern" that need not be transcendent or spiritual.[44] But as Philpott implies, that minimizes the unique force of spiritual devotions in human life and undercuts the rationale for recognizing religious freedom as a distinct human right.

For reasons explained in the next section, the ambit of "religious freedom" can reach a bit further.

WHAT IS RELIGIOUS FREEDOM?

International law provides the baseline definition of religious freedom. But much is implied in that definition that requires elaboration.

As noted, *The Universal Declaration on Human Rights* and implementing covenants recognize every person's "right to freedom of thought, conscience, and religion." This means, to each person, freedom *from coercion* in matters of transcendent purpose, identity, and obligation. Roger Williams, the seventeenth-century colonial leader of Rhode Island, called it "soul freedom." James Madison depicted it as the freedom to fulfill transcendent duties that are "precedent, both in order of time and degree of magnitude, to the claims of civil society." Cardinal Newman captured it with the epigram, "conscience has rights because it has duties."[45] Or as a Sikh advocate put it to me, religious liberty is *the right to be who you are*.[46] That implies a reciprocal obligation to accord that right to others, which makes individual religious freedom a potent human aspiration, whose denial reverberates in destructive ways.

Equally important, the right of conscience encompasses the seeker, the skeptic, the critic, and the reformer. The state has no business defining what is orthodox in faith or preventing nonconformity. While religious freedom protects the autonomy of religious institutions to define their faith and set criteria for their members or leaders, it also ensures the right of people to exit religious communities.[47] In violation of this principle, numerous states enforce apostasy and anti-conversion laws that prevent exit and thus empower religious leaders to suppress criticism, prevent competition, or maintain practices that subjugate women. Elastic anti-blasphemy laws, similarly, penalize religious dissent or prevent religious minorities from teaching their own truths.[48] As most faith traditions recognize, however, coerced faith is no faith at all. Or as Roger Williams colorfully proclaimed, "Forced worship stinks in God's nostrils![49]

Religious freedom also allows people to mix and match religious beliefs and practices, which is more common than expected. Religious freedom even defends the atheist. As stipulated in international law, genuine religious freedom protects freedom of religion "*or belief*," and thus includes the nonbeliever in its ambit. This may seem paradoxical, but the history of religion is filled with stories (or testaments) of former atheists making the journey to devout faith. The overt atheist, in a way, takes the idea of religion seriously enough to oppose or interrogate it; sometimes that interrogation leads to faith.

Perceptive readers will notice two distinct dimensions of religious freedom: (1) the individual's right to affirm and act on religious beliefs or mandates of conscience; and (2) the right of communal religious practice, which protects the autonomy of religious institutions to operate in civil society. Religion, for many, is rooted in community and bolstered by the shared experiences and religious instruction of faith institutions. This second dimension of institutional religious freedom is strongly linked to a host of other freedoms: the freedom of association; the right to own property and build houses of worship, schools, or charities; the freedom of the press; and the right to issue publications and communicate messages.

Though obviously related, these two categories are often treated differently by governments and comprehended differentially by international advocates. Indeed, scholar Lihui Zhang documents how the two dimensions are analytically distinct, with institutions more subject to state regulation but also more visible on the international stage, more capable of accessing international allies.[50] Recent scholarship, moreover, highlights why the protection of religious institutions matters deeply to the cause of individual religious expression.[51]

Equality is also central to religious freedom, a dimension too often overlooked. This is not surprising, since the language in Article 18 emphasizes rights and liberties, while equality is not explicitly mentioned. Moreover, international covenants and discourse heavily focus on "freedom of religion or belief" (shortened by the awkward acronym, FoRB).

The Preface to the *Universal Declaration*, however, proclaims the "*equal* and inalienable rights of all members of the human family." Protecting equal rights must entail equality under law, a principle widely violated by nations that privilege majority faiths. Many governments, in fact, funnel money to established or favored religions or grant them preferential access to public institutions such as schools, hospitals, prisons, and the military. As pluralism grows in societies around the world, religious majorities often seek to reclaim their cultural hegemony by gaining more state privileges under the guise of fighting for their "religious rights." We see this with Sunni Muslim theocrats in Saudi Arabia, Shia theocrats in Iran, Hindu nationalists in India, Christian nationalists in the West, Buddhist chauvinists in Burma, and Orthodox supremacists in Russia. This impulse leads to widespread discrimination against religious minorities and greater strife in societies.

When all religions enjoy equal freedom on a level playing field, on the other hand, we see interfaith amity instead of religious conflict. Paradoxically, state favoritism weakens the very religious communities granted such favors, sapping their zeal and industry, just as Adam Smith predicted over two centuries ago.[52] But state favoritism also makes majorities more militant and even violent, warping their spiritual core. I elaborate on these findings in chapters 5 and 6.

Finally, to be fully encompassing, religious freedom must protect indigenous and tribal peoples, whose spiritual lives are woven into the ancestral lands they inhabit. As discussed in chapter 6, international development agencies, religious advocacy groups, and nations must do a better job of incorporating and protecting this dimension of religious freedom.

Of course, religious liberty, like any right, is not absolute. The law can sanction actions animated by religion that harm others or operate by fraud, and it can require transparency in the finances of religious organizations. Societies can also enact reasonable regulations for the public good. For example, churches in the United States enjoy tax-exempt status; however, like other non-profits, they are barred by law from engaging in partisan political activity, such as endorsing candidates, though their leaders can speak out on political issues. While debated and recently tested, this provision is viewed by most religious citizens as reasonable, the stuff of normal politics.[53] Nonetheless, governments around the world often employ onerous registration requirements to prevent small faiths from functioning in society—from buying property, building houses of worship, and accessing media outlets.[54] Burdensome zoning or building regulations can also make it difficult for religious communities to expand houses of worship or even repair them.[55] These regulations mostly target religious minorities, testifying to the repressive motives behind them.

WHAT THIS BOOK IS AND IS NOT

This is not a policy book, except insofar as its cogent findings could guide nations and policy makers. Nor does it make specific recommendations about the *best ways* to promote international religious freedom. Other fine books and articles do just that.[56] The most recent and comprehensive is by Knox Thames, a veteran of two decades of advocacy within American government across multiple presidential administrations. That book, *Ending Persecution: Charting the Path to Global Religious Freedom*, documents the crisis of religious persecution afflicting the world today and offers informed strategies to address it. As Thames rightly observes, "The defining question of the twenty-first century will be whether we can defeat the age-old scourge of religious persecution."[57] High-level religious freedom commissions and institutes also offer informed recommendations to governments and international agencies on strategies to ameliorate the repression of religious exercise.[58]

Nor is this book a philosophical or normative treatise, though it certainly has implications for inquiries into the timeless ideals of liberty, equality, and justice. While I do not shy away from asserting the fundamental justice of religious freedom, that is not my primary aim.

Rather, this book is empirical. It marshals and synthesizes what vast global research tells us about why religious freedom matters, why violations of this universal right have such profound consequences. It also documents the specific pathways that produce these outcomes, and it provides an overarching theoretical explanation for why religious freedom matters so much to human flourishing today, to the kind of world most of us wish to inhabit. In a way, modern scholarship verifies what great thinkers of the past asserted: that religious freedom is a personal and social good, that religious freedom and equality serve as the antidote to religious strife and violence, and that violations of religious rights disrupt the social order.

ARGUMENT OF THE BOOK

Why is religious freedom such a potent human right? Why is it so critical to human flourishing? Why does it have such a huge impact on so many arenas of human life? *My central argument is that religious freedom uniquely matters to peaceful, democratic, and flourishing societies because it goes to the heart of human personhood and experience: the right to be who we are, to act on our ultimate commitments, and to be treated with equal worth and dignity.*[59] While I will probe specific empirical theories that link religious freedom to democracy, prosperity, women's empowerment, uplift, and peace, they all converge on this overarching theme.

Let me elaborate. Suppose I ask what is *ultimate* to you, what makes the greatest claim on your conscience. Then, I say, "You cannot live by that commitment. You cannot publicly affirm or act on it." You would see this as a violation of your identity and dignity, as fundamentally unjust.

This freedom to exercise one's transcendent duties—to seek truth about ultimate questions and act on them—is so central to humanity that government or social repression, along with unequal treatment that privileges religious majorities, will inevitably harm societies, governance, and economics.

If religious freedom is *the right to be who we are*, it is under siege in the world today, assaulted by theocratic movements, violated by authoritarian regimes, attacked by ethno-nationalists, curbed by aggressive secular policies, and undermined by elite hostility or misunderstanding. All reflect the hegemonic impulse of regime leaders and dominant social groups. For theocrats: *You must become us.* For ethno-nationalists: *You must be expelled from us.* For autocrats: *You must serve us before God.* For aggressive secularists: *You must hide your faith under a bushel.* And for regimes that privilege majority faiths: *You—religious minorities—must endure second-class status.*

These repressive impulses represent one of the greatest threats to more stable, democratic, prosperous, and peaceful societies in the twenty-first century.

In sum, empirically driven research demonstrates that restrictive laws, repressive societal practices, and state favoritism produce persecution and conflict, undermine democracy and civil liberties, contribute to terrorism and international conflict, and prevent the empowerment of women or the uplift of the poor. There are, in short, compelling reasons to see religious liberty as a fundamental and universal human right. *Justice demands it. Violations disrupt the social order.*

THE EMPIRICAL TURN: A LIMINAL MOMENT

The scholarly enterprise now underway represents a liminal moment in human history, a threshold to a new understanding of human dynamics. This statement may seem like hyperbole. But for centuries, even millennia, great thinkers have made assertions about the dangers of coercion in matters of religion, along with claims about why people should have the right to peacefully exercise transcendent duties unmolested by political authorities or hostile social groups. We now have the means to test such conjectures and derive theories that explain why society works the way it does, why stubborn facts back timeless normative ideals.

Let us explore that contention. Roger Finke, a leading sociologist of religion, made this observation: "Prior to 2000, there were no systematic data collections on religious freedoms and few studies attempted to understand either the origins or the consequences of these freedoms."[60] The decisive turn to empirical validation, therefore, required a way *to measure* global religious conditions. Enter two landmark scholars, Brian Grim and Jonathan Fox.

I begin with Brian Grim, a pioneering quantitative sociologist who developed the coding methodology used by the Pew Research Center to measure global restrictions on religion. Before his scholarly career, Grim spent two decades abroad as a curriculum developer in such diverse places as China, Kazakhstan, Saudi Arabia, Germany, and the United Arab Emirates. These experiences gave him an intuitive feel for the dynamics of religious culture, persecution, and interreligious conflict.[61]

As a doctoral student at Penn State, Grim worked with Roger Finke, an innovator in marshalling vast quantitative data to test theories about the relationship between religion and the state.[62] Rigorously trained in the latest social scientific methods, Grim understood the need for objective, verifiable, and replicable metrics.

So rather than attempt to measure some *indefinable quantity of freedom*, Grim developed a rigorous protocol to code and sum *actual restrictions on religion*, whether by governments or powerful social actors. If freedom itself is impossible to measure, *restrictions* on religious exercise are tangible, observable, and measurable. Moreover, such measures can be tracked across time (longitudinally) and compared by region, country, or religion, enabling empirical breakthroughs.

After developing the coding method in his dissertation, Grim refined and expanded it as a senior researcher for the Pew Research Center, which for a decade and a half has produced an annual report on the "global restrictions of religion."[63] Here is how the rigorous protocol works. The Pew Center employs coders who comb through some nineteen human rights reports—by the United Nations, the U.S. State Department, the U.S. Commission on International Religious Freedom, the European Union, other regional bodies, and reputable human rights organizations such as Freedom House and Amnesty International—to answer a battery of questions about the nature and degree of documented restrictions on religious exercise both by governments and hostile social actors. Two "double-blind" coders independently record their answers to minimize bias and provide what is called "inter-coder reliability."[64] The answers are scored and summed to produce an index between zero and ten, with ten being the highest level of restrictions on religion.[65]

Pew also groups national scores into percentiles that provide a vivid depiction of the nations with the most egregious restrictions on religion. Those in the top 5 percent are categorized as *very high*, those in the next 15 percent as *high*, the next 20 percent as *moderate*, and the bottom 60 percent as *low*.[66] Because many of the most populous countries on Earth are repressive, as many as 85 percent of the world's people live amidst high or very high restrictions on religion, either by governments or hostile social actors.[67]

For Pew's index of government restrictions, these are the kinds of questions coded with gradation points for how widespread or severe:

- Does the country's constitution or basic law recognize one or more favored religions?
- Does any level of government limit public preaching?
- Does any level of government formally ban any religious group?
- Does any level of government harass or intimidate religious groups?
- Has any level of government used force against religious groups that resulted in individuals being killed, physically abused, or imprisoned?

For Pew's index of social hostilities, these are the kinds of coded questions:

- Do social groups attempt to prevent others' religious practice?
- How many different types of crimes, malicious acts, or violence motivated by religious hatred or bias have occurred?
- Does religion-related mob violence occur, and, if so, how widespread is it?
- Are women harassed for violating religious codes?
- Are religion-related terrorist groups active in the country?
- Do individuals or groups use violence or the threat of violence, including so-called honor killings, to try to enforce religious norms?[68]

In other words, we are talking about real issues, progressively harsh conditions. One can quibble with this or that nuance in the indexes, but rising scores clearly indicate increasingly repressive conditions. The Pew Team scrupulously seeks out comparable indicators of repression, which leads them to omit from its reports only North Korea, whose isolation precludes accurate measurement.[69]

Brian Grim and Roger Finke provided a crucial early test of this method of measuring religious restrictions in their pathbreaking book, *The Price of Freedom Denied.* In this work, they develop a model that predicts and explains statistical relationships between restrictions on religion by governments or social actors and levels of religious persecution and violence. The robustness of their findings, followed by scores of other studies, buoy our confidence in the validity of the Pew coding methodology.[70]

Paralleling the Pew initiative, the Religion and State (RAS) project, under the direction of Israeli political scientist Jonathan Fox, serves as a huge repository of government religious policies around the world. For over two decades, Fox and his team have systematically collected and categorized every constitutional provision, statute, or regulation on religion, by national and provincial governments, for the largest 175 nations on Earth. This prodigious effort reveals an astonishing level of meddling in religion by most countries on Earth, a finding especially surprising to Americans accustomed to legal separation of religion and state.[71] In successive waves of coding, the RAS project tracks changes over time. It also added new measures, such as the degree of officially established religion, the degree of state favoritism to religious majorities, and, most poignantly, the amount of explicit discrimination against religious minorities, both by governments and societies. Fox is also a prolific author who has produced a succession of books that analyze and interpret the findings of successive RAS data waves.[72]

Like Pew, the RAS project is transparent in its protocols and makes its data freely accessible to researchers.[73] For measurement, Fox's coders commonly employ a four-point scale to score the degree of each indicator in each index: 0=None, 1=Low, 2=Moderate, and 3=High. As with the Pew coding, these scores are summed up to produce an overall index.[74]

The development and expansion of Pew and RAS measures over time coincide with expanding global databases on other dimensions, which provide an unprecedented opportunity for scholars. Religious measures can be statistically tested against levels and varieties of democracy, freedom indexes, civil liberties scores, terrorism and violent incidents databases, state fragility indexes, state corruption measures, gender equality rankings, economic freedom scores, national development indexes, comparative economic data, and global religious demographics.[75] Scholars can use either or both Pew and RAS metrics, depending on the question addressed. In addition, creative teams are experimenting with additional measures attuned to precise dimensions of international law.[76]

Researchers can also draw upon the voluminous qualitative record provided by the United Nations, the U.S. State Department, the U.S. Commission on International Religious Freedom, human rights organizations, and other global institutes. The International Institute for Religious Freedom, helpfully, maintains a clearinghouse of reports from these sources on the status of religious freedom in every nation on Earth.[77]

As noted, Pew and RAS do not measure religious freedom per se; rather, they document a wide range of religious restrictions, coercion, discrimination, favoritism, or violence against religious adherents and communities by governments or hostile social actors. Nonetheless, the range and weight of *positive* relationships between low levels of restrictions and socially beneficial outcomes suggest that we are not just measuring a negative thing, the absence of restrictions. Indeed, the findings presented throughout this book suggest that we are capturing the tangible benefits of religious freedom in the *lived experiences* of people. Sound constitutional provisions, protective laws, equal justice, flourishing civil society, and positive social norms conform to the definition of religious freedom in international law. As religious restrictions go down, and as the space for religious exercise expands, good things flow.

A MODEL OF SCHOLARSHIP

The global research enterprise underway represents a model of scholarship that mirrors the best attributes of modern science—theoretically driven, rigorous, quantitatively tested, and replicated over time and across the world.[78] Qualitative approaches, in turn, corroborate the findings of statistical tests, explain paradoxical results, and flesh out theoretical explanations. Innovative "participatory methods" also enable scholars to learn why religious freedom matters in the lived experience of poor, exploited, and marginalized peoples.[79] Such narrative methods, indeed, represent an indispensable dimension of global inquiry.[80]

The powerful findings presented in this book, therefore, emerge not from a single method or source but from a wide range of approaches. Historical accounts, comparative analyses, in-depth case studies, natural experiments, participatory investigations, immersive ethnographies, and rigorous statistical tests with multiple methods and diverse global databases all converge on the same lessons.

At the negative end, we can predict with confidence that countries with the highest restrictions on religion, the most discriminatory laws, or the most privilege for majorities will experience and incubate more violence, will lag in democracy and human rights, and will tend to suffer straggling economic performance. Conversely, we know that nations that protect religious free exercise and treat all religious communities equally will be far more likely to have thriving democracies and economies. In sum, religious freedom matters—for civil society, democracy, human rights, flourishing economics, interreligious amity, uplift of the poor, women's empowerment, and peace.

Religious freedom matters in such diverse arenas, as I argue, because it goes to the heart of human personhood and experience. My confidence in this theme stems from the fact that it explains so much in an elegant, parsimonious, and encompassing fashion—the very attributes of great scientific theories. As the reader will see, research findings on the value of religious freedom often initially seem paradoxical, but when theoretically explained, they shift the lens, or paradigm, through which we understand the world. That, too, mirrors the scientific enterprise at its best.[81] But it also should change the way political leaders, policymakers, and religious authorities approach the crucible of religious pluralism in a global age.

With this framework in mind, I now outline the key findings of the chapters to come.

CHAPTER 2: UNDERPINNINGS OF DEMOCRACY, CIVIL LIBERTIES, AND CIVIL SOCIETY

Chapter 2 documents how religious freedom helps underpin democracy by enhancing civil liberties, limiting the reach of government, and propelling a robust civil society. Research shows strong historical and statistical relationships between degrees of religious freedom and the longevity of democracy. Given that religious freedom is an essential civil liberty, these connections appear direct and obvious. By combining historical accounts with modern empirical analysis, I show how religious freedom is not just *associated* with democracy but serves as a crucial *agent* in propelling democratization. The chapter begins with the seventeenth-century quest by religious dissenters for greater religious tolerance and liberty, which spurred democratization in the Netherlands, England, and the American colonies. The transformation of the Catholic Church in the twentieth century then serves as a natural experiment of how a change in doctrine on religious freedom propelled the last wave of democratization on Earth. Turning to empirical research, I show how attempting to enforce religious uniformity on diverse societies, or extending privileges to majority faiths, produces strife, undermines equality before the law, and fuels despotism. That pattern explains the comparative deficit of democracy in most Muslim-majority countries, not the inherent tenets of Islam. When religious freedom is protected and religious pluralism promoted, we see more enduring democracy in those Muslim-majority societies. Finally, religious freedom serves as a crucial indicator of the direction "transitional regimes" are moving or as a harbinger of the erosion of democracies. Indeed, would-be autocrats often employ favoritism toward dominant religious groups and restrictions on minorities as tools to undermine democratic norms and consolidate power.

CHAPTER 3: THE FONT OF WEALTH: RELIGIOUS FREEDOM AND FLOURISHING ECONOMICS

Can religious liberty enhance material well-being and flourishing economics? Wide-ranging scholarship indicates that it does and in surprising ways. Protecting religious liberty and the pluralism it entails promotes conditions that help spark and sustain equitable economic growth. Repression and persecution, on the other hand, retard economic growth and distort outcomes. To chart the pathways that produce these outcomes, I synthesize historical accounts and econometric studies from around the world. Fascinatingly, the historical record shows how political economists of the past documented the economic and trading advantages gained by countries that practiced religious toleration, if not full religious freedom. As in the past, religiously free conditions act as a magnet to attract skilled craft workers and entrepreneurial risk-takers, unleashing their potential. As leaders in the American colonies learned, religious persecution is bad for trade and the wealth it produces. Another pathway entails contingent liberties that legal guarantees of religious freedom support, such as the rule of law, property rights, and the right to assemble, which underpin commercial enterprise. Econometric studies also show that religious repression represents a crucial *risk factor* for business investment, which redounds to the long-term benefit of religiously tolerant societies. When religious communities are free to build houses of worship, schools, charities, and other institutions, their investments produce multiplier effects for local economies. These societal contributions also generate social capital and trust that lubricate commercial enterprise. Some of the most fascinating research documents how state religious privilege and discrimination act to retard long-term economic progress. As sophisticated scholarship shows, the enforcement of rigid versions of Sharia law by Muslim empires impeded economic modernization for centuries. I end by examining the cases of India and China, which seem to defy global trends elsewhere. In India, we do see strong economic growth alongside heightened religious hostilities driven by Hindu nationalism, findings in need of deeper exploration. With China, on the other hand, we learn how the nation benefited economically from relaxed religious restrictions that accompanied economic modernization, which began with Deng Xiaoping and his successive leaders. The severe religious crackdown launched by Xi Jinping from 2018 onward, however, appears to be contributing to recent sluggish outcomes and a long-term demographic challenge.

CHAPTER 4: PATH TO EMPOWERMENT: UPLIFTING VULNERABLE COMMUNITIES

Mounting empirical research and in-depth ethnographic studies show that violations of religious freedom, both by governments and powerful social actors, reinforce oppressive structures that marginalize impoverished people, exploited women, migrants, and ethno-religious minorities. Indeed, religious restrictions tend to lock poor people, women, and outcasts in economic and social straitjackets. Protections of religious freedom, on the other hand—particularly the right to practice, interpret, criticize, or change one's faith—act as powerful engines of empowerment and integration of otherwise poor and marginalized people. Repression of this religious agency, moreover, produces cycles of persecution, societal instability, and violence that redound disproportionately on fragile economic and social institutions of integration. These findings may seem paradoxical given that religion is often portrayed as innately patriarchal and repressive of nonconforming beliefs. But as I will show, genuine religious freedom unleashes agency among the marginalized that extends far beyond religion. Indeed, some of the most stunning research shows how religious agency empowers women in developing societies and leads to improvements in their economic fortunes.

CHAPTER 5: WEAPON OF PEACE

One of the weightiest arguments for religious freedom is its vital link to international security and peace. Religious strife and violence represent major sources of global instability and conflict—undermining economic development and propelling massive refugee flows. The chapter begins by documenting the dramatic upsurge in the past few decades of religious violence and terrorism, sectarian civil wars, and religiously driven interstate conflict. Capitalizing on an unprecedented wealth of new global data, scholars have documented the robust causal relationships between rising levels of religious repression and these devastating outcomes. This empirical scholarship is corroborated by qualitative investigations of security threats. They show that *every* security threat to the United States is an egregious violator of religious freedom. On the other hand, no religiously free state represents such a threat, nor is there a single example in modern history of religiously free states fighting on opposing sides of a war. These patterns suggest that religious conditions inside a nation, like the proverbial canary in the coal mine, provide an early warning of new dangers to global security. The disruptive international ripples of state repression emerge in the powerful relationship between majority favoritism and religious violence. Landmark research shows that most religious violence stems from religious majorities emboldened by their privileged status in law and society. The chapter ends by recounting the pathways to peace facilitated by the protection of religious freedom and equality. By giving all a stake in the pluralist fabric of society, religious liberty cultivates inter-religious interactions and amity. It empowers global peacemakers. It is a weapon of peace.

CHAPTER 6: CHARTING THE WAY FORWARD

The concluding chapter refines the argument and carries its broader implications into the future. In pursuit of that aim, I qualify findings, clarify and summarize key themes, highlight slighted issues, explore challenges, and offer a vision for the way forward. I begin by clarifying the confused discourse on secularism to present an alternative way to capture the best regimes for protecting maximum religious freedom. I then elaborate on the *paradox of privilege* as one of the most consequential findings of global research—that state favoritism toward dominant religious majorities is uniquely disruptive to democracy and peace. This leads to the stunning realization that we may now possess insight into the timeless question of *what makes religion good or bad, compassionate or cruel, peaceful or violent.* Relatedly, research shows why inequality represents such a massive violation of religious liberty across the globe and why international law must incorporate *equality* more fully into formulations of religious freedom. I also make the case that governments and international organizations must recognize the special character of indigenous peoples, whose spiritual lives, tied to sacred lands, can be destroyed by large-scale development projects. Turning to a recent challenge, I frankly analyze emerging clashes between religious conscience claims and antidiscrimination laws on sexual identity and gender orientation. While sometimes depicted in zero-sum terms, I show that compromises exist to avoid culture wars and the stigmatization of religious freedom. I conclude by presenting an emerging vision for how diverse religious communities can accept the reality of pluralism—and live and work together—without giving up their religious truths or commitments. That vision, *covenantal pluralism*, serves as a crucial societal companion to constitutional provisions and statutes that protect religious freedom. Neither utopian nor relativistic, covenantal pluralism provides a way forward for societies to avoid religious strife, cultivate interfaith trust, and provide political support for legal guarantees of religious liberty and equality.

CHAPTER TWO

UNDERPINNINGS OF DEMOCRACY, CIVIL LIBERTIES, AND CIVIL SOCIETY

At one level, the connection between religious freedom and democracy seems obvious. Modern liberal democracy, after all, emerged from the European wars of religion and the conscious efforts of statesmen to craft regimes of toleration that would tamp down destabilizing religious strife. Current global scholarship, moreover, shows strong statistical relationships between religious freedom and other democratic underpinnings—political freedom, freedom of the press, and civil liberties (see figure 2.1).[1] These robust correlations suggest that religious freedom represents an integral part of what Brian Grim calls a "bundled commodity" of human freedoms.[2] Moreover, correlations between religious freedom and other aspects of a flourishing society, such as gender empowerment, reduced armed conflict, and improved health outcomes, help sustain the longevity of democracy.[3]

By combining historical accounts with modern empirical analysis, we can chart the pathways that produce these relationships. As we will see, attempting to enforce religious uniformity on religiously diverse societies produces strife, undermines equality before the law, and fuels despotism. On the other hand, protecting religious liberty checks abuses by government, reinforces civil liberties, and propels a vibrant civil society. The longevity of democracy likely depends on the survival of religious freedom. Indeed, I find no evidence that enduring (and full) democracy can coexist

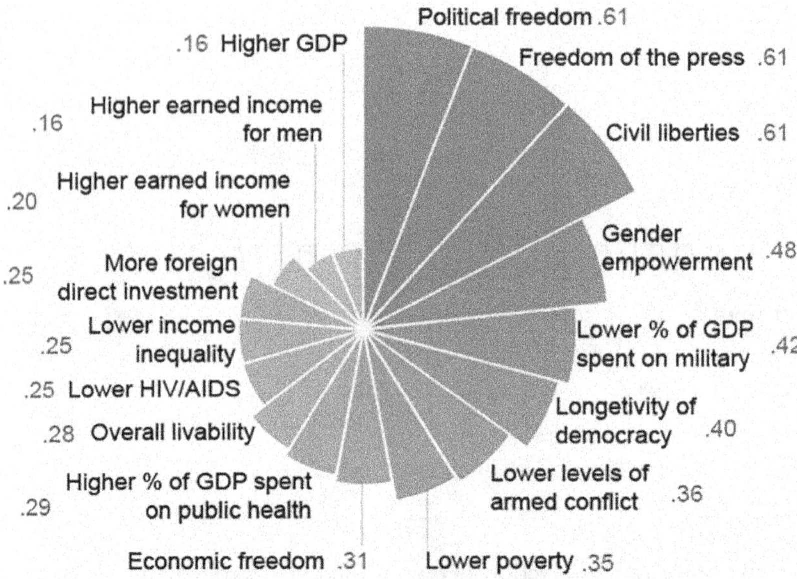

FIGURE 2.1. Correlations Between Religious Freedom and Other Global Measures, from Brian Grim, "Globally, Restrictions on Religion Reached 14-Year High," Religious Freedom and Business Foundation, March 21, 2024.

with significant religious repression. On the other hand, rising restrictions on religious liberty often signal or trigger a march toward authoritarianism.

The historical record illuminates these relationships. Take the English Civil War that led up to the Act of Toleration (1689). As with continental Europe, the Protestant Reformation unleashed divisive religious conflict in England, not only between Catholics and Protestants but among competing sects. Simmering conflict ignited into civil war when the English king, Charles I, tried to force religious uniformity throughout Britain by stamping out dissenters within the Church of England. The civil war that engulfed the nation turned into a political struggle between the monarchy and parliament. Crucial to ending the conflict was the act of Parliament that extended toleration to nonconforming Protestants. Because the act "legally bound the monarchy to respect dissenting religious beliefs," it also represented a decisive shift of power from the king to Parliament.[4] Here we see a direct link between nascent religious freedom and incipient democratic rule.

Similarly, one cannot understand the emergence of American democracy and civil liberties without grasping the role of colonial dissidents against state religious establishments. Government privileges for established churches and persecution of religious minorities seriously impeded democratization in colonial America. In varying ways, political leadership and citizenship rights depended on membership in the established church or the profession of religious oaths; minorities suffered discrimination and persecution. Sparked by this inequality and repression, Quakers, Baptists, and many others agitated for conscience rights and equal citizenship while developing theologies conducive to democracy. Across the world today, we see this same pattern: Minority religions often "prefer religious liberty" while dominant faiths seek "government-imposed restrictions on upstart sects."[5] Examining the link in American history between the struggle for religious liberty and democratization provides lessons for the contemporary world.

The seventeenth century (1659–1661) gives us the vivid example of Mary Dyer and other Quaker martyrs who were executed (hanged) on the Boston Common for insisting on freely practicing their faith. Offered banishment instead of execution, the indomitable Mary Dyer accepted death rather than compromise her right to do God's will as she saw it. The incident so shocked sensibilities that the English king ordered a stop to such executions, which chipped away at the Puritan theocratic hold on governance in New England.[6]

While such horrific persecution lapsed, privileges for established faiths and restrictions on competitors endured well into the eighteenth century in many colonies. Religious tests prevented dissenters from holding office, and tax assessments forced them to support established churches they did not attend. On the eve of the American Revolution, Baptists were jailed and flogged in Virginia for preaching without licenses and holding their own marriage ceremonies in violation of the Anglican establishment. This outraged the young James Madison, who waged a long fight against the fusion of church and state as inimical to conscience rights and republican governance.[7]

The reality of religious pluralism was also crucial to democratic experimentation in colonial America. Consider the case of Roger Williams, the fiercely independent pastor and theologian of the mid-seventeenth century.

Banished from Puritan Massachusetts in 1635 for preaching against state-enforced religion (and condemning colonial charters for failing to purchase land from native tribes), he went on to found the Providence colony (Rhode Island) in 1638 as a haven for religious liberty.

Or consider the enterprising William Penn, an early advocate of both democracy and religious freedom. As a Quaker, he had suffered persecution for his faith, including imprisonment for months in the Tower of London. But the irrepressible Penn ultimately secured a charter to found the Pennsylvania colony in 1681. Though envisioned as a haven for fellow Quakers, it became a hospitable place for Anabaptists, Lutherans, and a myriad of other sects, who contributed greatly to the economic vitality of the colony. Indeed, Penn made an explicit case for the value of religious freedom to trade and commerce. If you want to attract enterprising settlers and engage in mutual trade, as his "holy experiment" vividly showed, religious liberty is good for business.[8]

Other colonies, like New York, by virtue of their strategic economic location, became religiously diverse by default—a pluralism that included Jews who ultimately became an integral part of the cultural fabric of the great city.

The religious competition inherent in this pluralism played a crucial role in both shaking the foundations of religious establishments and fueling the egalitarian impulses of the nascent democratic society in America. Sparked by such great evangelists as George Whitfield and propelled by circuit-riding Methodist and Baptist ministers, the revivals of the Great Awakening democratized religious life. According to John Adams, this "radical change" in the "religious sentiments" of the people—especially the understanding that faith and conscience are independent of the Crown—sowed the seeds of the American Revolution. Sermons from independent preachers, such as John Witherspoon, inspired the revolutionary cause.[9]

During the nation-building era, James Madison joined with Baptists and other dissenters in successful campaigns to end Virginia's religious establishment and enshrine the free exercise of religion as a fundamental right in the new Constitution. As lingering religious establishments in the states were abolished, the American experiment in a deregulated religious market was fully launched.[10] Freed from the paternalistic hand of government, voluntary religion blossomed in the new nation, fueling the growth of a vibrant civil society, as Tocqueville so vividly chronicled.[11]

The record above shows the robust *long-term* interplay between religious freedom and democratic evolution. But historical analysis cautions against claiming too much in the *short term*. There can be costs and disruptions. Granting religious liberty too abruptly, for example, can sometimes generate a violent backlash against religious minorities by angry and intolerant members of the majority. In the 1560s, France was ruled by Catholics but had a growing Calvinist (Huguenot) minority, including some of the country's leading aristocrats. In 1562, France's Catholic Queen Regent, for political reasons, issued an edict of limited but real toleration of Huguenots. A militantly Catholic aristocratic family, the Guises, reacted by massacring a group of Huguenot worshippers in Paris, which sparked reprisals by Huguenot leaders and a spiral into civil war. In other words, the Queen Regent lacked the *capacity* to enforce toleration. The lesson is that new legal protections of religious freedom must be accompanied by the development of state capacity to enforce the rule of law.[12]

SOUL FREEDOM AND LIMITED GOVERNMENT

The crucible of religious strife in Europe and America produced seminal thought about the link between religious liberty and stable democratic government. Indeed, arguments for religious freedom (or at least toleration) were central to the grand liberal tradition, which emphasized consent of the governed, voluntary civil society, and proper limits on state authority.

In the Enlightenment view, however, these achievements required severing the political system from theological influences, even the privatization of religion.[13] Yet formative advocacy for religious freedom and conscience rights was deeply anchored in theological reasoning, not just Enlightenment thought. Moreover, because religious liberty advocates spoke the idioms of pervasively religious societies, they paved the way for modern democratic freedoms as surely as enlightenment skeptics, probably more so.

Consider these examples. John Smyth, an English separatist who left his country for a haven in Holland, penned in 1611 what may be the first claim for full religious liberty in the English language:

> The Magistrate is not by virtue of his office to meddle with religion, or matters of conscience, to force or compel men to this or that form of religion or doctrine; but to leave the Christian religion free to every man's conscience and to handle only civil transgressions, injuries and wrongs of men against men . . . for Christ only is the king and lawgiver of the Church and conscience.[14]

Roger Williams elaborated on this link between religious liberty and limits on the reach of political authority. In his famous tract, *The Bloudy Tenet of Persecution, for Cause of Conscience,* published in England in 1644, he asserted the doctrine of "soul freedom," that no temporal authority was entitled to coerce the "sacred haven of conscience."[15] As the path to God, conscience is inviolable and universal. It extends, Williams explicitly asserted, to Catholics, non-believers, women, Indians, and Muslims. It is the "fulcrum on which religion as a human activity and basic freedom rests."[16] Forcing belief, therefore, is "spiritual rape," which will inevitably unleash sectarian strife, turmoil, and war, and, by implication, render impossible the dream of limited government and free societies.

The Quaker William Penn echoed these arguments for religious liberty as both just and conducive to peaceful flourishing societies. In his 1670 work, *The Great Case of Liberty of Conscience*, he made a theological case that religious freedom serves as a shield against tyranny and bulwark of individual liberty.[17]

This brings us to the most influential thinker of the seventeenth century, John Locke, who saw religious freedom as a crucial pillar of the social contract. In his famous 1689 work, *A Letter Concerning Toleration*, Locke echoed Williams' theological themes that coercion is contrary to the gospel of love. Also, when the state attempts to enforce religious doctrine, it invites gross abuse by temporal authorities with no warrant or expertise in matters spiritual. Temporal power corrupts religion and thus undermines, even destroys, true faith. Moreover, because people form civil society out of voluntary consent to protect their liberties, no one should be deprived of "Terrestrial Enjoyments upon account of his religion."[18]

Significantly, Locke developed with equal vigor the argument that extending toleration to religious believers and communities ensures civil peace and a well-functioning state. When all enjoy freedom of worship according to the dictates of conscience, then peace, friendship, and justice can prevail. On the other hand, no peace or security can be gained if religion is enforced by arms, a theme corroborated by contemporary empirical scholarship.[19] Anticipating the contemporary arguments of sociologists, Locke acknowledged the ontological reality of plurality in religion. Thus, attempts to enforce a false unity would prove counterproductive. Moreover, extending broad toleration of faith is the best way for civil authorities to gain broad loyalty from citizens.

No figure developed the link between religious liberty and self-government as explicitly as James Madison, the "Father of the U.S. Constitution." Not only was Madison the principal author of the First Amendment, but he also provided the clearest, most robust justification for the defense of conscience rights and religious freedom of the founding generation. He echoed Locke's arguments that "torrents of blood have been spilt in the old world" by attempts of authorities to dictate what is orthodox in religion and that state establishment both corrupts religion and leads to despotic rule. More fundamentally, to Madison, religious liberty is the "first freedom" because it embodies a person's highest, especially transcendent obligations.[20]

We see this in how he consciously moved beyond Locke's argument for "toleration" to a full-fledged defense of "free exercise" of religion as a fundamental right. On the eve of independence, at the age of 25, Madison found himself embroiled in a battle to define religious liberty. A precursor to the American Declaration of Independence, the Virginia Declaration of Rights, drafted by George Mason in May of 1776, contained a provision stating that "all men should enjoy the fullest toleration in the exercise of religion according to the dictates of conscience." The language on "toleration" troubled James Madison because it implied a fragile condescension that could be removed at will. Believing that transcendent obligations impose limits on government, he successfully lobbied to replace the phrase on toleration with stronger language. The landmark Section 16 of the Virginia Declaration, which served as the foundation for the First Amendment, reads thusly:

> That religion, or the duty which we owe to our Creator, and the manner of discharging it, can be directed only by reason and conviction,

> not by force or violence; and therefore all men are equally entitled to *the free exercise of religion* [emphasis added], according to the dictates of conscience.[21]

A decade later, Madison would develop this sentiment in his famous 1785 essay *Memorial and Remonstrance Against Religious Assessments*, which serves as a kind of Ur text of American religious liberty. Once again, he anchored religious freedom in dictates of transcendent obligations. "Before any man can be considered a member of civil society, he must be considered as a subject of the Governor of the Universe." Consequently, "the duty which we owe to our creator . . . is precedent, both in order of time and in degree of obligation, to the claims of civil society." Religious liberty is inalienable because "no man's right is abridged by the institution" of government.[22]

Each of these figures charged that state-enforced religion is both wrong and destabilizing. It is wrong because the dignity of conscience is exclusively God's domain, not the temporal ruler's. It is destabilizing because it fuels despotism and religious strife. When political authorities exercise authority over religious affairs, they have warrant to crush dissidents and extend their prerogatives. On the other hand, the protection of religious conscience rights limits state power. Moreover, when religious communities are free to operate, civil society blossoms. As Robert Putnam documented a century and a half after Tocqueville, religious communities and charities constitute the most extensive and vibrant arena of voluntary initiative in the contemporary United States.[23]

In other words, champions of religious liberty advanced a potent theological case for limited government, checks on the authority of rulers, and the autonomy of civil society. These pillars of free and democratic societies thus owe a great debt to pivotal religious thinkers and heroes of conscience.

But is that legacy restricted to the West or to the past? Not at all. Today, heroes of conscience around the world suffer for their quest to live in accord with transcendent duties. And religious intellectuals from diverse traditions are linking that quest to democratic freedoms.

One of the most eloquent is Iranian Islamic philosopher Abdolkarim Soroush. Named by *Time Magazine* as one of the 100 most influential people in the world and by *Prospect* as the seventh most influential intellectual, Soroush initially supported the Iranian revolution. But its despotic turn made him a fierce critic of the clerical regime. Evoking the rich vocabulary of Persian poetry, his writings underscore the universality of spiritual aspiration with a freshness and originality to match a Williams, Locke, or Madison. To Soroush, because faith involves the individual assent to the divine, it "radiates like sunshine" and flows like an inner heat through "frosted limbs," producing enchantment and a "brisk," free, and "independent spirit." The "melodious song that emanates from the minaret of wisdom" intones that there is "no imposition in faith." Thus, a religious society, "based on free faith" and the "individual presence before God," "*cannot be but democratic*" (emphasis added).[24]

On the other hand, the attempt to coerce doctrine undermines true faith and retards societal progress. According to Soroush, a society of "fearful obedience" is "an oyster without the pearl, a face without the soul, an appearance without the essence." Theocracy will "paralyze minds with indoctrination, propaganda, and intimidation," creating "not a religious society but a monolithic and terrified mass of crippled, submissive, and hypocritical subjects." It "begets neither worldly prosperity nor otherworldly salvation." It throws "truth seekers into the pit of oblivion," snuffs out courage, and "ties down the feet and wings" of "inquisitive understanding." One can only base a "totalitarian" and "terrifying government on such premises"—which "neither God nor his Prophet desire." Soroush concludes that only democracy can secure and shelter authentic, examined faith from the despotism of "thought-killing rigidities."[25]

Soroush has backed up this eloquence with courageous challenges to the clerical authorities in Iran. In the aftermath of the rigged election in 2009, massive pro-democracy demonstrations rocked the clerical regime in what came to be known as the Green Movement. As a leading intellectual light of the movement, Soroush at the time was a visiting fellow at the U.S. Library of Congress. Knowing that speaking out would jeopardize his ability to return to Iran and reunite with his family, he nonetheless wrote scathing open letters to the regime. In sardonic prose, he "thanked" Ayatollah Khamenei for lifting the veil of the regime's religious tyranny. But he also had advice for how to govern a successful state: Adopt "auspicious freedom." Rather than send spies and informers among the people, Soroush recommended allowing "newspapers, associations, critics, commentators, teachers, writers, etc. to operate freely." Allowing "people to tell you what's on their minds" will "help you run the land and the State." Soroush later followed up with a more plaintive theological missive, appealing to the leader of Iran to embrace the Islamic principles of justice and free inquiry.[26] Soroush's voice refutes the view that religious freedom is a Western or imperialistic construct. Soroush's experience also illustrates the way religious coercion fuels political tyranny and the obverse, how religious liberty supports civil and political rights and democratic governance.

CONTEMPORARY SCHOLARSHIP

Global patterns show strong statistical correlations between religious freedom and the longevity of democracy around the world. Indeed, declines in democratic freedom track closely with rising religious restrictions. As measured by Freedom House, democratic freedom in the world reached a high point in 1998, after three decades of solid progress. It then stagnated and, ominously, has declined for nearly two decades, the longest decline in the forty-year history of Freedom House reporting.[27] During the same period, religious restrictions have risen markedly, as governments curbed religious civil society or extended privileges to majority faiths.[28] The "democratic recession" over the past two decades owes a lot to assaults on religious freedom.[29]

But skeptics ask: What will prevent powerful religious actors and movements from exploiting democratic openings to seize unfair prerogatives? Are not some state restrictions on religion necessary to prevent radicalization? Are there not examples of countries that failed to democratize because of religious divisions? The Arab Uprising, which left few democracies and enormous religious turmoil in its wake, seems to validate such concerns.

In response, advocates of religious freedom point out that it is precisely the absence of protection for vulnerable minorities and religious dissidents during transitions that emboldens radical movements and produces stillborn democracies. For example, Tunisia made the democratic transition during the Arab Uprising (at least initially) because it protected religious civil society.

Moreover, the role of religious freedom becomes clearer as scholars systematically chart the precise conditions and relationships conducive to enduring democratic governance. "Freedom of religion is deeply dependent on, and strongly promotes, other freedoms, such as property rights, rule of law, and freedom of assembly.[30]

Anthony Gill captures this symbiotic relationship by what he terms the "contingent liberties model." Vibrant religious communities need and will fight for a wide array of democratic freedoms: property rights to construct houses of worship, schools, seminaries, and charities; protections of assembly and association to gather for worship and other social activities; press rights for religious publications; legal security for contracts and charters that enable corporate functioning; and political rights to petition governments on behalf of these liberties.[31]

Moving to the crucial institutional level, the relationship between religion and democracy is best captured by the "twin tolerations" thesis. As developed by the late Alfred Stepan of Columbia University, this empirical theory shows how democracy hinges on a reciprocal bargain of mutual independence between the institutions of religion and state. The state protects and thus "tolerates" the freedom of religious institutions to operate in civil society; religious institutions, in turn, refrain from using the powers of the state to enhance their prerogatives and thus agree to "tolerate" (not squelch) competitors.[32]

As a keen analyst of comparative institutions, Stepan documented a wide array of religion-state relationships that conform to the twin tolerations model and which support enduring democracy.[33] A strict "separation of church and state" is not necessary, he observes, nor does democracy require the privatization of faith. Indeed, in Stepan's model, religious actors must enjoy the right to participate in public life on equal terms with other groups. Religion stops attempting to deploy the sword of the state for its ends and, in return, gains the autonomy to function in society and the right to civic and political engagement. That is the bargain. In a world of resurgent religion, this bargain offers a far better remedy to sectarian strife than the secularist vision of privatized faith.

Breaches of the twin tolerations, at either extreme, undermine democratic formation and longevity. Democracy is not sustainable where religion and state are fused, nor can democracy endure where the state exercises punitive control of religion. The first instance echoes Madison's argument that if dominant religious institutions can deploy state power to maintain their position, it both corrupts religion and undermines democracy. With good reason, one can mark the contemporary slide of Russia to authoritarianism by the 1997 religion law and subsequent amendments, pushed by Vladimir Putin, which empowered the state to restrict the activities of competitors to the Orthodox.[34] China illustrates the other extreme, in which increasing restrictions on religion serve the consolidation of centralized power by Xi Jinping, with devastating impact on Muslim Uyghurs and house church Christians, among others.

Taking the twin tolerations as his point of departure, Notre Dame Political Scientist Daniel Philpott elaborated on the link between religion-state relations, theology, and democracy. Democracy is best anchored where religion and state are differentiated, not fused, and where the "political theology" of religious actors eschews constitutional privileges or coercive state enforcement of doctrine.[35]

To illustrate his theory, Philpott points to the dramatic global impact of theological changes in the Catholic Church. For most of its history, the church enjoyed prerogatives of state establishment and opposed religious pluralism, which made Catholicism a net drag on democratization. The pattern of authoritarian Catholic-majority countries endured even after Pope Pius XII, in the wake of the Holocaust, endorsed democracy in his 1944 Christmas address. Throughout the 1950s, however, the Vatican continued to hold that because "error has no rights," the Catholic faith should be privileged or established by the state. As the twin tolerations thesis would suggest, this led the church often to support authoritarian regimes, which were happy to grant the church prerogatives in return for reciprocal legitimacy.

Influential Catholic intellectuals challenged the Church's position, making the case for the compatibility—even necessity—of freedom to authentic faith.[36] The Church officially embraced this idea in its "Declaration of Religious Liberty" at the Second Vatican Council. That declaration, *Dignitatis Humanae* (1965), which suggested that free pursuit of spiritual truth was anchored in the "sublime dignity" of humanity, stands as one of the pivotal documents of the twentieth century because it served as the hinge of change for global Catholicism. In a fascinating twist, the committee that drafted that document included two individuals with opposite experiences: the American theologian John Courtney Murray, who saw how a Catholic minority could thrive in a free pluralist society, and Bishop Wojtyla of Poland (later Pope John Paul II), who witnessed the church's existential struggle to survive amidst Nazi and Communist repression.[37]

Vatican II's embrace of religious freedom provided a singular natural experiment in the relation of political theology, religious freedom, and democracy. Indeed, social scientists could hardly have designed a better laboratory experiment: (1) a *pre-test* of conditions; (2) the intervention of the *experimental variable*; and (3) a *post-test* of impact. Before *Dignitatis Humanae,* most Catholic countries were authoritarian. After the church's embrace of religious freedom, its leaders were freed to challenge the legitimacy of authoritarian regimes, and with a few exceptions, most did just that, spurring democratization.

Moreover, a crucial intervening variable of *religious competition* helps to explain both the receptivity of Catholic leaders in embracing the message of *Dignitatis* and the exceptions of those who lagged in doing so. In Latin America, for example, the privileges of ecclesiastical establishment led church authorities, in many cases, to become complacent and unresponsive to the needs of their flocks, precisely what seminal thinkers like Locke and Madison predicted. But as church leaders faced growing competition from Pentecostals, they became more responsive to the poor and aware of conditions that exploited them.[38] Where such competition was lacking, as in Argentina, church authorities remained deeply in bed with authoritarian regimes and were slower to embrace the implications of Vatican II. But these democratic laggards were the exceptions.[39]

The first scholar to notice the impact of this great natural experiment was the late Harvard political scientist Samuel Huntington. In his book, *The Third Wave*, Huntington found that the last great wave of democratization on Earth was largely a Catholic Wave. Huntington documented how the theological shift of the Catholic Church at Vatican II enabled the church to catalyze democratization. Catholic leaders, from local priests and Bishops to Pope John Paul II, prominently defended human rights, shielded dissidents, and nurtured civil society. Like a great ocean liner that turns slowly but with tremendous force in its new direction, the church thus became the principal engine of democracy in the last quarter of the twentieth century. Beginning in 1974, it helped sweep away authoritarian regimes in the Iberian Peninsula, Latin America, Eastern Europe, and the

Philippines, leaving all but two Catholic countries in democratic hands by 1991.[40]

Philpott and colleagues Monica Duffy Toft and Timothy Shah have subsequently updated and deepened Huntington's work by systematically examining national cases where religious actors played a supportive or leading role in the democratization process. What they find is that the Catholic contribution continued past the period of the *Third Wave.* Even in countries with a Catholic minority, such as South Korea and Taiwan, Catholic leaders played a leading role in the democratization process. The autonomy of the church from state control, combined with a political theology that championed religious freedom for all, propelled democratization.[41] Moreover, Catholic majority nations today have the lowest average religious restrictions in the world, lower than the United States, the cradle of religious liberty.[42]

The role of religious competition in cultivating civil society is also revealed in research on how conversionary Protestants catalyzed democracy in a number of former Western colonies. By promoting mass literacy, printing, and voluntary organizations (for theological, not political reasons), these religious figures nurtured civil society. But they also sparked other religious groups to match their efforts, which served to propel a self-reinforcing democratization. Religious competition, under conditions of freedom and equality under the law, carves out space for civil society and reinforces it.[43]

ISLAM, RELIGIOUS PLURALISM, CIVIL SOCIETY, AND DEMOCRACY

The dramatic impact of the Catholic turnaround on religious freedom has led scholars to focus on the fate of religious freedom in Islamic societies, so fateful to democratic prospects. Is Islam inherently resistant to religious freedom (and democratization)? Or are there theological seeds that could lead Islamic societies to embrace pluralism, just as the Catholic Church developed a new theological doctrine?

At first glance, the picture is sobering, as Muslim-majority countries are among the most repressive in the world, and in the aggregate are significantly less religiously free than other societies. This pattern has led some to conclude that Islamic theology is inherently inimical to religious pluralism, civil society, and democracy.[44]

This satellite view of religious freedom in Islam, however, does not answer the profound question of whether Islam has the theological potential to *evolve* a principled commitment to living with people who adopt different answers to ultimate questions. A growing cadre of Muslim scholars advances the theological case for religious liberty and principled pluralism.[45]

Moreover, systematic investigation by Daniel Philpott finds both seeds of freedom within Islam and some promising empirical patterns. The seeds of religious freedom in Islam include key verses in the Quran[46] and features of the life of Mohammad that emphasize voluntary assent to the divine, the appearance of liberal Islam in the nineteenth and twentieth centuries, and present-day Muslim jurists who favor religious freedom.[47]

The empirical record also belies the assumption of the incompatibility of Islam and freedom, as nearly *one-fourth* of Muslim-majority countries are in fact "religiously-free."[48] In these countries, governments do not enforce Islamic law and eschew legal penalties for apostasy and blasphemy. Predominantly non-Arab, these societies range from sub-Saharan Africa to Southeast Asia, where conversions to Islam took place mostly through trading rather than military conquest and were often led by Sufi movements that stressed Sharia as a way of life, not a legal system. Thus, in a famous formulation coined by Stepan and Robertson, the problem is "an Arab more than a Muslim democracy gap."[49] As we will see, unique historical trajectories in the Arab Middle East produced repressive legal and social environments.

Not only are religiously free Muslim societies far more likely to be democracies than those with state-enforced Islamic law, but some also even "overachieve" given their levels of economic development. Based on the strong relationship between economic development and democracy, scholars can measure societies that either "underachieve" or "overachieve" on democratic governance, given their levels of economic advancement. In other words, poor democracies are overachievers while rich autocracies are underachievers. All the democratic overachievers in the Muslim world are religiously free states, highlighting the centrality of religious liberty to enduring democracy.[50]

The dramatic story of Indonesia, the world's largest Muslim-majority country, deserves special note in this discussion. In a landmark book on civil Islam, Robert Hefner documents how an Islamic movement, Nahdlatul Ulama, led by Abdurrahman Wahid, spearheaded the overthrow of the Suharto dictatorship and established electoral democracy in 1999. As Hefner shows, this Islamic reform movement repudiated state-enforced Sharia, backed women's rights, built ecumenical alliances, and defended democratic ideals.[51] While sectors of society, unfortunately, have been influenced by Saudi-financed Islamists since then, civil Islam in Indonesia continues to be championed by Nahdlatul Ulama, now the world's largest Muslim organization, which continues to emphasize public civility and pluralism.[52]

Among Muslim-majority nations that are religiously unfree, two patterns emerge: (1) "secular repressive" regimes that seek to control or privatize Islam; and (2) "religiously repressive" regimes that impose a harsh "Islamist" version of *sharia* on society. Comprising a third of all Muslim majority countries, secular repressive states provide further evidence that the lack of religious freedom in Muslim-majority countries is not simply Islam. Moreover, the evident failure of the Islamist project to produce just and economically flourishing societies may provide an opening for Islamic reformers to advance their case for religious freedom as a precondition for building such societies.[53]

In this light, the fate of the Arab uprisings of 2011 reflects the interplay between forces of religious freedom and secular or religious repression. As Philpott documents, the weakness of factions backing religious freedom helps account for the broad failure of democracy following the uprisings, although the relative strength of the forces backing religious freedom helps account for its advance in Tunisia. In sum, the status of, and constituency for, religious liberty strongly predicts democratic transitions in Islamic societies, just as we would expect from a growing body of empirical research.

While we see seeds of freedom in Islamic theology and promising variation in Muslim-majority societies, lagging conditions in the Middle East warrant deeper explanation. In particular, the Middle East/North Africa (MENA) region records the highest median scores of all regions on both government restrictions on religion and religious social hostilities.[54] This religious freedom gap coincides with poor political performance. The Middle East today is the least democratic region in the world, with disproportionately weak measures on civic participation, clean government, rule of law, social trust, and civil liberties.[55]

This pattern has led scholars to wonder how Islamic societies of the Middle East, which rivaled Europe up to the middle of the sixteenth century, suffered a marked downward slide to the present day. To answer that question, Timur Kuran provides a grand historical explanation of the underdevelopment of the Middle East. His systematic investigation uncovers social mechanisms that arose from the rigid enforcement of Islamic law by political authorities, which over time retarded political modernization.[56]

Kuran stresses that there were and are varying interpretations of Sharia by Islamic jurists, not all of which expect political authorities to enforce it through legal codes. But over time, from the pre-modern era into the Ottoman Empire, a detailed legal code emerged as the regnant interpretation.

Kuran's theme underscores a crucial insight, that the imposition *by law* of religious discipline produced adverse byproducts. What seemed beneficial to the Islamic community in the short run was devastating in the long term. In other words, deploying the sword of the state to support the dominant religion proved counterproductive, which is exactly what Roger Williams, John Locke, and James Madison predicted.

Take the Waqf, a system of highly regulated philanthropy in the Middle East. Typically produced by a land grant from a wealthy benefactor, each Waqf supported a particular educational or charitable function in perpetuity. Though not Quranic in origin, the Waqf system evolved into a rigidly enforced aspect of Islamic law, in part because it provided a means of sheltering wealth. Never independent of political authorities, it operated without transparency or accountability, which invited corruption. Assuming a fixed static world, it could not adapt to changing times, technologies, or evolving community needs. But most importantly, because it supplanted genuinely independent philanthropy, the system stunted civil society and fostered passivity and anemic civic participation, hardly conducive to democratic life.[57]

Another fateful legacy of Islamic law, penalties for apostasy and blasphemy, created a chilling climate for free thought and discussion. Though a variety of Quranic interpretations were possible, Kuran documents how Sultans and other political authorities opportunistically exploited charges of apostasy and blasphemy against their rivals, reinforcing autocratic rule.[58] Contemporary research confirms how apostasy and blasphemy codes choke freedoms, as they provide a ready means of targeting political dissidents, religious minorities, women, and even neighbors with property disputes.

Moreover, as Paul Marshall and Nina Shea document, Saudi oil wealth has been deployed to promote fundamentalist codes on apostasy and blasphemy beyond the Middle East, indicating how repressive ideas can spread if not confronted.[59]

By purporting to defend the faith and enforce Islamic law, political authorities in the Middle East operated without countervailing checks on their power. As Kuran shows, over time many Muslims came to accept behavioral restrictions imposed by the law as fundamental to Islam, from dress codes that limit female independence to bans on interest that frustrate economic development to curbs on criticizing or leaving Islam that fostered autocratic habits.[60]

In sum, the entanglement of religious and political authority in the Middle East produced social conditions that reinforced cycles of repression, undermined trust, fostered anemic civic participation, and stunted political development. Reversing these cycles requires an appreciation for how freedom will serve authentic Islamic practice, just as it did earlier in Western Christian societies.

A related line of research on the "Muslim democracy gap" examines patterns of religious regulations by all states with Muslim majority populations, including those outside the Middle East. Ani Sarkissian looks systematically at the types and levels of regulation in Muslim majority nations and analyzes those patterns against other common determinants of democracy. Except for Muslim societies in Sub-Saharan Africa (which generally preserve the free practice of religion), she finds that Muslim-majority countries tend to have significantly higher religious regulations than non-Muslim countries. But importantly, she finds that those regulations often target "Muslims who seek independence from state-controlled religion or who wish to challenge authoritarian governments."[61] In other words, governments regulate Islam to curb independent civil society and the political competition it might generate. While often portrayed as supporting Islam, restrictions on proselytization or public preaching also work to prevent independent voices from challenging the regime, not only of religious minorities but dissenters from the majority faith. Notably, her measures of religious regulation, when analyzed statistically with other factors, largely account for the democracy gap in Muslim majority countries.[62] Given the historic roots and contemporary motives for such regulations, they may be difficult to change; however, change is not impossible, as I show in the case of Uzbekistan in chapter 6.

A final line of research analyzes how global conditions shape the trajectories of states. In his book, *Confronting Political Islam: Six Lessons from the West's Past*, John Owen shows that majority-Muslim states are in fact more marked by violence, civil unrest, foreign intervention, and authoritarianism than the global average. But he argues that this is not because Islam is intrinsically less tolerant and less democratic than other religions (or the absence of religion). Rather, for nearly a century the Islamic world has been going through a contest over the oldest question in politics: What is the best form of government? The Western world itself went through similar prolonged contests—in the sixteenth and seventeenth centuries over established religion, in the late eighteenth and ninteenth centuries over monarchism and republicanism, and in the twentieth century over communism, fascism, and liberal democracy. Each of those periods was marked by the same kinds of violence. Ultimately, it was the comparative success of liberal democratic states—in terms of wealth and stability—that consolidated their model.[63]

The contemporary struggle between Islamist, authoritarian secularist, democratic, and hybrid forms of governance in Muslim-majority societies looks to be a lengthy one. It will be determined mostly by Muslim leaders and civil society actors, and the success of the models they fashion. Western historical experience indicates reasons for long-term hope but cautions us about short-term expectations.

RELIGION IN AUTHORITARIAN REGIMES

Authoritarian leaders often have a keener, if perverse, understanding of the power of religion than secular democrats and thus seek to control or co-opt it. Autonomous religious communities and institutions present a threat to the power base of an autocratic regime. Indeed, Chinese authorities viewed with alarm the pivotal role churches played in the downfall of communism in Eastern Europe.[64] From Poland to Czechoslovakia and East Germany, churches provided a haven for dissidents, inspired solidarity, and eased peaceful democratic transitions.[65]

The symbiotic relationships between freedom of religion, civil liberties, and civil society are being captured, ironically, by contemporary investigations into autocratic or mixed regimes. Moreover, the status of religion provides a key indicator of the trajectory of such societies, whether they are democratizing or slipping deeper into authoritarian rule.

As scholars apply modern methodologies and global data to such regimes, the picture that emerges is one of tremendous complexity and variation. This owes to the fact that different authoritarian regimes employ diverse tools to co-opt dominant religions for legitimacy, restrict religious groups to contain emerging civil society, or both.[66] Religious groups, in turn, develop a variety of adaptive strategies, often with great local variation, to survive within authoritarian contexts.

Russia and China present vivid laboratories of the relationships between growing religious movements and post-Communist regimes. Our guide here is Karrie Koesel, a comparative politics scholar from Notre Dame University. She notes that since religion and the state can represent competing centers of authority in these regimes, authoritarian leaders may attempt to co-opt religious leaders and institutions to enhance their base of support in the quest for popular legitimacy. We see a dramatic illustration with Vladimir Putin, whose privileging of the Russian Orthodox Church so co-opted its leaders that they blessed his brutal invasion of Ukraine in 2022 and continue to parrot Putin's rationale for it.[67] But autocratic regimes may also strive to restrict or regulate religion to prevent the emergence of an opposing civil society sector, as we see in China.

What makes Koesel's field research especially insightful is her ability to look at the motivations and strategies of both state authorities and religious actors.[68] At the national level, she finds that both Moscow and Beijing initially created a more hospitable environment for religious expression in the restructuring periods of the 1980s and 1990s. But as religious revivals grew in size and diversity, the regimes saw the need to retighten control over religion. This forced religious actors to come up with diverse strategies to navigate restrictions.

While both China and Russia employed national strategies to contain religious civil society, Koesel finds that they deferred regulation to local discretion, with often vague and contradictory national laws.[69] Thus, religious groups commonly find themselves engaged in complex bargaining with local authorities to maintain church property or carve out zones of partial autonomy for their operations. Authorities can provide selective accommodations, creating incentives for some religious groups to accept regulation while others find themselves in opposition.

But by dividing and entangling religious groups, regimes can prevent co-ordinated religious challenges—the kind that undermined repressive regimes in the past. As Koesel's research shows, some religious actors accede to co-optation by the state in return for favored treatment, while other religious actors accept restrictions on their competitors, which authoritarian regimes are often happy to grant. In other words, religious actors are not always fully supportive of religious freedom or democratization. Their posture depends upon strategic relations with the state. While Koesel's research focuses on authoritarian strategies of control, she confirms that expanding religious freedom helps propel civil society and democratization.[70]

Ani Sarkissian extends this inquiry for a broader range of autocratic regimes to understand how and why they restrict religious organizations and activity. In *The Varieties of Religious Repression: Why Governments Restrict Religion*, she documents how authoritarian regimes especially target religious civil society "as a means of restricting political competition and extending non-democratic rule."[71] Indeed, she finds that the degree of religious repression in a state—necessarily linked to the freedom of its civil society—is a more accurate measure of its authoritarianism than the presence of free or fair elections. For example, until recently Turkey held relatively free elections for its government, but it repressed all religions except for the majority population of Sunni Muslims. That privileging, over time, enabled the Erdoğan regime to tilt elections in its favor and assert greater autocratic control.[72]

Rather than measuring the quality of elections, therefore, Sarkissian argues that "democracy-promotion programs can emphasize religious freedom as an aspect of good-governance." Indeed, the types of religious repression she catalogues provide a crucial "indicator of the potential for more violent religious persecution and conflict in the future." Sarkissian poses her work, therefore, not only as a new means to understanding authoritarianism but as a scale with which to predict future conflict or relative improvement in civil society's freedom.[73]

One of the most common means of targeting civil society, Sarkissian finds, is restrictions on the right to proselytize—in the interest of supporting the dominant religion. The right to proselytize is one of the more controversial dimensions of religious freedom. A basic definition of proselytization is the process of trying to persuade another individual to change his or her religion. But popular usage has given the term negative connotations, as it is often thought of as incentivized or coerced attempts at conversion. Moreover, the status of proselytization among other religious freedoms in international law is hotly debated within individual states, among scholars, and within religious traditions.

Autocratic states often justify restrictions on proselytization in the interest of preserving social order or protecting citizens from force, coercion, and fraud. Sarkissian approaches the issue empirically. Using data from nearly two decades and covering 175 countries,[74] she tests whether restrictions on proselytization affect the protection of religious freedom in general, as well as whether these restrictions have larger impacts on civil liberties unrelated to religion. Using sophisticated statistical analysis with numerous controls, she finds that state restrictions on proselytization are a strong predictor of increased restrictions on religion, especially for religious minorities. Proselytization restrictions are also associated with greater restrictions on civil liberties more generally, even when controlling for other factors that explain state repression. In other words, political leaders with authoritarian tendencies employ anti-conversion laws to curry favor with majority faiths by repressing religious minorities. These findings lead to the conclusion that, when considered as an empirical issue, proselytization rights do belong among the larger categories of both religious and civil liberties.[75]

RELIGIOUS FREEDOM AND THE AUTHORITARIAN TOOLKIT

Autocratic systems cover a wide spectrum, from fully authoritarian regimes to regimes that mix democratic institutions with autocratic practices, which are increasingly common across the world. How do such different regimes deal with the potential competition of religious loyalties? What lessons do we learn from them? In the latest investigation to date, Koesel and Sarkissian team up to explore what they call "authoritarian toolkit"—the blend of carrots and sticks that autocrats employ to tame or control religion.[76]

Their inquiry challenges the notion that carrots replace sticks in that toolkit, or that co-optation replaces repression. Rather, different regimes blend the instruments of control, rewards, and concessions in highly diverse ways. That variation, along with new global data,[77] enables Koesel and Sarkissian to probe the relationship between strategies of co-optation and the status of religious freedom and other democratic liberties in autocratic or mixed regimes.

Those co-optation tools include: (1) providing patronage, or such material benefits as funding for religious schools or even salaries of clergy, normally to the dominant faiths; (2) policy concessions sought by major religious leaders, such as laws on marriage, divorce, abortion, or anti-conversion; (3) allowing religious political parties to function in society; and (4) creating bureaucracies to regulate or support religious communities.[78]

Their empirical analysis finds that patronage and policy concessions do not replace the use of repressive sticks in the authoritarian toolkit. Rather, they go hand in hand with restrictions on civil and political liberties, especially of religious minorities. Repressive tools must be used in conjunction with patronage because buying off majority religious communities with material benefits can produce a backlash from other religious groups that either receive no support or resist co-optation for theological or practical reasons. In other words, when autocrats or would-be autocrats use patronage and policy concessions to co-opt majorities, they continue to use sticks, especially against religious dissenters, minorities, and independent civil society actors.[79]

These findings corroborate the theory of "bundled liberties" that intimately links religious freedom with other rights. Religious free exercises support civil and political rights more generally. Moreover, regimes that ban religious political parties tend to restrict religious freedoms more than those that allow for some religious competition in politics.[80] This finding supports those who argue that full religious freedom must include the right of religious groups to participate in the public square on equal terms with others.

This research also provides lessons to both policy makers and scholars: Gauging the trajectory of religious freedom may predict the democratization of an autocratic or mixed regime, or the backsliding of a democratic one, as we see below.

RELIGIOUS PRIVILEGE AND DEMOCRATIC BACKSLIDING

As noted earlier, from 2005 onward, the world has been experiencing a democratic recession, with an unbroken, nineteen-year-long decline in country-by-country Freedom House scores on political rights and civil liberties.[81] While assaults on freedom have intensified from secularist regimes such as China, most backsliding stems from the rising influence of religious nationalists who seek to tie the dominant faith to national identity. Powerful forces of globalization, migration, and rapid cultural change have unmoored historically dominant religions from their prior status in many societies. This ferment leads "historically dominant religious communities to throw their support behind authoritarian political elites" who enact policies that privilege the dominant religion and link it to national identity.[82]

An especially notable example of this phenomenon occurred with the collapse of communism in countries of the Warsaw Pact and the former Soviet Union. Initially, many of the new democratic governments in these countries, especially in central and eastern Europe and even in Russia, established constitutions and laws that embraced religious freedom and pluralism. But the unsettling competition led religious majorities to press for state privileges and restrictions on competitors, which led to less free societies and democratic backsliding.[83]

For autocrats, the co-optation of the majority religion helps them stay in power and provides cover for their quest to overcome constitutional checks. For religious nationalists, this means legal curbs against competitors. As described by Nilay Saiya, the global rise of religious nationalism—affecting Christian, Islamic, Buddhist, Hindu, and Jewish societies alike—represents a threat to religious freedom and democracy.[84]

A survey of the world finds a wide array of examples. Autocrats and would-be autocrats who rose to power as defenders of the "national" faith include Vladimir Putin of Russia, Recep Erdoğan of Turkey, Viktor Orban of Hungary, Narendra Modi in India, Jair Bolsonaro in Brazil, Benjamin Netanyahu of Israel, and Donald Trump in the United States. Concerning Trump, Christian nationalists featured prominently in the Capitol insurrection in 2021, aimed at keeping him in power despite his loss in the 2020 presidential election. Indeed, Nilay Saiya claims that "the January 6 siege was largely a Christian insurrection."[85]

Elsewhere, we see democratic backsliding where religious nationalism comes to embody the regime, as militant Buddhists achieved in Myanmar. Or where insurgent groups make inroads at claiming the authentic mantle of the faith, as hardline Islamists have done in Indonesia. Fear of cultural displacement, in turn, fuels extreme right-wing, anti-immigrant parties throughout Europe. A key dynamic is often the quest to reclaim identification of the faith with the nation. But the ultimate result is greater state privilege for the dominant faith. Saiya's statistical analysis of the phenomenon, moreover, demonstrates that "as majoritarian privilege increases, so does repression of basic democratic rights."[86] As we will see in chapter 5, majority privilege is a key driver of religious violence in the world. And as I will discuss in chapter 6, state privilege, though tempting to religious communities, inevitably compromises the faith.

SUMMARY LESSONS AND PATHWAYS

A central challenge of governance is working out the relationship between the institutions of religion and the institutions of government, both of which can claim the ultimate allegiance of people. Stepan's "twin tolerations" provides the crucial formula for how that relationship promotes the longevity of democracy. In turn, that formulation represents a central aspect of religious freedom, that faith communities enjoy functional autonomy in society but cannot wield the sword of the state to restrict competitors. The historical record represents a kind of grand laboratory in which persecuted religious minorities pushed for the twin tolerations bargain, and the successes of that bargain helped birth modern democracy.

Both historical excavations and contemporary research, moreover, help us understand the specific pathways that strongly link religious freedom to democracy. Let us look at these pathways.

Religious liberty serves democracy by providing a crucial check on government. Religious institutions represent a competing source of authority that limits the hegemonic reach of modern states. For sustainable democracy, political authorities must not be armed with the power to dictate on matters of conscience and religious exercise or to grant privileges to dominant faiths. It is no accident that the status of religious exercise is one of the best predictors of the democratic or authoritarian trajectories of societies.

Because religious freedom is such a potent human right, it reinforces and underpins other civil liberties and democratic rights. While some see tension between religious rights and other liberties, that is not what the empirical case shows. Religious communities need and will press for the freedom of expression, assembly, and press; the right to own property; the autonomy to select their own leaders and norms; and the ability to form their own institutions for mutual support, education, and humanitarian aims.

Religious freedom nurtures the vibrant civil society so essential to democracy. Giving all religious groups a stake in the system fosters healthy competition and inter-religious amity. Such participation serves as a school of citizenship. It cultivates civic skills, generates social capital, and fosters trust. By taming religious strife, it facilitates self-government.

Finally, authentic religious liberty limits the capacity of powerful religions to dominate society. A common misunderstanding is that religious freedom inordinately empowers majority faiths. The opposite is the case. Equality before the law, inherent in the definition of religious freedom, serves as a barrier to such privilege. History and social science confirm that tyrannies often co-opt majority religions by patronage, anti-conversion laws, and curbs on competitors. But the price for that majority privilege is greater state control of religion and less vibrant faith. Privileging dominant majorities, therefore, stunts civil society and undermines democratic norms. Moreover, research confirms that religiously free societies are, in fact, more congenial to the skeptic, seeker, reformer, or non-believer. Religious freedom, in fact, creates the space for these voices.

These findings provide a clue to why religious freedom is also pivotal to societal peace, as we see in chapter 5, and pivotal to the protection and integration of vulnerable and marginalized people—ethnic and religious minorities, women, the poor, refugees, and migrants—as we will see in chapter 4. But first, I turn to the role of religious freedom in propelling flourishing economics, which may surprise modern readers but made sense to keen observers of political economy in the past.

CHAPTER THREE

THE FONT OF WEALTH

Religious Freedom and Flourishing Economics

A free Exercise of Religion is so valuable a branch of true liberty, and so essential to the enriching and improving of a Trading Nation, it should ever be held sacred in His Majesty's Colonies.

—English Lords of Trade, circa 1750[1]

Chapter 2 documents how religious freedom supports political democracy by enhancing civil liberties and strengthening civil society. Given that religious freedom itself is an essential civil liberty, this connection appears direct and obvious. But what about economic growth and equitable development? Can religious liberty enhance material well-being and flourishing economics? The answer is "yes." Religious freedom improves economic growth and equitable outcomes. To be sure, this impact comes out over the long term and in combination with other factors. The pathways between religious liberty and material prosperity are not as direct as with political liberalization, but mounting research suggests the impact is real. This chapter shows that protecting religious liberty, and the pluralism it entails, promotes conditions that help spark and sustain economic growth. Combined with the empowerment that spiritual freedom unleashes among marginal communities (discussed in the next chapter), religious freedom propels more equitable economic development.

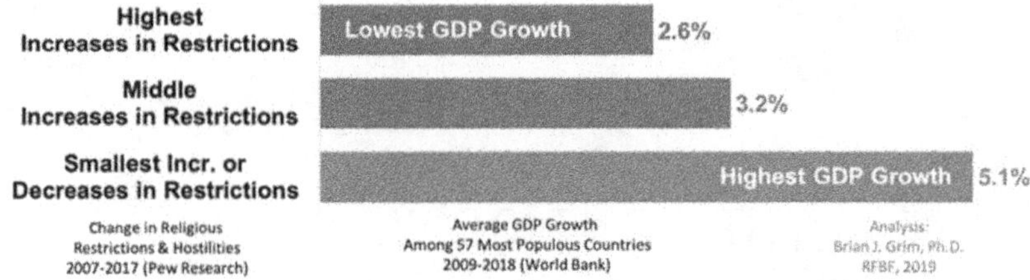

FIGURE 3.1. Impact of Religious Restrictions on Country GDP Growth, from Brian Grim, "Economic Growth Slowed by Decline in Religious Freedom," Religious Freedom and Business Foundation, 2019.

The most compelling evidence of the link between religious freedom and flourishing economies is as follows: In the world today, the nations that rank most highly on religious liberty, with few exceptions, tend to be the wealthiest, most economically vibrant, and advanced.[2] As figure 3.1 shows, there is a strong statistical relationship between low levels of restrictions on religion and economic growth, along with strong evidence that religiously repressive nations suffered retarded economic growth in the decade after 2008.[3]

But skeptics rightly ask of this relationship: Is it causal? Just as scientific theories gain strength from the diversity of tests, the causal link between religious liberty and economic vitality is now being tested, elaborated, refined, and corroborated. Historical accounts, case studies, statistical controls, and econometric analyses converge to suggest powerful causality, though often indirect and in combination with other factors. But equally important, theoretical frameworks suggest why religiously free, tolerant, and pluralistic environments promote entrepreneurial risk-taking, human development, social capital, trade, foreign direct investment, skilled immigration, and creative synergies.

PATHWAYS

Anthony Gill and coauthors systematically proposed and developed the specific causal mechanisms that produce the link between religious liberty and economic development.[4] For example, the *religious economy model* posits that because religious activity is economic activity (hiring pastors, building churches, etc.), more religious freedom leads to more religious activity, which necessarily contributes to economic growth, especially for local economies. Recent research suggests that this activity is considerable, but it even underestimates the religious impact by not accounting for the market value of in-kind and volunteer contributions by religious organizations.[5]

Gill's *Religious Ideas Model* suggests that at least some religious ideas promote attributes that are conducive to economic development, ideas that can only produce that result under the conditions of freedom.[6] The most dramatic instance of this is Robert Woodberry's research on the role of missionaries in supporting literacy and printing (to enable biblical understanding), which, as documented in the previous chapter, propelled democracy in developing nations. As we will see, this same theology-driven drive for literacy and printing produced long-term economic impacts.[7]

Another pathway is the *Civic Skills Model,* which suggests that religious groups in conditions of freedom promote human capital skills among members, such as education, cooperation, social capital, and training. Relatedly, a line of research indicates that independent religious communities not only counteract crime, addiction, and delinquency but also cultivate more stable families. Religious groups also promote direct charitable causes, which can free up resources that a society devotes to other productive uses. Gill terms this the *Charitable Giving Model,* which is illustrated later in this chapter.[8]

One of the more intriguing pathways is the *Migratory Magnet and Merchant Model,* which suggests that a national climate of religious toleration and freedom attracts migrants and industrious citizens with entrepreneurial skills. That pathway, as we will see, operated powerfully in history, and does so today.[9]

Finally, the *Contingent Liberty Model* suggests that religious freedom is dependent on and promotes other freedoms, such as property rights, rule of law, and freedom of assembly. This model deserves elaboration because it goes to the definition and practical lineaments of religious freedom. As Brian Grim notes, religious freedom is inextricably woven into a bundled commodity of liberties. Vibrant religious communities need property rights to construct houses of worship, schools, seminaries, or charities;

protections of assembly and association to gather and conduct collective activities; press rights for religious presses and publications; legal security for contracts and charters that enable corporate functioning; and political rights to petition governments on behalf of these liberties. So, while religious freedom alone may not promote economic growth, these other freedoms, which it inculcates, do.

As we will see, from the historical record to contemporary econometric investigations, religious freedom contributes to flourishing economies through a blend of these pathways and the depressive impact of religious persecution and strife on economic life.

FOUNDATIONAL THINKERS AND HISTORICAL EXAMPLES

While it seems implausible to secularists of our day that religious freedom could help propel flourishing economies, such was not the case for thinkers and actors of the past. Indeed, foundational figures of the sixteenth and seventeenth centuries—such as John Locke, William Penn, David Hume, Adam Smith, and Voltaire—explicitly saw religious toleration as being central to economic flourishing.[10] They thought so in part because their concrete experience taught them that *persecution is bad for business*, and that religious toleration facilitated peaceful and productive trade.

Indeed, in his foundational book, *The Wealth of Nations*, Adam Smith devoted an entire section to the free exercise of religion.[11] Religious tolerance was viewed by Smith and others as central to the free flow of trade among religiously diverse nations, firms, and peoples. Similarly, Voltaire famously saw a natural symbiotic relationship between vibrant economic enterprise and religious toleration:

> Go to the Royal Exchange in London, a place more respectable than many courts; there you will see the representatives of all nations assembled for the benefit of mankind. There the Jew, the Mahometan [Muslim], and the Christian transact business together, as though they were all of the same religion, and give the name of infidels only to bankrupts; there the Presbyterian confides in the Anabaptist, and the Anglican depends on the Quaker's word.[12]

The quote by the English Lords of Trade that begins this chapter epitomizes this view. Formed to regulate colonial affairs in the interest of imperial trade policies, this trade board took a cold-eyed stance toward anything that would inhibit flourishing trade and tax revenue for the Crown. In Virginia, the Anglican religious establishment employed discriminatory laws and pinched legal interpretations to inhibit faith competitors, which produced a crackdown on new congregations planted by a prominent Presbyterian minister. Seeing this action as harmful to trade and migration among the religiously diverse American colonies, the Lords of Trade vetoed the Virginia policy and urged that the governing council of the colony do nothing "which can in the least affect that great point." Remarkably, the board employed the more robust language of "a free exercise of religion"—rather than mere religious toleration—as essential to "enriching and improving a Trading Nation."[13]

One of the key contemporary scholars to probe the historic links between religious freedom and flourishing economics is Anthony Gill. Gill began his career exploring what he calls the "political origins" of religious liberty by first examining the expansion of religious freedom in the Netherlands, England, and the American colonies, then the growth of religious competition in Latin America and elsewhere. Applying a rational economic calculus to explain the expansion of religious liberty, he theorized that tangible economic incentives help explain why political leaders in certain times and places decided to relax religious restrictions and extend toleration.[14]

Repression and persecution, it turns out, are costly to a state because they inhibit trade, cause industrious people to flee, and require a large and expensive enforcement apparatus. Moreover, as societies become more religiously pluralistic, the costs of enforcing religious uniformity will mount, leading officials to see the value of deregulation. Lower government restrictions, in turn, lead to more religious vitality and diversity, which expand the constituency for religious rights. As a natural outgrowth of liberty, religious pluralism itself provides economic benefits because it lubricates trade and facilitates entrepreneurial synergies, especially with the advent of the commercial and global ages. For political leaders, this economic boon serves their concrete interests by replenishing the state's tax coffers.

To explore some of these theoretical propositions, Gill teamed up with John Owen and documented the historical link between religious liberty and economic flourishing. Gill and Owen, in fact, show that the growth of religious toleration and pluralism arose conterminously with the commercial age. But more than this, they demonstrate that the extension, first of religious toleration and then of broader religious freedoms, served as a crucial catalyst of the economic boon in the seventeenth and eighteenth centuries. They probe how a liberal commercial culture emerged in Northwest Europe in the seventeenth century, particularly in the Netherlands and England (and England's colonies), then spread. What are the lessons from the past?

RELIGIOUS PLURALISM

The first lesson is that freedom of religion was pioneered slowly by religious people and political leaders who accepted the inevitable permanence of religious pluralism as a foundation for secure and prosperous societies. "Religious pluralism is an essential ingredient to religious liberty," Gill and Owen observe.[15] Here they echo the sociologist Peter Berger, who argues that plurality is the default condition of religion.[16] When the Protestant Reformation shattered the illusion of religious unity in Europe, some states doubled down on repression, which stifled commercial development. Others, such as the Dutch, responded to the burgeoning religious pluralism by extending toleration to the different faith communities. A live-and-let-live religious consensus emerged, which made the Netherlands a crossroads of trade and a great place to build a business. Indeed, Gill and Owen make a compelling case that religious toleration helped the Dutch to punch above their weight economically and become a great commercial empire.

RELIGIOUS FREEDOM, ENTREPRENEURIAL MIGRATION, AND TECHNOLOGICAL DIFFUSION

A key lesson of history is that freedom of religion attracts the very people—"creative, risk-taking, pioneering, and entrepreneurial"—who propel economic growth and flourishing societies.[17] Human capital—in the form of educated, industrious, skilled, and entrepreneurial people—is a major driver of economic enterprise. Societies that attract the migration of such people will benefit enormously; conversely, societies that make life "odious" for such people will see them flee. As Gill and Owen show, in the seventeenth and eighteenth centuries, national policies toward religion served as the key reason for migration flows of skilled tradesmen and entrepreneurs.[18]

The Netherlands, as the birthplace of modern notions of religious freedom, benefited enormously from its tolerance of diverse religious communities. It served as a haven for the persecuted fleeing other nations, including Jews from Spain and Portugal and Protestants from France and elsewhere. It gained their talents and wealth at the expense of the persecuting nations.

France provided a natural experiment of this phenomenon. Following the Protestant Reformation, France was beset by bloody religious conflicts in the sixteenth century, which ended after King Henry IV issued the Edict of Nantes in 1598, granting a measure of freedom to Protestant Huguenots.[19] A recognition that religious violence tended to "devastate the king's forces and the French economy" provided an economic justification for the Edict.[20] As a result of this religious truce, the French economy grew for nearly a century after the Edict, with Huguenots playing a crucial role in economic enterprise.

When King Louis XIV assumed the throne of France in the middle of the next century, he came to see the independence of Huguenots as a threat to his absolute power and authority. He renewed discriminatory pressure on Huguenots, and then formally revoked the Edict of Nantes in 1685. This brought a reign of persecution against Huguenots, including forced conversion. Thousands fled, many to the Netherlands, some to England, and eventually to her colonies in America. Since only the most skilled, wealthy, and enterprising were able to migrate, the recipient nations gained an immediate infusion of such people.[21]

The Dutch economy gained from this emigration at the expense of the French. As a major study documented, the Huguenots propelled the diffusion of new technologies to host countries, especially Holland. While France previously enjoyed a competitive advantage in crucial technologies, fleeing Huguenots changed that equation. Dutch cities competed to attract Huguenot entrepreneurs and skilled craftsmen, who brought with them technologies for producing fine silk, velvet, linen, sailcloth, document paper, glassware, crystalware, and even beaver furs. Huguenot printers and book publishers also emigrated, along with skilled goldsmiths, silversmiths, jewelers, and watchmakers.[22] Huguenot sailors and shipbuilders, in turn, spurred the growth of Dutch shipping and whaling and helped expand the Dutch navy. Finally, because "the most prosperous merchants and the wealthiest among the Protestants fled to Holland," they provided an infusion of liquid capital into Dutch banks, which measurably lowered interest rates.[23]

King Louis XIV and his ministers noticed troubling economic trends but failed to understand their roots in his own policy of religious repression. For example, Louis XIV asked a minister "why the Dutch had lately ceased to buy as much French linen as they formerly did for the East Indian trade." A strong hint came when another minister reported that "Huguenots had opened a factory at Rotterdam that turned out coarse woolen cloth, which France had formerly been selling in large quantities throughout the world." Lamely, a top French diplomat was dispatched to Holland and ordered to "spare no expense" to persuade the workers to return to France. But why would they do so when returning meant facing a powerful state coercing them to violate transcendent obligations? Like some economists today who see only economic motives behind choices, the king and his ministers could not fathom the pricelessness of religious liberty. While the Dutch economy boomed in the wake of the revocation of the Edict of Nantes, France stagnated.[24]

In sum, the geographically small Netherlands became a major commercial and maritime power in the seventeenth and eighteenth centuries because its religious freedom acted as a magnet for risk-taking entrepreneurs and skilled tradesmen and fostered a competitive advantage for thriving trade with diverse religious nations and businessmen. As Gill and Owen also show, keen observers drew on the Dutch experience in crafting regimes of greater religious toleration.

Attracting immigrants to the fledgling American colonies made the link between religious toleration and economics a matter of survival and buoyed theological defenses of the liberty of conscience. No one made this dual case for religious freedom as explicit as William Penn. As a Quaker, he embraced the liberty of conscience, but as the founder of Pennsylvania, he explicitly used its guarantee of religious freedom to attract enterprising immigrants. His advertisements for new settlers made explicit appeals to those persecuted elsewhere.

Penn also recognized the value of religious toleration to trade and wealth creation. Persecution harasses merchants, produces colonial trade wars, and ruins estates. But Penn's genius rested on his insight into the benefits of religious toleration to the crown's tax coffers, a theme of Gill's research. As Penn wrote, "Peace, Plenty, and Safety" are the "best Allurements to Foreigners to trade," while rewarding "men of industry" whose labors "maintain the Poor" and contribute to the "King's Revenue."[25]

Once entrenched in a country, religious freedom tends to spread to neighboring countries through demonstration effects. A great question of the commercial age was this: How could the tiny Netherlands become Europe's largest economy and biggest trader in the seventeenth century? Perplexed by this success, other nations sought answers, which were supplied in abundance by religious dissenters. Baptist founder Thomas Helwys (1575–1616), who relocated to the Netherlands, observed that the most flourishing and prosperous nations "under the heavens" are those where "freedom of religion is permitted." Other English admirers of the Netherlands wrote about the salutary impact of Dutch toleration, including John Locke, who took refuge in Holland where he penned his famous *Letter Concerning Toleration* in 1685. He returned four years later to see the British Parliament pass the Toleration Act of 1689, which marked a pivotal hinge in the expansion of religious rights in the English-speaking world.

As Gill and Owen conclude, "The connection between the Netherlands, John Locke, the English Toleration Act, and subsequent religious freedoms that flourished in the British American colonies cannot be underestimated."[26] In other words, the economic boon of religious toleration and pluralism helps propel crucial milestones in the expansion of religious rights.

CONTEMPORARY ECONOMIC RESEARCH

One of the most active scholars on the economics of religious liberty is Brian Grim. After directing the landmark annual reports for the Pew Research

Center on global restrictions, Grim left in 2014 to establish the Religious Freedom & Business Foundation. Through this foundation, the peripatetic Grim has focused his efforts on twin objectives: (1) documenting the quantitative and causal relationships between religious liberty, thriving businesses, and sustainable economic development; and (2) making the case for corporations to use their leverage to promote religious freedom while working with business partners to articulate and model best practices.[27]

Grim anchors this research in the UN definition of sustainable development: "Development that meets the needs of the present without compromising the ability of future generations to meet their own needs."[28] He then prodigiously tests (and controls for) virtually every other explanation that could explain the strong relationships he finds between low restrictions on religion and sustainable economic development. He concludes that "religious freedom contributes to human flourishing and sustainable development—and their underlying socioeconomic conditions—in at least seven ways":

(1) Religious freedom fosters respect for differing faiths and beliefs, which is crucial to stable societies in a world in which eight of ten people identify with a religious faith and which produces the societal diversity shown to be beneficial to economic growth.
(2) It helps reduce corruption, which is a key ingredient in sustainable development. Laws and practices that burden religion are strongly related to higher levels of corruption, and they prevent faith-based values from checking corruption in business.
(3) It engenders peace by diffusing religious tensions and reducing religion-related violence, a huge drag on foreign investment and business growth that relies on stability and predictability.
(4) It encourages broader freedoms that contribute to positive socioeconomic development by removing what Amartya Sen calls the sources of "unfreedom." For example, research shows a strong link between religious freedom and the protection of property rights.
(5) It enables religious groups to play a measurable role in the human and social development of countries, especially the development of human capital through education, health care, and agricultural development.
(6) It overcomes government overregulation associated with such things as coercive blasphemy and anti-conversion laws. Repressive religious

environments inhibit entrepreneurial activity, foreign direct investment, and economic synergies. Persecution is bad for business.

(7) It multiplies trust among employees whose faiths and beliefs are respected, which improves workplace morale, encourages creative input, and signals to stakeholders that the company is ethical. Global consulting firm McKinsey has shown the value of ethical branding to business.[29]

To be sure, Grim and his co-authors acknowledge that diverse factors produce positive economic and social outcomes, and that religious freedom is not a "silver bullet" or a "secret solution to the world's ills." Nonetheless, their research suggests that the tandem effects of governmental restrictions on religion and social hostilities inhibit economic growth.[30]

RELIGIOUS DIVERSITY AND FLOURISHING ECONOMICS

If there were only one religion in England, there would be fear of despotism; if there were but two, the people would cut one another's throats, but there are thirty, and they all live happy and in peace.

—Voltaire, *Letters*, "Letter 6: On the Presbyterians"

Viewing life in England after the passage of the Act of Toleration (1689), French philosopher Voltaire saw numerous societal and economic advantages of the religious pluralism that the Act propelled. This theme of the social and economic advantages of religious diversity enjoys contemporary resonance and corroboration. Religious diversity, for example, is strongly associated with increased foreign direct investment and economic growth.[31] A team of economists suggests that the positive relationship between religious diversity and economic growth "probably stems from the presence of more competition for ideas and beliefs, which in turn promote divergent thinking and a greater capacity for innovation." They point to the remarkable religious and cultural diversity of Silicon Valley as a prime example of this engine of innovation.[32]

Other research finds that religious diversity correlates with an array of positive social and economic outcomes, particularly regarding gender equality. Greater religious diversity apparently helps produce higher enrollment of girls in school, higher female literacy rates, and higher labor force participation for women.[33] As we will see in the next chapter, the empowerment of women flows from the natural link between religious freedom, religious pluralism, and individual agency.

In a shrinking globe, religious pluralism will be one of the dominant features of life in the twenty-first century. Through his foundation, Brian Grim seeks to demonstrate to companies, communities, and nations how they can capitalize on religious diversity as an economic asset. Companies that promote and celebrate their religious diversity, he shows, will experience tangible benefits in improved employee morale, retention, and productivity. When employees and executives bring their whole selves to their jobs, the enterprise enjoys better teamwork, creativity, and innovation. Diverse perspectives produce better outcomes, especially over the long term. An ethical culture also springs more naturally when employees can share and know each other's foundational beliefs. Because most businesses operate internationally, religiously diverse teams also bring enhanced cultural sensitivity to suppliers and customers around the world, avoiding blunders. Similar dynamics can operate for communities and nations. When fully respected and protected, religious freedom enables the natural diversity to blossom in societies. Such societies are better poised to operate productively on a global scale.[34]

By modeling best practices for businesses and entrepreneurs, Grim features companies that score highly on an index he created of Religious Equity, Diversity, and Inclusion (REDI). Initiatives like this will serve as natural experiments going forward, helping foster business success in a world of vibrant religious pluralism. Ironically, this work collides with the assault on DEI (Diversity, Equity, and Inclusion) by the MAGA movement in the United States. Grim's research finds unintended harm to religious freedom with the wholesale repudiation of efforts to include and celebrate diverse workforces in business and government.[35]

RELIGIOUS FREEDOM, RISK ASSESSMENT, AND ECONOMIC GROWTH

One of the most promising developments in economic research incorporates the religious environment into econometric models, which document the impact of religious restrictions on economic growth and provide tangible guidance to companies and investors, such as assessing investment risk. A leading scholar in this arena is Ilan Alon, professor of Strategy and International Marketing at the University of Agder, Norway, and a global consultant on franchising, marketing, and political risk assessment. Along with his co-authors, Alon has documented the statistical relationships between religious freedom and business environments.

Alon and Chase begin with the well-documented relationship between economic freedom and investment risk by incorporating religious liberty as an independent variable in econometric models. Their positive findings suggest that it makes sense for multinational corporations and venture capitalists to employ religious restrictions as a risk factor. Specifically, they posit a two-way relationship between multinational companies and host markets. Governments can create more amenable host markets by relaxing needless religious regulations and the social strife they produce, while multinational companies acting in their own interest can promote religious freedom in host countries.[36]

One of the more tangible connections involves risk assessment in global investing. In today's global economy, the need for capital is vital and ubiquitous. Developing nations and nascent companies must have access to capital, and international banks and investment firms employ risk calculations in determining where investment loans are made and at what interest rates. Obviously, political instability can increase default rates, and as I show in chapter 5, religious repression is a key driver of strife and violence. Yet until recently, risk assessments relied on a relatively narrow set of factors with modest predictive power, ignoring religious conditions as an aspect of risk. Recent research suggests that incorporating measures of religious repression into risk models enhances the predictive power of risk assessment. In particular, Alon and Spitzer find that as scores on religious freedom increase, risk diminishes. Moreover, they offer a theory for why this relationship exists. Because religion is an unavoidable aspect of the political and social life of a nation, it will inevitably shape the business climate. Businesses value and need a modicum of stability: Religious repression produces instability.[37]

In other words, for purely self-interested reasons, global corporations and international investors should factor religious conditions, especially repression, into their risk calculations. National leaders, in turn, should promote policies that protect religious free exercise and treat religious groups equally under the law, because doing so will foster a better long-term climate for foreign direct investment.

A vivid example of the profound risk of ignoring religious conditions occurred two decades ago during an international human rights campaign against the Islamist regime of Sudan, which had waged a two-decade genocidal war against the minority African peoples of its south.[38] One strategy of Western activists involved targeting the oil industry of Sudan with capital market sanctions. At the time, the China National Petroleum Company was working with Goldman Sachs to raise capital through an initial public offering (IPO) to develop Sudan's oil infrastructure. A dramatic public awareness campaign about "genocide fueled by oil"[39] enabled activists to convince potential investors to avoid the IPO, and they raised the specter of future U.S. government action to deny access to American capital markets. Because of this pressure, the Chinese company's plan to raise money from American investors was cut by nearly $7 billion,[40] and the congressional Sudan Peace Act (2002) conditioned future access to capital markets on whether the Sudanese regime ceased its atrocities.[41] This vivid example illustrates how violations of religious freedom impair the economic prospects of nations and global corporations.

RELIGIOUS REPRESSION AND ECONOMIC GROWTH

Economists Alon, Li, and Wu produced one of the most rigorous and systematic statistical examinations of the link between religious freedom and economic growth, using data from 198 countries over a seven-year time span. Even controlling for an array of traditional factors of economic growth, they find that "government guarantees of equal civil rights across all religious groups" plays a positive role in economic growth. Conversely, government discrimination against minority religions "exerts a statistically significant negative effect on economic growth.[42]

Helpfully, this study probes the impact of different *types* of religious regulation by states. Such fine-grained analysis is enabled by global data that charts the multitude of ways governments restrict religion, from the most prosaic or reasonable regulation to the most draconian or preferential policy. For example, government policies that favor one religion or repress them all act as a drag on economic performance. On the other hand, reasonable government regulations that prevent unfair advantages by majority religious groups or blunt sectarian conflict are conducive to economic growth.[43] These findings make intuitive theoretical sense and conform to provisions of international law on religious freedom.

So, in response to skeptics who suspect weak or complex causal relationships between religious freedom and economically flourishing societies, a cadre of scholars have developed clear conceptual theories, tested them repeatedly, controlled for all other factors and explanations, and arrived at a plausible case for religious freedom as a powerful contributing factor, along with others to be sure, of sustainable economic growth.

STATE-ENFORCED ORTHODOXY AND LAGGING ECONOMIC PERFORMANCE IN ISLAMIC SOCIETIES

As we see in this chapter, a growing scholarship shows how restrictions on religious freedom can impair economic fortunes. This finding is particularly momentous for Islamic societies because state-enforced orthodoxy, and the denial of religious choice that goes with it, appears to be the crucial explanation for lagging economic fortunes in many Muslim-majority nations.

Foremost in this scholarship are two Turkish-American scholars, Ahmet Kuru and Timur Kuran. Both probe the question of why Muslim-majority societies, especially in the Middle East and despite oil wealth, lag behind other nations in economic development and produce net incomes far below their share of the global population.[44] That question is especially poignant because Islamic societies flourished intellectually and economically during the first centuries of Islam's geographic expansion, then began to stagnate and decline, especially relative to Europe.[45]

To Kuru and Kuran, Islamic history serves as a grand laboratory of the impact of state-enforced religious orthodoxy on socioeconomic development. Their distinct but complementary historical and empirical accounts show decisively that the emergence of religion-state alliances in Islamic societies and empires, not Islamic teachings per se, represented the crucial variable separating flourishing intellectual and economic life from stagnation. This prodigious research underscores a central theme of this book, that the fusion of religion and government not only undermines democracy and sparks repression and violence but also retards economic development.

Let us begin with Kuru, who traces how Islamic societies flourished during the first centuries of the faith's growth. As he shows, between the 8th and 11th centuries, Muslim societies "produced major achievements in science and economics,"[46] with "characteristics similar to what Western European societies would gain during the Renaissance—creative intellectuals and influential merchants."[47] Independence from the state fostered a symbiosis between merchants, who valued flourishing trade with diverse societies, and Islamic scholars who arose from, and were supported by, the merchant class.[48] Islamic scholars "avoided serving the state; they were funded by trade revenue and regarded interactions with rulers as corrupting."[49]

An atmosphere of open intellectual life, combined with the wealth flowing from innovations in industry and commerce, produced a virtuous cycle of intellectual and economic progress. Because "they ascribed high status to scholars and merchants," Muslim societies during this era were "scientifically and economically superior to Christian societies in Europe."[50] Both merchants and scholars lived in a reality of pluralism that included cultural and business exchanges with Christians and Jews. As with other commercial societies, religious toleration facilitated trade and wealth creation. This wealth, combined with flourishing intellectual life, fostered innovations in science, mathematics, astronomy, cartography, hygiene, medicine, technology, and agriculture (including dams, irrigation, and underground canals).[51] Consequently, compared to Europe of the 12th century, the Muslim world enjoyed superior socioeconomic conditions and was more urbanized and more literate.[52]

That favorable position owed to the high status accorded to independent scholars and merchants in Muslim societies, while Europe was under clerical and military hegemony. From the 12th century onward, however, those positions reversed. Independent scholars and merchants became more important in Western Europe, while Islamic scholars lost their independence and merchants were marginalized by militarized states.[53]

The crucial hinge of Islamic history, as Kuru documents, was the emergence in the 11th century of an alliance between the ulema (orthodox Islamic scholars, jurists, and mosque administrators) and military states. This "ulema-state alliance," as Kuru terms it, gradually stifled intellectual and economic creativity, ultimately producing economic stagnation and political authoritarianism.[54]

This alliance emerged from a combination of military and religious challenges in the Seljuk empire. As military rulers struggled to govern an expanding empire, they found it valuable to seek identification with Sunni Islam for cultural support and solidarity. Sunni ulema, in turn, confronted divisions among themselves and fierce competition from Shias. Faced with these challenges, the ulema and military rulers forged a fateful alliance. The ulema provided a source of legitimacy to the military state; in return, the state patronized Islamic scholars and enforced their favored version of Sunni Islam. In other words, state power was employed to codify and enforce Sunni orthodoxy. Simultaneously, the military state increasingly relied on wealth extracted from the conquests of other lands, marginalizing the role of merchants. The ulema, once independent and supported by merchants, "increasingly became state servants."[55]

Like many Orthodox clerics in Russia today, the ulema cooperated with and were co-opted by state rulers.[56] Around the world today, we see the same deleterious impact of religious authorities succumbing to the temptation to accept state support or sanction for their faith—whether Christian, Hindu, or Buddhist nationalists—a cautionary lesson of global significance.[57]

The crucial tool of this ulema-state alliance in Islamic lands was the extravagant use of apostasy laws against adversaries of the state or competitors of Sunni orthodoxy. Prior to this era, a Muslim could not be killed for apostasy unless he "explicitly and publicly renounced Islam," a rare occurrence. With the ulema-state alliance, however, we see the "killing of self-defined Muslims based on *charges* of apostasy."[58] Not surprisingly, this threat to religious choice stifled free inquiry, intellectual creativity, and commercial relations with non-Muslims. Today, apostasy and blasphemy laws in many Muslim-majority societies continue to stifle free thought and civil society.[59]

The full impact of the ulema-state alliance took centuries to fully manifest, but as subsequent empires copied the Seljuk religion-state pattern, economic and technological progress slowed, then stagnated.[60] An early egalitarian ethos was replaced by hierarchy and stratification, merchants were marginalized, scholars were co-opted, and "people became more docile."[61]

But Kuru concludes on a hopeful note: "Islam is not responsible for Muslims' problems, but certain quasi-Islamic theories are."[62] Thus, nothing prevents Muslims from redesigning "the relationship between their religion and their states in a way that would promote intellectual and economic creativity." As Kuru concludes, "Muslims need creative intellectuals and an independent bourgeoisie, who can balance the power of the ulema and state authorities."[63]

Confidence in the findings of social science is strengthened when scholars across different fields, marshalling different data and ranging widely through historical epochs, come to similar conclusions. That is what we find in the scholarship of Timur Kuran, which corroborates, clarifies, and elaborates on Kuru's findings. While Kuru is a political scientist, Timur Kuran is an economic historian of enormous range, whose research focuses on the relationships between religious, political, and economic institutions in the Middle East. Through a succession of studies, he traces the impact of Islamic law (or its dominant interpretation) on economic practices.[64] Like Kuru, he shows how Islamic law, especially the state-enforced ban on religious choice and agency, became more rigid over time, making Islamic institutions less adaptable to changing economic conditions.

Helpfully, Kuran focuses exclusively on the Middle East, where the codification and expansion of Islamic law came primarily through military conquest. As he notes, Islam reached outside the Middle East primarily through traders, not military conquest. This meant that the Middle East had the longest exposure and most robust practice of state-enforced Islamic law. Beyond the Middle East, as Kuran and other scholars document, we often see less rigid religion-state regimes.[65] This variation provides an opportunity for quasi-experimental studies measuring the economic impact of greater or lesser conditions of religious freedom in Muslim-majority nations, as we will see.

Kuran probes two related and momentous questions. First, why are religious freedoms in Muslim-governed societies stubbornly weak in relation both to other societies and to Muslim freedoms in other domains? Second, what are the economic consequences of this reality? His findings go a long way in explaining both the political instability and the lagging economic performance in many Middle Eastern societies. The linchpin of his explanation lies in the emergence and impact of apostasy and blasphemy laws enforced by governments, which were codified as part of the ulema-state alliance that Kuru documents. Kuran shows that the ban on leaving Islam or questioning its interpretation, in fact, produces perverse and enduring economic consequences.[66]

Like Kuru, Kuran rejects the essentialist argument that Islamic doctrine is inherently antithetical to freedom of religion. Indeed, they join with other contemporary scholars in showing how faithful Islamic interpretations support religious toleration and freedom of conscience. Kuran's own textual analysis of the Quran shows that both individually and collectively, its relevant verses lend themselves to an interpretation consistent with full freedom of exit from Islam. People accused of apostasy and blasphemy can legitimately argue that objecting to an interpretation of Islam does not amount to polytheism, that in Muhammad's time Muslim opinions were never uniform, and that the Quran bars ideological compulsion.[67] Indeed, Kuran shows how severe interpretations of Islamic law were codified generations after the founding.

So, what accounts for the emergence and endurance of Islamic rules against exit or voice? The answer lies in the incentives of rulers to co-opt religious scholars and the weakness of constituencies to challenge those arrangements. Over time, rulers in Islamic states found it beneficial to form alliances with clerics to augment their power, just as Kuru argued. By enhancing the credibility of apostasy charges, rulers enhanced their capacity to control public discourse and tarnish the reputation of opponents. Nothing surprising here. As Gill and others have shown, throughout history, rulers have often employed religious levers for political control, even when relaxing religious restrictions would have brought economic benefits.

Kuran provides vivid elaboration on how social and political forces "routinized the apostasy charge" and made it a contentious and "potent weapon of social control."[68] Thus, when the state was empowered to enforce apostasy laws, it opened a Pandora's box. Rivals employed "opportunistic use of the apostasy charge" to settle scores. Sunni and Shia charged each other with apostasy. Blasphemy and heresy were subsumed into apostasy charges to demonize "rival religious camps." As Islamic empires encompassed increasingly diverse populations, apostasy charges were often employed against religious minorities. Apostasy charges also extended to independent thinkers, as prominent Islamic scholars urged the state to execute philosophers.[69]

Rulers themselves found the apostasy charge a convenient tool against opponents or dissidents, which Kuran sees as analogous to the Spanish Inquisition. "Just as inquisitors targeted ostensibly deviant Christians who threatened the Spanish Crown, Church authority, or simply social harmony, so Ottoman clerics were primarily concerned with Muslims who irritated the broader Ottoman establishment."[70]

As the state increasingly enforced intolerant forms of Islamic orthodoxy, huge numbers of Muslims perished for offending Orthodox Sunni sensibilities. Indeed, at the height of the Ottoman Empire in the sixteenth century, thousands of Muslims were executed for apostasy.[71] This atmosphere, understandably, stunted free inquiry, independent civil society, and commercial innovation at the very time that religiously tolerant European states, such as the Netherlands, capitalized on those traits. Commercial societies thrive in environments where ideas are shared and critiqued. By crushing religious choice, state laws against apostasy undermined the foundations for flourishing economic growth in the Middle East.

Kuran also elaborates on how the "uncompromising literalism" of Islamic schools of jurisprudence bled over into explicitly economic institutions, preventing them from adapting to changing conditions.[72] These economic institutions included an Islamic tax system that did not generate reliable funds or protect property rights, and a system of permanent endowments, waqfs, that kept these organizations politically powerless to adapt to new circumstances.

Consider, for example, the mandate for almsgiving, the Zakat, one of the five pillars of Islam. As a charitable responsibility for all believers, the Zakat not only served the needy but developed into a huge system of financing education and other public benefits for the Islamic community, often expected as an annual contribution based on wealth. As the state expanded, however, the Zakat became ineffective as a tax system. But because innovations in Islamic practice could be viewed as apostasy, reforms were stifled. Over time, a new form of private endowment, the waqf, made in perpetuity by wealthy donors, emerged as an alternative because it avoided charges of sacrilege. The system of waqfs generated enormous sums to finance education and other public benefits. But waqf trusts, mandated to serve designated purposes in perpetuity, could not be altered to suit changing needs. Indeed, Islamic courts enforced original charters and denied waqf the flexibility to respond to the evolving needs of beneficiaries. Even with vastly different circumstances, caretakers were forced to blindly follow original instructions. Educational systems funded by waqfs, for example, often kept curricula fixed, the only safe route when innovators could be charged with apostasy.[73]

As Kuran shows, the waqf structure inhibited Islamic nations from establishing the legal infrastructure for modern corporations and nongovernmental organizations, which in the West spurred economic innovations and civil society activity. Under the strictures of Islamic law, however, waqfs were weak civil society actors, incapable of challenging an overweening state.[74] In contrast, during the Renaissance, the West saw the emergence of independent universities, cities, guilds, and religious orders, which asserted their associational rights against the state.

In sum, restrictions on religious choice in Islamic law, which emerged centuries after the founding, also served to freeze in place economic and educational institutions, preventing them from adapting to changing conditions or global competition.[75]

As an economist, Kuran is not content with developing theories that rely on detailed historical corroboration; he also seeks to *measure* how the ban on religious choice precisely affected economic fortunes. To attain such statistical confirmation, Kuran and his co-author Jared Rubin probe the empirical impact of Islamic law on prosaic economic phenomena, such as credit markets and business contracts. The result is one of the most stunning empirical findings of the new research on religious freedom and economics.[76]

Kuran first provides a bit of historical background. Once apostasy and blasphemy laws were codified by the ulema-state alliance, Muslims lacked the choice-of-law granted to Christians and Jews from the early years of Islam (as religious minorities in Islamic societies were often allowed to operate their own courts for family and contract law). Thus, a Christian or Jew was free to do business under Islamic or non-Islamic law. By contrast, a

Muslim was required to do business under Islamic rules, because turning to non-Muslim courts amounted to apostasy, which was punishable by death.

Here is the rub. Muslims enjoyed preferential treatment in Islamic courts, which, over time, produced perverse outcomes. Because Muslim borrowers could more easily break contracts, creditors did what they always do with higher risk clients: *charged them higher interest rates.* Jewish or Christian businessmen, because they could not as easily break contracts, were seen as more trustworthy and thus were charged lower interest.

Muslim business owners, therefore, paid a real cost for the ban on choice in religion. To measure this cost, Kuran and Rubin discovered and analyzed a massive data source from the meticulous records of Ottoman courts. This entailed all the contracts recorded in Istanbul's leading Islamic courts governing the private credit market between 1602 and 1799, nearly 200 years. The procedures of these courts were openly rigged against non-Muslims; for instance, whereas Muslims could testify against anyone, non-Muslims could not testify against a Muslim. Because the law was markedly biased in favor of Muslims, Muslim borrowers paid a surcharge for capital. That is because Muslim borrowers posed a greater risk to lenders who had limited means of punishing them if they failed to pay. Even Muslim lenders charged higher interest to fellow Muslims than they did to Christians and Jews. Critically, individual Muslim borrowers could not avoid the surcharge by agreeing to have disputes settled outside the Islamic court system (as that would be judged apostasy).

This handicap put Muslim merchants at a disadvantage vis-à-vis their local Christian and Jewish counterparts. Higher credit costs rendered them uncompetitive in the key economic sectors of the new economy that began forming in the industrial era. Unable to raise the capital necessary to compete in mass production, mass communications, or mass transportation, Muslim businesses lagged behind others. The divergence of Muslim economic fortunes from those of non-Muslims set the stage for intercommunal tensions that have led, in stages, to the departure of most non-Muslims from the Muslim-governed countries of the Middle East.

As Kuran and Rubin show, this perverse outcome bled over into other business relationships throughout the Middle East, undermining the fundamentals of a modern economy—property rights, business trust, legally protected contracts, and entrepreneurial risk taking.[77]

Here, we can see the interaction between humanitarian concerns and good business practices. Human rights groups and religious advocates document the enormous abuses of apostasy and blasphemy laws around the world.[78] Kuran and Rubin, on the other hand, documented their profound and enduring economic price.

RELIGIOUS ECONOMIC ACTIVITIES AND CONTRIBUTIONS TO FLOURISHING COMMUNITIES

The most direct relationship between religious freedom and economic flourishing is the fact that religious activity *is* economic activity. Think for a moment about the vast number of houses of worship that are constructed and maintained by religious communities and the vast number of employees who work in religious ministries—such as clerics, youth directors, teachers, secretaries, and janitors. Think also of the huge number of people working for religious charities, schools, colleges, youth programs, hospitals, and other religious organizations. Religious activity constitutes a substantial economic engine, particularly in local communities where religion is independent of the state and not subsidized or restricted by government.

We might use the analogy of healthy religious competition in a voluntary environment to a free market in economics, as opposed to a command economy of religion, where states either subsidize or restrict religious activity. That lack of freedom leads to less economic activity by religious organizations and less economic flourishing. When people must own and operate their houses of worship and other religious institutions, what they invest in those organizations constitutes a real measurement of the value they place in religion for their lives. As we learn in introductory textbooks, economics focuses on how *value* is accorded in the economic marketplace, based on what people are willing to pay for certain goods and services. Where religion is free and independent of the state, we have a good measure of how profoundly people value religion by the billions of dollars (in the United States, for example) that they contribute freely to houses of worship and other religious institutions because they are willing to pay for them through their voluntary contributions.

Here, again, we benefit from sophisticated scholarship that measures this economic contribution. In a landmark study, Brian Grim and Melissa Grim measured the tangible economic contributions of religion to American society. Their estimate of the annual contributions of religion in the United States was $378 billion in 2016. This figure consisted of concrete data: the annual income of religious congregations, annual tuition payments to religious schools and colleges, and annual operating revenues of faith-based charities, hospitals, and the like.[79] This is a conservative estimate because it does not measure the in-kind contributions of congregations to flourishing community life, the enormous voluntary investment in uplift for the poor, or the cultivation of pro-social and moral behavior that leads individuals to be more productive members of society. Reasonable estimates of this dimension push the total religious contribution to nearly $419 billion annually.[80] Let us elaborate.

A unique benefit of religious activity as economic activity is that it predominantly takes place at the local level. Whether in churches, synagogues, mosques, temples, cathedrals, or gurdwaras, religious activity is decentralized. Unlike the consolidation that has occurred in many sectors of the economy, which leaves urban neighborhoods and rural communities economically hollowed out, religious investment continues to ripple in local economies. Religious activity is intensely local and thus is an investment in local economies. If we think about houses of worship alone—consider all the local construction workers needed to build and repair them, the local venders who provide goods and services, and all the wages paid to employees who live locally and spend locally—we gain a sense of what economists term the "multiplier effect" of local religious activity for local economies.

A singular contribution of religious freedom to economic flourishing is that houses of worship (religious buildings and programs) become resources for local communities. In the United States especially but also in many other parts of the world, religious communities provide, often free of charge, the use of their buildings to community groups for a host of beneficial services. Often, this entails direct uplift to the most vulnerable members of society. In a non-bureaucratic and humane way, congregations provide rent assistance to the poor, sponsor soup kitchens and food banks, host literacy programs, provide language classes for immigrants, and offer tutoring for school students. They also provide or contract with governments to run day care centers and health clinics, delinquency prevention after-school programs, drug and alcohol treatment initiatives, support for people living with HIV-AIDS, educational and job training for adults, prisoner reentry programs, refugee resettlement, and the like. As Grim and Grim observe, this collective effort contributes tangibly to more productive citizens and healthier communities.[81] We see this not only in the United States, with its vibrancy of religious congregations and volunteer contributions, but also elsewhere in the world. In parts of Africa, for example, religious congregations often supply much of the education and health care services that weak governments are unable to provide.[82]

Scholars have coined the term "halo effect" to capture the healthy ripple effect of independent religious congregations in urban communities. In addition to providing a setting for education, health care, childcare, and job training, as noted above, local houses of worship provide islands of stability, repose, beauty, and green space in otherwise bereft inner cities. They host weddings, music, lectures, social clubs, art, and other forms of vibrant social activity. The halo effect of this contribution is substantial.[83]

These numerous contributions of religion to flourishing communities happen especially under conditions of freedom and independence from the state. Where religious institutions are privileged by the state or subsidized by the government, they do not have the same incentives to provide voluntary services. Where they are restricted, discriminated against, or harassed, they do not have the capacity or freedom to supply these services and prosocial community investments. Where they are co-opted by the state, they cease to function as independent local community groups.

RELIGION, RELIGIOUS FREEDOM, AND BROADER HUMAN FLOURISHING

The halo effect hints at potential wider contributions of religion to vibrant economic and social life. Tyler VanderWeele, director of Harvard University's Human Flourishing Project, notes that a voluminous body of research indicates that "religious community contributes profoundly to numerous aspects of human flourishing." He summarizes that scholarship in this way:

> Large well-designed longitudinal research studies have indicated that religious service attendance is associated with greater longevity, less depression, less suicide, less smoking, less substance abuse, better cancer and cardiovascular disease survival, less divorce, greater social support, greater meaning and purpose in life, greater life satisfaction, more charitable giving, less crime, more volunteering, more prosocial behavior, and greater civic engagement.[84]

While much of this research focuses on the United States and some western European nations, scholarship is expanding internationally.[85] Many of these attributes contribute to equitable economic growth, but they also serve as important indicators of broader human flourishing. Let us explore some of them.

As we have seen, religious communities contribute to social capital, the norms and networks of reciprocity and trust that make societies function and serve as lubricants to healthy economic enterprises. As Robert Putnam documented, in the United States, fully half of the social capital is generated by religious communities, including half of all donations to nonprofit organizations and half of all volunteering in local civic groups.[86] Broader research documents how faith communities generate valuable social trust that enable even strangers to cooperate.[87]

Another robust line of scholarship documents how religious observance contributes to pro-social behavior. Extensive empirical research shows that religious observance produces less crime, teenage delinquency, and drug abuse.[88] Prisoners who complete a spiritually-based rehabilitation program while incarcerated have lower levels of recidivism, particularly when they are incorporated into a faith community after leaving jail.[89]

Religious observance also contributes to physical and mental health. Surveys also show that religious practitioners experience lower rates of dementia and depression.[90] Religious practice and belief tend to reduce hypertension, bolster the immune system, and limit the likelihood of contracting some cancers and Alzheimer's disease.[91] A Harvard longitudinal study found that regular worship attendance reduces mortality between 20 and 30 percent over a fifteen-year period, while simultaneously producing a wide array of other positive health impacts. As the researchers observed, if a single elixir that produces such profound results existed, people would rightly clamor to receive it.[92] Regular church attendance is even associated with higher levels of reading and support for high culture.[93]

All these things—better physical and mental health, lower crime rates, and appreciation for intellectual pursuits—are widely recognized to have positive effects on economic productivity and civic participation. Society, in general (including the nonreligious), benefits from a healthier, happier, more trustworthy, and better-informed public.

Finally, because many persons value religion in and of itself, religious liberty facilitates the satisfaction of preferences akin to, though not necessarily measurable by, economic analysis. As Anthony Gill and Timothy Shah have written, "to the extent that increased religious activity is what people desire, religious freedom contributes directly to the overall economic well-being and flourishing of a society—on a broad understanding of economic well-being."[94]

This broader idea of "human flourishing" can be captured by global surveys of self-reported happiness and satisfaction. Sophisticated cross-national studies show that religious liberty produces measurable increases in such self-reported happiness. One measure is the U.N. World Happiness Report,[95] which presents diverse measures of human happiness for every country on Earth. As Gill and Shah show, the highest levels of citizen happiness are overwhelmingly in those nations that respect religious liberty.[96]

The key element of the World Happiness Report is the Gallup World Survey, which reports on self-reported life evaluations from nationally representative surveys conducted in 99 percent of the countries on Earth, using comparable metrics. Respondents report on their life satisfaction and expected future life satisfaction in five years, both on a ten-point scale. Drawing upon that Gallup measure, a major study analyzed the statistical links between life satisfaction and religious liberty for 150 countries, controlling for other variables. The findings were stunning. For example, "the countries that experienced the greatest growth in religious liberty between 2006 and 2018 also experienced the greatest growth in human flourishing." Moreover, statistical tests were robust. An increase in religious liberty produced a correspondingly measurable increase in both self-reported life satisfaction and expected future life satisfaction. Crucially, these improvements were concentrated among religious minorities, who tend to suffer disproportionate discrimination and persecution, confirming that something real is happening here. Religious minorities who experience greater freedom of religion report greater levels of life satisfaction.[97]

The ability to improve human well-being (flourishing) by allowing greater freedom of choice is bolstered by another growing field of study. According to the "capabilities approach" to human development promoted by Amartya Sen, Martha Nussbaum, and Sabina Alkire, the expanding capability of humans to exercise choice and freedom—including religious matters—enhances human development and flourishing intrinsically.[98] Promoting religious liberty, therefore, enhances this kind of human development and societal flourishing.

A much larger research enterprise is now underway to develop and measure a broader index of human flourishing, which will provide new avenues for exploring the relationship between religion, religious freedom, and thriving peoples. Sponsored by a consortium of academic and survey institutes, The Global Flourishing Study is a five-year panel survey of over 200,000 participants in 22 geographically and culturally diverse countries. It expands upon the World Happiness Survey by developing a broader measure of human flourishing and tracking it over time with the same respondents. It conceptualizes human flourishing as "a state of complete physical, social, emotional, cognitive, volitional, and spiritual wellbeing." It includes six dimensions: Happiness and Life Satisfaction, Mental and Physical Health, Meaning and Purpose, Character and Virtue, Close Social Relationships, and Financial and Material Stability.[99]

Not surprisingly, the first wave of the study shows that financial/material security is a strong contributor to flourishing, though with great variability among different countries. One of the most intriguing findings concerns the relationship between religious service attendance and overall flourishing. It is generally and strongly positive, but with some exceptions. Among those exceptions are countries that restrict religious freedom, experience social hostilities, or favor the dominant religion.[100]

This latter finding suggests a caveat about the conditions under which religion plays the positive roles described in this section. We know that overt state sponsorship or government repression undercuts religion's positive contributions, thus supporting the thesis that religious freedom fuels flourishing economic and social life. But another peril is politicization of religion—the fusion of faith with tribes, parties, or ideological movements, or what scholars describe as religious nationalism. Religious nationalists seek state privileges for the majority faith, often by tying it to national identity. To the extent they gain such privileges, religious freedom is reduced for religious minorities, nonbelievers, or dissenters from the ideological program of the nationalists. No surprise here, as state privilege violates the very definition of religious freedom. But even if they are not successful, politicized religious nationalists undercut the pro-social tendencies of religious communities by introducing divisive religious conflict into civil society. In recent times, we have witnessed a huge volume of scholarship and commentary about the rise of Christian Nationalism in the United States, particularly with the infusion (or co-optation) of white evangelicals into Donald Trump's MAGA movement.[101] But as Nilay Saiya documents, Christian nationalism is a global phenomenon.[102] Moreover, he shows that religious nationalist movements, whether Christian, Muslim, Buddhist, Hindu, or Jewish, tend to undercut democracy and increase violence, which saps economic performance.[103] We will explore the implications of this profound finding in later chapters and the conclusion.

WHAT ABOUT CHINA?

In the world today, we see exceptions to the general patterns reported in this chapter. India's robust growth, for example, despite rising religious restrictions, requires further exploration. A huge and growing population is a key economic engine. But perhaps regional differences in restrictions, which vary widely, might help explain why a religiously restrictive environment does not do more economic harm.

Of all the countries on Earth, however, China clearly defies many of the propositions presented in this book, especially on economics. While Russia, Iran, North Korea, and other nations with repressive religious environments conform to our theory—that they will be economic laggards, not to mention oppressive and violent—China seems exceptional, an extremely autocratic regime with a booming economic engine to rival the United States.

Recent research and trends, however, suggest that China's increasing repression of religion under Xi Jinping is eroding the foundations of its economic engine. Indeed, in the wake of the COVID-19 lockdown, China's economic performance continued to lag on several fronts.[104]

One strand of research suggests that the Chinese economy benefited enormously from the relaxation of religious repression after Mao's death and the greater degree of de facto religious freedom provided by Deng Xiaoping and his successors (before Xi Jinping).[105] In other words, China partly deregulated its religious sector at the same time it began deregulating its economy, sometimes officially but sometimes in a relaxed administration of religious laws, which varied from region to region.

This benefited the Chinese economy in several ways. The greater spiritual freedom enjoyed by Chinese entrepreneurs and employees boosted morale, creativity, and productivity, as expected from previous research. It helped unleash the industrious culture of the Chinese population.[106]

China's economy also benefited from religious diversity. As previously documented, companies and nations benefit economically from the religious diversity that freedom nurtures. But some nations enjoy greater innate religious diversity, assuming favorable government policies allow that diversity to blossom and function. As Brian Grim shows, in the post-Mao era, China capitalized on its innate diversity to become one of the world's most religiously diverse societies, unintentionally enjoying the benefits of global religious networks and relationships. By 2015, China was "home to the world's largest Buddhist population, largest folk religionist population, largest Taoist population, seventh largest Christian population, and seventeenth largest Muslim population."[107] Rather than continue to capitalize on this phenomenon, however, the Xi regime launched a repressive campaign against religion, including a genocidal effort to eradicate Uyghur culture.[108] The stalling of the Chinese economic engine in the 2020s, even after the end of the COVID-19 lockdowns, indicates a real cost of this repression.[109]

One of the most surprising benefits of the era of relative religious freedom in China entailed the unique contribution of Christianity to the modern Chinese economic engine, as documented by Chinese scholars. Understanding this contribution requires some background. In the post-Mao era, Christianity grew dramatically, especially among unregistered (or "house church") Protestants. Indeed, by 2016, the annual growth rates of Christianity led to projections that it would become the most popular faith in China in the coming decades, perhaps even reaching half of the

Chinese population by 2050.[110] Why was it taking off? It seemed to provide a deeper sense of meaning, purpose, and moral restraint than the hyper-commercialism and consumerism that replaced Marxist ideology. And because the Maoist era assaulted and undermined Confucian culture, Christianity seemed to provide a more tangible, modern alternative.[111]

Christianity's contribution to the Chinese economy is multifaceted. Capitalizing on international Christian networks, Chinese entrepreneurs played a prominent role in propelling booming growth, especially in enterprise zones where they enjoyed greater latitude to operate. Nanlai Cao documented how Christian entrepreneurs transformed Wenzhou "from an impoverished rural town to a dynamic regional center of global capitalism."[112]

One of the great assets enjoyed by Christian entrepreneurs is their reputation for ethical behavior and trustworthiness. As China rapidly plunged into the profit-driven fever of capitalism, corruption and unethical practices became major concerns, both for Chinese leaders and among the general public. In this environment, Christian entrepreneurs, particularly Protestants, earned reputations for trustworthiness and integrity, which enabled them to play a disproportionate role in building loyalty among employees and social trust among business partners, suppliers, and customers. To put it another way, Christian business leaders cultivated beneficial social capital—the norms and networks of reciprocity and trust that lubricate efficient operations of modern enterprise.[113]

An astute reader might notice that much of the research just presented on Christianity and the Chinese economy was led by sociologists. What do economists have to say? As it happens, they provide remarkable verification and corroboration. Given the innate skepticism of most Western economists to religious explanations for economic outcomes, it is ironic that Chinese economists, operating in an officially atheist regime, appear to have no such hesitation. Two economists from China's top university programs conducted a sophisticated econometric analysis of the role of religious beliefs on economic growth, using provincial-level data to capitalize on the wide variation that exists across the sprawling country. They concluded that Christianity and Christian institutions produced a significant positive impact on economic growth in China. Employing a variety of measures and approaches, their findings were "consistent among different estimators and robust with stability over time."[114]

What accounts for this finding? Wang and Lin attribute certain Christian teachings and ethics as beneficial to the development of a healthy market economy. For example, China's rapid plunge into capitalist economics resulted in speculative get-rich-quick schemes and risky investment behavior. On the other hand, Christian ethics promoted prudent investment behavior "rather than speculation." Christian morality also fostered honest comportment in business practices, which counteracted rampant and inefficient corruption. Christian teachings about "loving one's neighbor" supported the "all round development" of human beings and people-oriented economic development policies. Christian leaders and institutions also promoted healthy free markets by defending private property rights and economic freedom. While this economic freedom enabled entrepreneurs to generate wealth for themselves, the Christian ethic also enforced a sense of relevant obligations to others and the wider society, even a view that one should use wealth to the glory of God and the benefit of others. This benevolent impulse promoted the development of human capital, a central component of economic flourishing.[115] In sum, Christianity in China, while a relatively small portion of the population, contributed measurably to China's economic miracle.[116]

More broadly, we know that religion, religious diversity, and relative religious freedom helped fuel economic growth in China. This pattern led Brian Grim to conclude in 2015 that further deregulation of religion would help sustain the Chinese economic engine, a recommendation echoed by a prominent Chinese religious scholar.[117] But that was the road not taken by the regime, as it launched a massive crackdown on religion from 2018 onward. According to Pew, China's government restrictions on religion rose to the highest in the world, to the long-term detriment of China's economy and society.[118]

There is a final link between the status of religious freedom and the economy in China. In January of 2023, on the eve of the Chinese New Year, a news story rocked the image of China's economic colossus: China reported fewer births than deaths in 2022, marking an inexorable demographic trend of declining population. With a growing elderly cohort and shrinking youth cohort, China will face a shortage of workers to support its aging population, a huge challenge to sustaining its exceptional economic growth and societal stability. This report coincided with data showing that the Chinese economy had its worst annual performance since 1976.[119]

There is a religious dimension to this. As Pew research shows, religious people tend to have far more children than secular people, which explains why many secular Europeans have children below replacement levels, with only immigration sustaining population levels in some societies.[120] If China wanted to sustain healthy population growth, it would have allowed the natural growth of religion, which would have resulted in a dramatic expansion of its dynamic Christian population.[121] Instead, Xi Jinping launched a severity of religious repression not seen since the Maoist era, including the deployment of a massive surveillance infrastructure against religious communities. By stemming the natural growth of religion, particularly of Christianity, the regime undercut the potential religious motivation for families to have more children and cultivate healthy communities. Once the regime recognized its looming demographic challenge and relaxed its one-child policy, its more secularized population did not respond. By impeding religious aspirations and growth, the regime may have cut itself off from the only potential amelioration of its long-term demographic time bomb.

CHAPTER FOUR

PATH TO EMPOWERMENT

Uplifting Vulnerable Communities

A successful democracy and flourishing society must protect the civil and economic rights of all, especially women, ethnic and religious minorities, the poor, the disabled, and other vulnerable communities. Promoting religious liberty helps accomplish this. This assertion may appear paradoxical given that religion is often portrayed as innately patriarchal and repressive of nonconforming beliefs, but the protection of religious minorities to believe and organize as they best see fit enhances the ability of other communities to do the same. The emphasis here is not defending religion per se, but *religious freedom*—the right to enter *and exit* a confession of one's own choosing. A lack of organizational exit rights (e.g., anti-apostasy and anti-conversion laws) traps individuals within oppressive institutions, including patriarchal or exclusionary religious structures. Freedom of association tied to exit rights reduces the power such institutions have over the downtrodden. Such rights promote greater agency amongst the historically weak in society, allowing them to organize to defend their interests and achieve their full potential. The ability to exercise agency in matters of ultimate (transcendent) concern serves to build confidence and efficacy in other arenas of life.

Mounting empirical research suggests that violations of religious freedom, both by governments and powerful social actors, tend to reinforce oppressive structures that marginalize impoverished people, exploited women, migrants, ethnic and religious minorities, sexual minorities, and outcasts.

On the other hand, protections of religious freedom—particularly the right to practice, interpret, criticize, or change one's faith—act as powerful engines of empowerment and integration of otherwise marginalized people. Repression of this religious agency, moreover, produces cycles of persecution, societal instability, and violence that redound disproportionately on fragile economic and social institutions of integration. Sadly, in many places around the world, we see massive repression of this empowering religious agency. Indeed, religious discrimination serves as a major driver of marginalization and repression in numerous societies.

This chapter features the role of *religious agency* as a vital dimension of religious freedom. Agency represents the active dimension of religious freedom as defined in international law. Agency suggests the capacity to act on—or change—one's beliefs, commitments, relationships, and religious practices. This capacity helps explain the powerful impact of religious freedom on human development, good governance, women's empowerment, and integration of vulnerable minorities.

As in other chapters, I not only marshal empirical evidence for this theme but also illuminate the specific pathways through which religious freedom facilitates empowerment and uplift for the most vulnerable members of societies. Briefly described, those interrelated pathways include:

- *Opening civic space.* Religious liberty embraces and protects religious pluralism, which, in turn, allows different groups in society to carve out social space for themselves and make beneficial societal contributions. Allowing religious communities to organize themselves acts as a check on state power and opens civic space for other marginalized communities. Emergent civil society, as history shows, opens a potential door to full citizenship for those treated as second-class or stateless on account of their religion, ethnicity, caste, or gender. On the other hand, when a society's dominant religion works with the state to restrict the rights of religious minorities, that prevents the opening of civic space and cements the marginal status of all sorts of marginalized people, whether self-consciously religious or not.
- *Building social capital.* A vibrant civil society of diverse and independent religious communities facilitates the building of social capital. As popularized by Robert Putnam, social capital constitutes "the norms

and networks of reciprocity and trust" that enable people to engage in cooperative and mutually beneficial enterprises.[1] Social capital is generated through relationships of voluntary engagement, which flow naturally from self-organizing religious communities independent of state power. A voluminous literature documents how the trust generated through social capital acts as a lubricant for all sorts of cooperative ventures and empowers average people with the confidence and capacity to shape their collective lives. A crucial "hidden dimension" of social capital is spiritual capital.[2] Spiritual commitments—transcendent obligations—can inspire people to forgo short-term pleasure for long-term gain, supply the motivation to sacrifice for the common good, and buoy generosity and charity.

- *Fostering healthy competition.* As in classical economics, religious monopolies or oligopolies often serve the spiritual needs of people poorly. But even more pertinent to our purposes, such state-backed religions tend to cement social hierarchies. When religious authorities must compete for adherents, they tend to better serve both the spiritual and temporal needs of their flocks. As we will see, such competition propels wider social and political uplift, empowering the poor and women in developing societies and providing leverage to other marginalized groups.
- *Unleashing powerful agency.* Spiritual uplift, as I will show, leads to empowerment in other sectors. We see this agency in peasant social movements for justice and poor women's emancipation from stultifying economic and social strictures.

WHY RELIGIOUS AGENCY MATTERS

Religion will powerfully anchor forms of identity, meaning, community, and purpose for an increasing majority of the global population well into the future. This is fateful for religious and ethnic minorities, but especially for poor women, the doubly marginalized. Given that these women in developing societies often disproportionately belong to religious communities and adhere to faith commitments, guaranteeing or expanding their agency in religion is pivotal to their broader integration.

Solutions to exclusion and marginalization, therefore, cannot rely on the secular assumptions of economic factors, but must flow from a proper "anthropological" framework. As Timothy Shah documents, anthropological (and psychological) research suggests "that the capacity for religious belief is natural; that belief appears early and easily in the lives of individuals; that it appeared full-blown at the dawn of human civilization; and that the suppression of religious belief, expression, and practice runs against the grain of human nature and experience."[3] Repression of what people experience as fundamental to their human dignity fuels division, destabilizes societies, and undermines integration.

International law suggests the importance of religious agency. Recall Article 18 of the *Universal Declaration of Human Rights*, adopted by the United Nations in 1948, which reads as follows:

> Everyone has the right to freedom of thought, conscience, and religion. This right includes freedom to change his religion or belief, and freedom, either alone or in community with others and in public or private, to manifest his religion or belief in teaching, practice, worship, and observance.

Notice the emphasis on active agency in the definition, with active verbs such as change and manifest. Similar language is found in the *International Covenant on Civil and Political Rights*, the *Helsinki Accords*, the *Declaration on the Elimination of All Forms of Intolerance and Discrimination Based on Religion or Belief*, and the *European Convention for the Protection of Human Rights and Fundamental Freedoms.*

As with the foundational Vatican II proclamation on religious freedom, *Dignitatis Humanae*, the *Universal Declaration* anchors religious agency in *human dignity* and its correlates. Indeed, the preface to the *Declaration* roots all rights in the "inherent dignity" and "worth of the human person," and in the "equal and inalienable rights of all members of the human family" who are "endowed with reason and conscience." Article 18 also emphasizes the relational aspect of human life, that people must be free "in community with others" to manifest their faith or beliefs. *Dignity, equal worth, reason, conscience, and community*—these traits of common humanity provide the clues to why religious freedom can powerfully serve to uplift the poor and other marginalized people.

Religious agency also matters because it is massively denied. As noted in Chapter 1, Pew Global Measures reports that up to 85 percent of the world's population lives amidst high restrictions on their religious practice, either by repressive government actions or hostile social agents.[4] Companion global data from the Religion and State (RAS) Project documents an astonishing array of repressive government practices against religion, especially targeting religious and ethnic minorities who are uniquely vulnerable to marginalization.[5] If the default condition of religion is diversity, and if freedom to exercise one's transcendent duties—to seek truth about ultimate questions and act on them—is a near universal aspiration, then government or social repression will inevitably cause harm to societies, governance, and economics. We see this in the devastating marginalization of Baha'is in Iran, where theocratic leaders treat them as a contagion to be eradicated. We see it in the efforts of Hindu nationalists in India to marginalize non-Hindu minorities. We see it in the brutal cleansing of Rohingya Muslims from Myanmar. We see it in the Chinese government's brutal and high-tech campaign to eradicate Uyghur Muslim culture. We see it in the destructive reign of Vladimir Putin, whose first steps to autocracy in Russia entailed backing the Orthodox monopoly and clamping down on religious minorities. The list goes on. Indeed, the Pew Research Center finds that government restrictions on religion are strongly related to social hostilities and violent religious extremism. It is thus unlikely that societies can erect structures and build norms of inclusion and uplift if wracked by such forces.

With this as a backdrop, let us turn to specific examples of how religious liberty and the agency it provides serve to uplift and empower.

RELIGIOUS AGENCY AND WOMEN'S EMPOWERMENT

As we see in the "Contemporary Economic Research" section of Chapter 3, a growing literature documents how religious freedom contributes to sustainable and inclusive development in at least seven ways.[6] Religious agency lies at the center of these mechanisms.

The role of religious agency—as illustrated by Robert Woodberry's landmark research on the impact of Protestant missionary activity in fueling democratization—also shows up in economic uplift. Missionary initiatives that promoted literacy (especially for girls), overall human development, and anti-corruption campaigns contributed to the rule of law and protection of indigenous property rights in developing nations. All these factors support long-term economic growth. Astonishingly, Woodberry found that conversionary Protestant activity prior to 1960 still had a strong positive association with national income levels 75 years later.[7]

These findings dovetail with a special concern of development economists: the status and uplift of women, whose repression operates as a drag on sustainable economic growth. Grim and Finke's analysis of global data reveals a strong statistical relationship between religious freedom and women's empowerment, as illustrated in figure 2.1 in chapter 2. This finding supports their broader theory that protecting religious rights contributes to peaceful, flourishing societies and the integration of marginalized people.[8] Moreover, measures of the UN Human Development Report's *Gender Inequality Index* show a direct correlation between religious tolerance and gender equality.[9]

The obverse also emerges robustly from the data. As Brian Grim and Jo-Ann Lyon document, "The denial of religious freedom contributes to gender inequality throughout the world."[10] Higher government and social restrictions on religion, as they document, are strongly associated with gender inequality. Indeed, the nations with the highest religious restrictions also show the highest levels of such inequality. In other words, women's status is lowest where restrictions on religious freedom are greatest.[11]

One cannot understate the potential significance of these findings. Global oppression of women not only represents a massive human rights violation, but it also serves as a key barrier to economic development and the eradication of extreme poverty. In their book, *Half the Sky: Turning Oppression into Opportunity for Women Worldwide*, Nicholas Kristof and Sheryl WuDunn catalogue the devastating oppression of women and girls in the developing world and show how female empowerment will unleash economic progress and uplift for the poor.[12]

To be sure, no one contends that extending religious rights is more important than other economic, social, and educational levers of women's empowerment. But as we will see, fascinating new research reveals how restrictive government religious policies are intimately linked with structures that constrict opportunities for women. Expanding religious choices, on the other hand, produces tangible improvement in women's status.

Of all the relationships developed by scholars, this seems the most paradoxical or counterintuitive because religion itself is often seen as a major barrier to gender parity. How could religious freedom enhance women's status when religion justifies, if not propels, much of the institutionalized discrimination against women around the world today? Why would one want to empower the very patriarchal institutions that repress women and constrict girls' horizons?

These questions reflect a profound misunderstanding about what religious freedom is and is not. Protection of religious rights signifies the opposite of favoring or empowering a dominant faith. Full religious freedom entails the right to criticize or leave one's inherited religion. As Brian Grim, Rebecca Shah, and others have shown, extending these options of "exit and voice" empowers women in traditional societies. This crucial dynamic is particularly potent for devout women in highly religious societies.

The freedom and agency to criticize, reform, reinterpret, or change one's religion; the right to form new religious associations for mutual support; and the ability to teach new ideas about faith are the dimensions of religious freedom that facilitate women's participation in civil society, expand girls' educational opportunities, and spur female economic enterprise. In regimes of general religious freedom, no one sect can monopolize discourse, making it harder to enforce a single anti-female narrative or sustain hierarchies detrimental to women's advancement. Moreover, greater agency in religious matters can powerfully translate into other social and economic initiatives. Religious rights build upon and buoy the rights to speech, assembly, and property ownership so essential to the social and economic advancement of the marginalized.

On the other hand, various forms of government and social restrictions on religion tend to cement oppressive structures against women. The collusion of states with dominant religions—a remarkably common practice—prevents women from leaving repressive situations, narrows their societal options, and constricts their economic participation. This is obvious with theocratic nations like Saudi Arabia. But even in democratic states, such as India, state laws that favor the dominant religion tend to freeze low-status women in rigid caste structures, as research by Rebecca Shah shows.[13]

As we would expect from Grim and Finke's *religious violence cycle*, government restrictions on religion also invite social hostilities against vulnerable people, often under the guise of protecting traditional culture.[14]

When dominant social groups can act with impunity against religious minorities or dissenters, mob violence and intimidation fall disproportionately on women, the doubly marginalized.

The rise of extremist religious ideologies represents the most dramatic example of this dynamic and illuminates how violations of religious freedom disproportionately redound against women and girls. Indeed, it is the twin rejection of religious pluralism and women's agency that helps define jihadist ideology. Not surprisingly, the prime victims of such extremist groups as ISIS, Boko Haram, and the Taliban are religious minorities, women, and girls. Indeed, pushing back on women's rights is a key component of their deadly strategy. Under the sway of their theocratic ideology, we see dramatic reversals in women's status and a descent into grotesque forms of sexual violence, trafficking, and bondage.

In sum, places with the greatest measurable religious freedom also demonstrate the greatest empowerment and participation by women in all sectors of society. Nations with the highest government and social restrictions on religion show the opposite.

For those who question whether these correlations really imply causality, path-breaking research by Rebecca Shah and others uncovers some of the most intriguing causal mechanisms and pathways that operate with religious agency. The capacity to exercise religious voice, choice, and exit propels agency in other dimensions of social and economic life. Spiritual capital and supportive religious networks work to empower marginalized women.

A former World Bank development economist, Rebecca Shah, anchors her work in behavioral economics on the importance of such attributes as dignity, agency, hope for the future, and self-control in the uplift of the impoverished. Amartya Sen demonstrates, for example, that poverty alleviation hinges not only on material factors but also on the capacities of the poor to make choices and the freedom to act on what they value.[15] To a surprising extent, the poor not only value material assets or education, but relationships with family and community, growth in their faith, and harmony with the transcendent.[16] These values or aspirations can facilitate the social capital that we know facilitates cooperative enterprises, access to credit markets, and economic development. But Shah and others also point to the ways that religious participation also generates *spiritual capital,* which can buoy uplift and the broader inclusion of the poor and marginalized. As Shah observes, spiritual capital is "generated through attitudes and perceptions of people toward themselves," particularly through a sense of agency before God, "to improve their lives, the lives of their families and the lives of the wider community."[17] To the extent that spiritual awakening can promote a positive, even transcendent, sense of oneself and one's agency, it provides a source of hope and future-orientation essential to take advantage of development initiatives, such as microloans, training programs, craft guilds, and the like.

Freedom to practice one's faith, thus, can be central to economic development and inclusion because of the debilitating impact of extreme poverty. Caught in a vicious cycle of desperation and hopelessness, the poor often indulge in self-destructive activities or give up entirely. Religious agency, on the other hand, can supply a sense of hope, as well as cultivate attributes of thrift and planning essential to breaking free from the poverty cycle.

How do we know this? Shah and her research teams have followed the trajectories of thousands of poor women in Asia and Africa, with a special emphasis on India and now Sri Lanka. From this ongoing research, Shah concludes that spiritual capital is indeed a "fungible resource" that is "accumulated in the religious domain by specifically religious means, but which can be 'spent' or leveraged to advance non-religious domains like governance and the economy."[18] Surprisingly, Shah finds that the practice of religious tithing can not only help build social networks of mutual support but also help foster a culture of self-discipline and future orientation. She points to Muslim Dalit women, whose visits (and tiny contributions) to Sufi dargah shrines empower them with a sense of hope and agency. Crucial to this empowerment is the freedom to make one's religious decisions, which is vulnerable to theocratic pressures, whether from Islamist Sunni clerics or Hindu nationalists who reject such choices.[19]

To explore the causal pathways of exclusion and inclusion, Rebecca Shah focused her research on Dalit women involved in microenterprises. Indian Dalits comprise one of the largest discrete classes of people in the world subject to systematic exclusion, and Dalit women are doubly marginalized. The term Dalit literally means "broken" and is used to describe those traditionally regarded as untouchables or outcasts in the Hindu caste system. Referred to as "scheduled castes" by the Indian government, they comprise at least 200 million people (or over 16 percent of India), but Dalit advocates estimate a much higher figure.[20]

Given Dalit exclusion from broader Indian or Hindu society, religious switching for them can serve as a potent form of agency, and large numbers have become Buddhists, Muslims, or Christians. Quite by accident, Rebecca Shah's research on Dalit women unearthed a large sample of women who were converting from Hinduism to other faiths, particularly revivalist Christianity. This enabled her to conduct a fine-grained comparison of these women to their peers in the same slums, and thus to track the impact of religious choice on economic betterment.

The results were dramatic. The ability to *break free and break out* of cultural and legal straitjackets—to exercise religious choice and agency—spurred these women to take initiative in other aspects of their lives. They were more likely to take part in microenterprises and be successful in them, more likely to report domestic abuse, more likely to invest in their children's education, and more likely to save and eventually own their homes. Participation in face-to-face religious communities also gave them access to networks of mutual support and accountability that yielded significant economic and social benefits. Notably, Shah finds these impacts especially strong for Christian converts, whose identities are transformed by the Christian idea of their transcendent worth and dignity. As a deeply marginalized group, Dalits have even developed their own empowering theology by identifying Christ on the cross as literally one of them, a Dalit, a broken one.[21]

These findings suggest that the *nature* of religious belief, especially theologies of hope versus fatalism, could magnify the impact of religious agency on economic uplift and women's empowerment. This hypothesis is guiding different experimental research projects. One team, for example, conducted a spiritually based intervention with 600 indigenous women who were part of a faith-based microfinance program in Oaxaca, Mexico. Based on prior research showing that dimensions of hope facilitate transitions out of poverty, researchers randomly placed participants in control and intervention groups. The intervention group was engaged with a biblically based curriculum that emphasized hope and agency—having goals and aspirations, recognizing gifts and abilities, and conceptualizing pathways out of poverty. The study found that evangelical Protestant women already enjoyed higher levels of aspirations, agency, and optimism at baseline, but that the intervention significantly enhanced these attributes among Catholic women, narrowing their differences with their evangelical sisters.[22]

In turn, Rebecca Shah and her local collaborators have undertaken an even more ambitious project to test the impact of religiously based hope and agency on poverty alleviation. The study entails household surveys of thousands of persons in different sites in India and Sri Lanka, oversamples of Dalit and tribal women, and case studies of Dalit women entrepreneurs. Employing a rigorous methodology of quasi-experimental controls (places where conversion is allowed and where it is not), the study tracks the longitudinal impacts of religious conversion and other aspects of agency on poverty alleviation.[23]

This research shows that when marginalized persons exercise agency in religion, they tend to develop "deeply held and personally appropriated" beliefs and practices, as opposed to formal and routinized religion. These vibrant beliefs and practices produce positive social and economic outcomes.[24] Individuals who exercise choice in religion—who switch religious traditions—are more likely to own a business and less likely to get drunk, to smoke, or, for men, to abuse their wives.[25] Fascinatingly, persons with strong religious commitment and practices were more likely to have reasonably sound knowledge of interest rates on loans and act accordingly.[26] Greater religious participation also creates community networks that enable marginalized persons, such as Dalits, to break out of prescribed roles in stratified societies. Such community networks, in turn, provide social and economic support to help people weather disruptions, such as the shocks of COVID-19 lockdowns. Ironically, while Muslims and Christians reported receiving some community support during the pandemic, Hindus faced only locked temples. Because their temples receive state patronage, Hindus had not developed their own local community resources,[27] a vivid example of the "paradox of privilege" in action.[28]

Contrary to common expectations, respondents with higher reported levels of religious commitment and practice were more likely to be *tolerant* of people from other religious communities than those respondents with lower or routinized levels of religiosity. Part of this greater toleration flowed from the fact that significant numbers of respondents, especially women, have "multiple religious identities, beliefs, and practices" that they mix and match to suit their lives.[29] These collective findings suggest the intrinsic value of human choice and religious freedom in economic development and uplift for the poor.[30]

The striking findings of this new line of research also shed light on previous studies. Indeed, older studies gain new meaning and traction as they fit into new streams of research on the empowering role of choice and agency in religion. This is nicely illustrated by the 1995 inquiry into the impact of evangelical conversion on women in Colombia. Elizabeth Brusco sought to understand the rapid growth of evangelical (especially Pentecostal) churches in Latin America, and particularly their popularity among poor women. The catalyst for the burst of evangelical growth was a constitutional reform in 1991 in Colombia that separated church and state, ending the state Catholic monopoly. Brusco conducted an anthropological study of Pentecostal conversions in Colombia, driven primarily by women, and discovered how these conversions reattached men to the family, increased family income, and empowered women to take on new roles in society. In particular, she found that the ascetically demanding tenets of evangelical faith—against drinking, smoking, and extramarital sex—redirected male income back into the household and thus raised the standards of women and children. So dramatic was the impact of evangelical conversion that Brusco concluded that it represented a "strategic" women's movement. Contrary to the common view of "Christian fundamentalism" as antithetical to women's empowerment, Brusco documented how evangelical conversion challenged prevailing forms of gender subordination within the culture of machismo. It did so by serving the practical interests of women, especially mothers. While Brusco emphasized traits of Pentecostal culture, her research also supports the broader theory about how women's agency in religion is uniquely empowering.[31]

In summary, cutting-edge research on women's empowerment and faith underscores the value of religious freedom—understood as full equality before the law, the right of exit and voice, associational rights, and social dignity. Expanding religious agency cultivates moral and social capital, unleashes economic enterprise, and spurs the uplift of the poor in traditional societies. These empirical findings also call into question the fashionable valorization by some Western scholars of fixed indigenous religious identities, and the attendant criticism of conversion as a transitive act, rather than a potentially liberating one.

The broader significance of this line of research is in its documentation of the importance of recognizing religious choice and pluralism. Where states or societies restrict the right of religious change, they unintentionally undercut the kind of agency that choice can propel. In contrast, when poor and marginalized women can exercise their agency in religion—making their own religious choices, cultivating their own religious communities, reforming or challenging interpretations of their religion that oppress them, or changing their religion—this freedom unleashes their agency in broader economic and social realms of life.

RELIGIOUS COMPETITION, UPLIFT, AND EMPOWERMENT OF THE POOR

A growing body of research shows that religious competition in a society results in more religious vitality and better provision of religious goods. Just as businesses are more responsive to consumers when they must compete for loyalty, religious institutions and clerics better serve the spiritual and physical needs of their flock when they face competition for the faithful. On the other hand, religious monopolies and oligopolies become complacent and arrogant, resulting in poor service and restrictions on competitors.[32]

As we will see in this section, religious competition plays a uniquely powerful role in the empowerment of the poor, who appear to benefit disproportionately when religions must vie for their loyalty.

The landmark examination of the role of religious competition in uplift for the poor came out of Latin America. In *Rendering Unto Caesar: The Catholic Church and the State in Latin America*, Anthony Gill empirically documents how competition from Protestants sparked leaders of the Catholic Church in Latin America to mount unprecedented initiatives of solidarity and uplift for the poor.[33]

Gill concluded that religious liberty accounted for the differential rates of Protestants throughout Latin America, which, as he showed, provided the competition that led Catholic leaders to serve the poor more assiduously. In other words, in countries where competition for the faithful was the greatest, Catholic authorities responded with the most vibrant ministries for the poor and publicly challenged their exploitation. On the other hand, where competition was blocked by continued state patronage for Catholicism, church services for the poor were limited, and social justice voices were muted. Related research shows democracy also lagged in such countries. Daniel Philpott documents that where the Catholic Church enjoyed continued government patronage, those countries tended to be laggards in religious freedom and democracy.[34] Genuine religious freedom, which allows free people to change their faith, tends to promote a free marketplace in religion, where different religious communities and institutions must compete for the loyalty of the faithful.

This pathway of competition is illustrated in the previously cited research by Robert Woodberry on the role of conversionary missionaries in developing countries. While Woodberry primarily focused on the unique contributions of Protestant missionaries—owing to their emphasis on education and printing for biblical literacy—he also showed how Protestant successes spurred other religions to copy their initiatives. Religious competition, in other words, induced dominant religions (and others) to copy Protestant initiatives in education, health care, development assistance, and spiritual succor. Competition led all religious communities to better serve the needs of the poor.[35]

As elsewhere in this book, theories about the value of religious freedom, in this case competition, are corroborated by diverse and sophisticated empirical studies. Gill's theory about the powerful role of religious competition in Latin America, for example, was tested by Guillermo Trejo's later study of indigenous rebellion in Mexico.[36] Trejo was intrigued by the general question of "how the poor take charge of their destiny themselves and collectively defy authoritarian rulers."[37] In particular, he wanted to know how the poor and exploited peoples of Mexico, after centuries of repression and marginalization, suddenly mobilized and demanded their rights. Prior to his study, conventional scholarship attributed indigenous mobilization, like the Zapatista rebellion of the mid-1990s, to economic globalization or international advocacy of indigenous rights. On the other hand, Trejo found that religious competition enabled and propelled indigenous mobilization against oppression, just as Gill's theory suggested.

Trejo's study illustrates how innovative scholars blend sophisticated statistical methods, natural experiments, and on-the-ground observation to test theories with compelling findings. To explore the causes of indigenous mobilization in Mexico, Trejo assembled a massive database of thousands of acts of indigenous protest and rebellion from 1970 to 2000, which empowered the poor, earned greater autonomy for indigenous communities, and democratized the country.[38] This database enabled Trejo to correlate eruptions of protest with the transformation of the religious environment from a Catholic monopoly to a competitive market, in which Catholic authorities had to compete with Protestants for allegiance of the flock.

Trejo supplements his statistical analysis with qualitative field research to demonstrate exactly how the Catholic response to Protestant competition changed power structures in rural communities, empowered new indigenous leaders, and fostered organizational networks that spearheaded movements for land redistribution and indigenous rights.[39] Trejo was even able to identify "natural experiments."[40] Based on extensive interviews with Catholic clergy, he was able to document the transformation of an influential Catholic Bishop from protector of the status quo to champion of indigenous people. The "experimental variable" in this instance was the Vatican's transfer of the Bishop from a Catholic-dominated diocese to a diocese marked by rising levels of competition.[41] The Bishop only became a "promoter of indigenous mobilization and ethnic identities" after he faced intense competition from Protestants.[42]

Trejo documents the "major wave of U.S. Protestant missionary activity in Mexico's poor rural indigenous regions in the last quarter of the twentieth century," which triggered "unprecedented" religious competition between Catholic and Protestant churches. In an echo of Woodberry's research, Trejo shows how Protestant missionaries in Mexico "translated Bibles into indigenous languages, developed literacy programs, and established local churches led by indigenous leaders." Where the previously monopolistic Catholic Church had "underserved poor rural indigenous villagers for centuries," this decentralized Protestant approach drew thousands of young villagers away from Catholic parishes.[43]

In response, the Catholic Church developed parallel decentralized and horizontal networks and empowered local peasant leaders. Catholic bishops and clergy created thousands of local Bible study groups led by newly trained indigenous catechists, promoted cooperatives, and advocated for land reform and indigenous rights.[44] In addition, the competitive religious environment empowered parishioners to demand that the Church serve their needs rather than the interests of the state or the rich.[45] This response to religious competition facilitated social movement mobilization, not only by creating a cadre of indigenous leaders but by linking them in dense networks across regions. Ironically, these same networks also facilitated armed rebellion by reducing "the risks associated with rebel recruitment."[46]

Trejo also shows that politicized ethnic identities were driven by religious competition. Where the Catholic church faced the greatest competition, Catholic leaders promoted ethnic identities through the doctrine of inculturation "to keep indigenous souls in the Catholic fold."[47] Unintentionally, but powerfully, this facilitated the creation of the armed Zapatista rebellion that forced Mexico to grant autonomy and rights to indigenous peoples.

One of the hallmarks of great science is replication, when scholars use different methodologies to arrive at similar theoretical conclusions. A 2020 book on religion and collective action in Mexico by Christopher Hale, *Divined Intervention*, illustrates this. Hale analyzed national survey data to show that the decentralization of the Catholic Church documented by Trejo was strongly associated with greater political activism across Mexico, not just in indigenous communities. Supplementing this survey with case studies, Hale found that religious decentralization facilitated cooperative interactions (social capital) and promoted the growth of grassroots organizational capacities. These capacities enhanced the political clout of the poor and leveraged better services.[48]

There are crucial lessons here. Because religion constitutes a fundamental aspect of culture, particularly in poor societies, the breakdown of religious monopolies creates spaces for autonomous associations independent of state power structures. Religious competition makes church authorities more responsive to the needs of the poor, empowers local leaders, and fosters social movement networks. Religious competition produces better religion, and, with respect to Christianity, we might say more authentic expressions of a faith called to proclaim "good news" to the poor. Moreover, as emerging theories of religion and the state suggest, the independence of religious institutions from state control, often fueled by religious competition, acts as a check on autocratic abuses.

RELIGIOUS EQUALITY, LIVED RELIGION, AND INDIGENOUS UPLIFT

As I briefly discuss in Chapter 1, religious equality, although central to religious freedom, is often overlooked in international law and advocacy. The emphasis on "freedom of religion and belief," with the awkward acronym (FoRB), tends to focus initiatives mostly on *liberty* but less on *equality*. But as growing scholarship documents, one cannot ameliorate poverty, exclusion, and hardship without redressing religious inequalities. This redressing must incorporate indigenous peoples, whose way of life in the natural world is infused with spiritual meaning. The encroachment on, or destruction of, ancestral lands, revered forests, and sacred burial grounds, which displaces and immiserates indigenous peoples, also represents a fundamental violation of religious freedom.

Thankfully, pioneering scholarship has begun to document and redress inequalities in the treatment of the lived religion of marginalized and indigenous peoples around the world. A leader in this endeavor is Mariz Tadros, a United Kingdom scholar of religious equality and inclusive development.[49] A native of Egypt, Tadros brings the insights of her deep roots in the life and struggles of the Coptic Christian minority in that nation.[50] That experience made her aware of the need for scholars to uncover hidden inequalities by immersion in the daily life of local religious communities. This means immersion in the lives of the marginalized: listening to what people say, watching their interactions with government authorities, or witnessing the impact of religious vigilantes on the lives of minority communities. As she observed, the simple act of seeking to renovate a Coptic church not only confronts enervating bureaucratic hurdles but also sparks assaults and property destruction by Salafi Islamists. The simple act of a woman wearing a cross on a necklace can provoke harassment and intimidation.[51]

In addition to her own scholarship, Tadros leads the Coalition for Religious Equality and Inclusive Development (CREID), sponsored by the Institute for Development Studies at the University of Sussex in England.

It seeks to integrate understanding of religious inequalities into development policy, practice, and studies.[52] Through CREID, Tadros assembles an international group of scholars and advocates to investigate religious inequalities and exclusion in an array of countries and settings. With on-the-ground knowledge from immersive or ethnographic approaches, they show why "redressing religious inequalities" represents a crucial dimension of advancing religious freedom today.[53] And how such redressing provides leverage to marginalized people and magnifies uplift for the poor in development initiatives.

This research illustrates both the negative side of ignoring religious inequalities and the positive impact of addressing them. On the negative side, religious marginality worsens poverty and undermines development efforts. In Pakistan, researchers found that development efforts faltered because they did not incorporate minority communities, which suffer disproportionate poverty.[54] In Uganda, indigenous populations were denied access to conservation programs from the outside, when incorporating them is essential to sustainable conservation and development.[55] In South Africa, ignorance of indigenous ways of life led to displacement from development projects.[56] Elsewhere, public health programs failed to achieve their potential because clinicians lacked knowledge of religious practices and cultural identities of communities served.[57]

The COVID-19 pandemic, which rippled through the world in the spring of 2020, represented a natural experiment. As researchers followed the fortunes of different groups, they found that the pandemic exacerbated religious and gender inequities and exposed the blinders of policy makers to these dimensions of society.[58]

On the positive side, as we learned earlier, Dalits gain leverage to fight against entrenched discrimination when they can exercise agency in religion.[59] We see similar results for India's large tribal (or Adivasi) population. One study found that accentuating and celebrating Adivasi spirituality galvanized solidarity across diverse tribal groups and empowered them to assert their rights. For a population of over 100 million people, these findings deserve greater international attention.[60]

The rich insights from this broad line of inquiry often flow from the use of "participatory methods" that involve immersion in the lives of marginalized religious communities and listening to the actual voices of the persecuted. The CREID program at the University of Sussex has emerged as a leading center in sponsoring experiments in such participatory research, another example of how diverse research approaches uncover hidden benefits of religious freedom.[61]

THE TOUGH CASES? ATHEISTS AND SEXUAL MINORITIES

In the United States, and increasingly in the West, we see cleavages between religious and secular voters or clashes between champions of LGBT rights and defenders of religious liberty. These patterns lead to the common view that religious liberty is not for atheists or that religious freedom is "incompatible with the growing public acceptance of LGBT (lesbian, gay, bisexual, and transgender) people, lifestyles, and rights."[62] While one cannot deny policy differences between advocates of religious liberty and those of nonbelievers or sexual minorities, global data suggests that religious freedom for all is strongly associated with expansive rights generally. Conversely, religious minorities, LGBT persons, and nonbelievers are often victimized by the same repressive regimes.

Concerning atheists, governments that privilege a dominant religion or discriminate against minority faiths also tend to be inhospitable to nonbelievers. Pew studies find the harassment of unaffiliated people growing in many countries that also restrict religious freedom. Indeed, the countries with the greatest harassment of unaffiliated people include those with the highest religious restrictions, such as Iran, Russia, and Saudi Arabia.[63] Conversely, countries with strong protections for religious exercise, along with societal acceptance of religious diversity, are more hospitable places for nonbelievers. The few exceptions to this pattern are nations in the communist remnant, like China and North Korea, that promote—and thus privilege—an atheist ideology. On the other hand, the strong correspondence between the harassment of religious believers and nonbelievers alike should not surprise us, as they both reflect state authorities who arrogate to themselves the prerogative to curb freedom of thought and violate the "sacred haven of conscience."[64]

Moreover, the definition of religious freedom in international law explicitly entails the "freedom of thought, conscience, and religion," and the

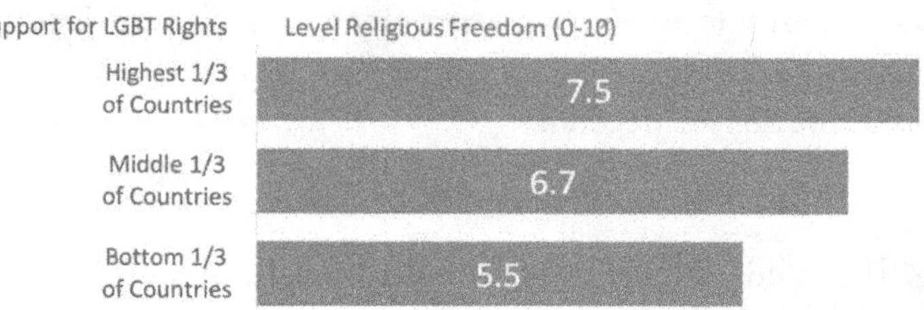

Analysis: Religious Freedom & Business Foundation, 2019; Religious Freedom Data: Inverse of the Pew Research Center's 2017 Government Restrictions on Religion Index (GRI); LGBT Data: The Williams Institute, UCLA School of Law, 2009-2013 Global Acceptance Index (GAI). Number of countries in both data sets, 137.

FIGURE 4.1. Religious Freedom and Support for LGBT Rights

right to hold or change one's "religion or *belief*" (emphasis added).[65] In other words, to protect freedom of religion, one must defend the sincere conscience rights of atheists and agnostics, along with a host of religious skeptics, critics, seekers, and reformers. Indeed, great stories of religious conversion often involve the spiritual journey from unbelief to belief. Without the freedom to question, explore, and seek spiritual truth, such quests are impossible.

With respect to LGBT rights, high-profile clashes have erupted with traditionalist religious believers over same-sex marriage and antidiscrimination proposals.[66] Indeed, some see the push for new "equality" legislation for sexual minorities as a grave threat to religious liberty in America.[67] But global data suggests a different pattern. Here, again, scholars benefit from new sources of global data and measures, such as the LGBT Global Acceptance Index, which provides scores for public support for sexual minorities in numerous countries in the world, along with the Pew Global Measures of restrictions on religion. Marshaling these indexes with sophisticated statistical analysis, Brian Grim found that countries with the strongest public support for LGBT persons were also those with the highest levels of religious freedom (see figure 4.1). In fact, he found that public support for LGBT rights was 38 percent higher in countries with robust religious freedom than in those with low levels of religious freedom. In tracking change over time, Grim also discovered that all but one of the dozen countries with the lowest levels of religious freedom also registered *declines* in support for

LGBT people. In other words, even as acceptance of LGBT persons grew in many countries in the first decades of the twenty-first century, public acceptance *declined* in nations that restrict religious freedom.[68]

This relationship is even stronger with respect to societal hostilities involving religion. Societies rent by religious hostilities and strife are deeply inhospitable places for sexual minorities.[69] As we see below, such religious repression also propels destabilizing violence that falls disproportionately on the poor, women, and other marginalized persons.

THE LOCUST EFFECT: RELIGIOUS RESTRICTIONS AND VIOLENCE AGAINST THE VULNERABLE

In his book, *The Locust Effect: Why the End of Poverty Requires the End of Violence*, Gary Haugen, President of the International Justice Mission (IJM), describes the origins and nature of violence that pervades the lives of many of the world's impoverished people, keeping them marginalized. Seared by the experience of investigating the Rwanda genocide, Haugen developed a global initiative to address the lack of justice for victims of violent exploitation, trafficking, and expropriation of property. His advocacy and research led him to conclude that widespread violence against the poor, rooted in the impunity of the victimizers, constituted one of the greatest barriers to their uplift and broader inclusion in social and political life. He likens this phenomenon to a plague of locusts that devour ripe fields just before harvest. Agricultural development initiatives or microenterprise projects may be taking root in a developing society, but these can be wiped out by "locusts of predatory violence" that "lay waste to all that the vulnerable poor had otherwise struggled to scrape together to secure their lives."[70] The lack of avenues in many developing societies for legal recourse, he shows, creates an environment of impunity that emboldens those who would enslave or steal from the poor.

As Haugen and his team show, the poor's endemic vulnerability to violence results in massive sexual exploitation, forced labor, illegal detention, land theft, assault, and police abuse. Such violent exploitation endures because victimizers have little reason to fear legal retribution in inadequate or corrupt justice systems.[71] Much of this exploitation and marginalization is sparked or exacerbated by religious repression.

A formidable scholarship now documents how apostasy and blasphemy statutes or anti-conversion laws, often passed under pressure from dominant religious groups, serve to intimidate and marginalize religious minorities and women. The mere accusation of apostasy, blasphemy, or conversion can spark mob violence against marginalized minority communities, resulting in massive loss of life and destruction of property. Often, local government authorities look the other way or fail to prosecute leaders of these orchestrated assaults. In Pakistan, the victims are often Christians or Ahmadis; in India, Christians and Muslims; in Sri Lanka, Hindus.[72]

Not well appreciated is how such government laws against blasphemy, apostasy, and conversion, along with other restrictions on religious minorities, serve to undermine the economic advancement of poor and marginalized persons. These restrictions often provide a pretext to steal a neighbor's property, to destroy a competitor's business, or to impress workers into indentured labor. Here we see how scholarship on religious repression intersects with the Locust Effect. Envy of even the modest success of ethnoreligious minorities can invite vigilante action by dominant groups and destroy gains by vulnerable workers or peasants. Property rights and worker protections are not secure under these conditions.

As we will see in the next chapter, religious repression by states and social actors, acting with impunity, also fuels a disproportionate number of violent conflicts, civil wars, and terrorist incidents in the contemporary era. These conflicts devastate the economic and civic fabric of societies, leading development agencies to conclude that they must counteract this violence to provide uplift for the poor. Otherwise, initiatives by the United Nations and NGOs that provide women's education, microenterprise initiatives, land reform, or agricultural development will be wiped out by the eruption of religious violence and sectarian civil wars. The denial of religious freedom fuels the locust effect.

RELIGIOUS FREEDOM AND SOCIAL INCLUSION OF REFUGEES, MIGRANTS, AND GUEST WORKERS

The world in the twenty-first century is awash with refugees and migrants, many fleeing religious repression and violence, as shown above, or propelled by economic privation. These are joined by millions of guest workers and legal immigrants, making those living outside of their national homes a key feature of our global era. Migrants and refugees often suffer various degrees of social and economic exclusion, which led the late Pope Francis to call upon global leaders to seek means of authentic inclusion for the millions living on the margins of host societies. Greatly compounding exclusion is the fact that so many migrants are religious "others," perceived as alien to dominant cultures and thus subject to restrictions, discrimination, and social hostilities. Government protections of religious freedom and social acceptance of diverse religious identities provide crucial leverage for the inclusion of newcomers. On the other hand, the denial of religious rights reinforces exclusion.

Saudi Arabia provides a vivid example of how this works with guest workers. Such workers comprise a significant percentage of the Saudi population (over 30 percent), and most are not adherents of its austere Wahhabi form of Sunni Islam. Christian worship is illegal, and other religious minorities face severe religious restrictions. The appalling exploitation that guest workers often experience, therefore, is compounded by the religious exclusion they face. Religious observance often must take place in secret, and thus the denial of the right of corporate worship and fraternal organization atomizes guest workers and prevents empowering solidarity.

The social exclusion of "religious others" can also operate in more benign national contexts. Japan is a democratic nation with legal protections for religious freedom. But guest workers, because they are viewed as alien to Japanese culture, continue to be marginalized and excluded in significant ways. A broader social acceptance of religious pluralism would aid in the inclusion of these workers.[73] The struggle of the Turkish minority in Germany illustrates this dynamic as well. While multigenerational Turkish families have lived in Germany for decades, it was not until this century that German law provided avenues for their inclusion as citizens. The identity of Turks as cultural and religious "others" proved a barrier to this change in law and social recognition. In sum, to have one's religious identity recognized and validated by a host country serves to open avenues of inclusion hitherto closed.

The flood of refugees from Syria and Afghanistan, themselves the victims of religious repression and strife, represents the greatest refugee crisis since the end of the Second World War. This influx of mostly Muslim refugees is driving a new politics of nativist nationalism in the West, with huge implications for questions of inclusion and national identity. Moreover, it appears that the growth of Muslim immigration in Europe and North America is leading to an increase in both government restrictions and social hostilities. According to a recent Pew Report, "government harassment and use of force against religious groups" has surged "as record number of refugees enter Europe," which recorded the largest increase in religious restrictions in the world since 2015. But the report also recorded increases in government restrictions in the United States, mostly in local zoning resistance to mosque construction, as well as growing social hostilities.[74] On the other hand, restive Muslim minorities in Europe seem to be driving some of the increases in anti-Semitic assaults and terrorist incidents. The great migrations have given rise to nativism and ethno-nationalism in Western nations, challenging the pluralist fabric of their societies. Clearly, Western nations face dramatic new challenges to the vision of an inclusive society. Again, religious repression or government favoritism exacerbates the refugee crisis, while religious freedom provides avenues for inclusion and hospitality to the millions on the move in our world.

Russia's invasion of Ukraine, which forced millions of Ukrainians to flee to neighboring countries, illustrates how such hospitality can operate powerfully. The people and governments of Poland, Germany, and the Czech Republic, among other nations of the West, have provided extraordinary succor for these refugees, many of whom have been welcomed into homes rather than camps. To be sure, this response is driven in part by kindred religious and cultural affinities, but it illustrates how respect for broad religious freedom can facilitate both government and civil society responses to tragedy.

RELIGIOUS SUCCOR AND GLOBAL ADVOCACY FOR THE POOR AND EXPLOITED

From the end of the Second World War onward, we have seen the dramatic growth of global religious humanitarian organizations. These nongovernmental organizations (NGOs) provide extensive development aid, disease control, medical care, education, and famine relief in some of the poorest places on Earth. Fueled by the charitable impulse of religious people, these NGOs operate multi-billion-dollar enterprises. Impressive in scope, sophistication, and on-the-ground reach, they fill a crucial niche in global development. Indeed, the major development programs operated by the United Nations, the United States, and the European Union routinely contract with religious NGOs to implement local projects or deliver emergency relief.[75]

An enumeration of some of the major religious humanitarian organizations suggests their ecumenical range and depth: Adventist Relief and Development Agency, Buddhist Global Relief, Caritas Internationalis (the global Catholic federation), Catholic Relief Services, Church World Service, Islamic Relief, Jesuit Refugee Services, Jewish Refugee Services, Lutheran World Relief, Mercy Corps, Samaritan's Purse, and World Vision among many others.

With some of the best indigenous networks in developing nations, religious NGOs also generate valuable information on emerging problems and possible remedies, as well as early warnings of crises. Their global linkages, in turn, equip them to convey this information to high-level policy makers. Indeed, their offices at the United Nations, the European Union, and Washington, DC, enjoy natural access to policy makers and a reputation for providing credible information about conditions in some of the most remote and forbidding places on Earth. Leaders of these organizations have emerged as forceful champions for the world's poor, refugees, exploited ethnic and religious minorities, and vulnerable women, both inside developing nations and at the highest levels of policy making in the West.

Religious freedom is central to this development work and advocacy because it enables the autonomous development and independent operation of transnational religious institutions. In other words, religious humanitarian and advocacy organizations first emerged, and now thrive, where they enjoy the greatest operational freedom from national government constraints, where they enjoy religious freedom.

Not surprisingly, the most extensive humanitarian infrastructure emerged in the United States, where the long-standing independence of religious institutions propelled a vibrant entrepreneurial and competitive civil society uniquely conducive to the creation and expansion of religious

NGOs. While mostly sustained by charitable contributions of Americans, these NGOs have become truly global enterprises, with international boards, operations through regional and national affiliates in more than one hundred countries, and large international staffs. Wander the halls of NGO headquarters or country offices, and you will see a veritable UN of faces. In addition, these organizations have undergone what Andrew Natsios describes as decolonization, the process of turning over control of field programs to people in the beneficiary countries.[76] Today, the vast bulk of personnel of religious NGOs are indigenous staff living amidst suffering or exploited people. This enhances knowledge of local conditions and propels effective advocacy.

Take the example of Jesuit Refugee Services. Staff members on the ground are often themselves refugees living in camps in Africa or Asia. Global communication enables them to relay policy concerns instantaneously to their leaders in the United States, who in turn act as advocates for the refugees with U.S. government agencies or at the United Nations. Those leaders, in effect, see themselves as advocates, indeed as lobbyists, for exploited refugees.[77]

Among the numerous examples of international advocacy by humanitarian religious organizations, momentous recent campaigns relieved debt burdens on developing nations, successfully reduced the AIDS epidemic in Africa, and erected a global infrastructure against human trafficking. Let us look at these.

From the 1980s onward, development experts bemoaned how debt burden in developing nations undermined economic progress. Often incurred decades earlier by dictators no longer in power, debt service swallowed up funds needed for education, health care, economic infrastructure, and agricultural development. Keenly aware of how this burden was undermining their own development efforts, leaders of religious NGOs seized on the coming millennium in 2000 to launch a campaign for global debt relief, lobbying Western governments and international agencies to cancel debts on poor nations. Invoking the powerful imagery of a "Year of Jubilee" when debts are forgiven, religious groups and leaders in the United States and around the world, notably Pope John Paul II, joined secular organizations and celebrities like Bono (lead singer of the band U2) in the campaign to write off debts burdening poor countries. In the United States, this entailed a successful effort to gain a huge congressional appropriation that helped leverage the write-off debts held by banks and international monetary organizations. The impact on the ground of the Jubilee campaign was immediate and long-lasting. This is how one religious insider described the effort:

> I think the great story of the last generation has been the Jubilee movement. Economists had talked about debt relief for decades . . . [but] when the religious communities, hitting the year 2000, began to bring into the public consciousness this idea of the Jubilee year, the cancellation of debts as being a profound moral obligation that people had, it really helped drive the argument in a very deep and profound way. It gave it a political traction that it didn't have otherwise, and it transformed the debate.[78]

The AIDS epidemic that burst into public consciousness in the 1980s was initially treated as a problem of unprotected homosexual sex and intravenous drug use in the West. But as the disease spread, it became clear to development experts that it was exploding in vastly different conditions in the developing world, especially in Africa, where it originated. Prominent Christian development organizations such as World Vision and Catholic Relief Services saw firsthand the devastating impact of HIV/AIDS in Africa, and they witnessed how their own treatment programmes in the 1990s were being swamped by the spread of the disease, which was producing a generation of orphans. By 2000, they were raising the alarm with international agencies and governments. Employing the unique access they enjoyed with the newly elected President George W. Bush, evangelical leaders joined with Catholic and Jewish groups to lobby the president on HIV/AIDS. President Bush ultimately made it a signature issue. The President's Emergency Plan for AIDS Relief (PEPFAR) was launched in 2004.[79] In the first years of the PEPFAR initiative, U.S. AIDS funding more than tripled. A striking success, the program delivered antiretroviral treatment to more than 2 million HIV-positive Africans by 2008 (up from just 50,000 before PEPFAR), saving many lives and contributing to economic development.[80] A more recent summary of the ongoing program notes that "through PEPFAR, the U.S. government has invested over $100 billion in the global HIV/AIDS response, the largest commitment by any nation to address a single disease in history, saving 25 million lives, preventing millions of HIV infections, and accelerating progress toward controlling the global HIV/AIDS pandemic in more than 50 countries."[81] Global religious NGOs and religious advocates were central to this achievement.

Modern slavery—the sexual exploitation of trafficked women and children, forced labor, debt bondage, chattel birth, and other forms of servitude—represents an enormous violation of human dignity. The wide scope of modern slavery and trafficking—encompassing over 20 million people—is due in part to the involvement of dangerous organized criminal syndicates that specialize in trafficking and labor exploitation. They employ intricate systems to move individuals within countries and across borders, and they employ violence and intimidation to keep them in bondage.[82]

Because traffickers purposefully take advantage of weak governments and ineffective law enforcement, transnational religious NGOs have provided some of the best documentation, rescue, rehabilitation, and justice advocacy for trafficking victims.[83] Pivotal here were Christian advocacy organizations focused on justice for victims. A prominent example of this anti-trafficking advocacy is the work of the International Justice Mission, led by Gary Haugen, whose work on violent injustice was previously cited.[84] Haugen, an evangelical Christian, sees the fight for global justice as a central tenet of the Christian faith.[85] With a network of investigators and attorneys around the world, IJM directly frees victims, educates law enforcement officials, exposes corruption, and presses for more effective national and international laws and policies.

Another anti-trafficking initiative is the Catholic women's organization, Talitha Kum: The International Network of Consecrated Life Against Trafficking in Persons. Talitha Kum draws inspiration from the biblical stories of Ruth and the Samaritan woman to inspire solidarity with female victims of trafficking.[86] Sponsored by the International Union of Superiors General, Talitha Kum draws on this vast network of women in Catholic religious orders to address human rights abuses globally.[87]

Advocacy groups like these have built a new global regime to attack human trafficking. They provided the crucial information and anchored the coalition (which included secular feminist groups) behind the landmark American law, the Trafficking Victims Protection Act of 2000, along with subsequent strengthening legislation.[88] The law created a major State Department office on trafficking with annual reports on the situation in every country on Earth and with real enforcement teeth, the withdrawal of aid for nations that fail to crack down on trafficking. This robust program helped spark expanded attention by other governments, the United Nations, and international law enforcement agencies. By placing human dignity at the center of their advocacy, religious actors helped catalyze broader attention to this global challenge.[89]

Without religious freedom—without the autonomy to create and operate transnational organizations—religious communities could not act as effectively, if at all, on their humanitarian impulses to provide succor to the poor and justice for the exploited.

SUMMARY LESSONS

The enormous range and diversity of research findings presented in this chapter lend weight to the argument that religious freedom plays a key role in the path to empowerment for poor and marginalized people around the world. Environments of religious freedom facilitate uplift for the poor, agency for women, and succor for outcasts and refugees. In contrast, religiously repressive nations and places not only afflict their own people but also export destabilizing forces. In our global era, what happens inside a nation—especially its religious environment—matters to the rest of us who value a world of greater peace and equity, as we see in the next chapter.

This chapter also illustrates the importance of understanding the lived reality of poor, female, lower-caste, indigenous, and other marginalized persons in societies around the world. Only when researchers immerse themselves in the milieus of these people and use creative participatory methods that let them speak for themselves do we fully grasp the centrality of religious freedom and agency as paths to empowerment.

CHAPTER FIVE

WEAPON OF PEACE

One of the weightiest arguments for religious freedom concerns its vital link to international security and peace. Religious strife and violence represent a major source of global instability and conflict—undermining economic development and propelling massive refugee flows. Indeed, since 9/11, we have seen a huge increase in religiously inspired terrorist attacks, while devastating sectarian wars have fractured societies and international order.[1]

It seems as if major regions of the world are living through a time akin to the seventeenth century, when religious wars engulfed Europe. Those wars ended with the Westphalian settlement of 1648, in which European powers sought to contain religious strife through a system of sovereign nations that agreed to forswear exploiting religious divisions in neighboring countries. In effect, European powers sought to "tame" religious passions by co-opting and controlling confessional communities. Today, the Westphalian system has broken down, unleashing transnational religious conflict.[2]

The most dramatic instances of such conflicts are religious civil wars that devastate the economic and civic fabric of societies. As tragically illustrated by the protracted Syrian conflagration, religious civil wars are especially brutish, lethal, and intractable. They often become proxy conflicts between nations with competing religious aims, and they represent a growing reality on the global stage. In the 1940s, religious civil wars constituted only 19 percent of all such conflicts. That proportion increased to 36 percent in the 1970s, 45 percent in the 1990s, and 50 percent in the first decades of the twenty-first century.[3]

We see similar trends with terrorism. Drawing upon the Global Terrorism Database, Nilay Saiya identifies all terrorist incidents in which the perpetrators operated with clear religious motivations. He then tracks the dramatic increase of religious-based terrorism in the first two decades of the twenty-first century. He observes: "In the year preceding the 9/11 attacks, the world witnessed only 255 identifiable religious terrorist attacks. By the year 2014, that number had risen nearly tenfold to 2,237."[4] In contrast to politically motivated terrorism, religious-based terrorism is more ruthless and resilient, harder to stop, and less amenable to negotiated settlements.[5]

Given the rise of religious civil wars, terrorism, and religiously driven interstate conflict, one can understand why leaders of nations respond by imposing greater restrictions on religion. To government authorities, it seems logical to control religious strife by restricting religious freedom. But that strategy produces the very thing most states wish to avoid. "Regimes that repress religion," as Saiya documents, "invite the very belligerency they seek to thwart through such restrictions." Indeed, repressive environments that "choke religious liberty" serve as "the natural breeding ground for terrorism."[6] Put another way, repression of assertive religion by governments and societal actors nurtures the fanaticism they fear and propels the transnational religious violence they seek to escape.

On the positive side, nations that generally protect religious freedom produce far less internal violence and transnational terrorism, and they do not spark interstate conflicts, especially with each other. To understand why and how this works, we must trace key global trends that help frame this discussion.

GLOBAL TRENDS

The first trend is the global resurgence of religion, especially its public and transnational power. As Toft, Philpott, and Shah show, globalization enables religious actors to operate beyond the constraints of state control. On the global stage, religious actors today employ more resources, operate with more boldness, and maneuver more internationally than ever before, making this "God's Century."[7]

Thus, religious freedom matters to international security because religion matters, and increasingly so. Religion remains "an ineradicable aspect of human anthropology and culture," as Durham and Clark observe. Protecting peaceful expressions of this religious impulse, therefore, "is a more powerful stabilizing force than is often realized," because it cultivates "enhanced loyalty to the state flowing from gratitude felt by those whose core rights are secure." Protecting religious freedom, therefore, "yields a peace dividend."[8]

The second trend, also fueled by globalization, is the dramatic diffusion of religious pluralism. While religious diversity is an innate aspect of human life, modern forces dramatically expand the intermixture of people of diverse faiths. Once a major proponent of the theory that modernization produces secularization, famed sociologist Peter Berger came to a profoundly different view of the dynamics of modern societies. Modernization and globalization do not bring secularity, he argued; rather, they propel plurality, as people increasingly live cheek-to-jowl with religious others. In our global age, he quips, "everyone is everywhere."[9]

States and societies once expected (and many still strive to impose) religious uniformity, based on the mistaken assumption that enforced religious unity will produce political and societal cohesion. But that assumption was questioned long before the hyper-pluralism of the global age. In the eighteenth century, for example, French intellectual Voltaire contrasted the despotism of state-enforced monopoly he saw in France with the peace of plurality he noticed at the Royal Exchange in London. Adam Smith, similarly, contended that if the government allowed religions to operate freely, their natural tendency to subdivide would prevent any one or two from dominating society and enlisting the sword of the state to repress competitors. David Hume expanded on this insight by noting that to ensure public liberty, tranquility, and thriving industry, a wise magistrate must avoid extending favoritism to dominant sects and instead require that they leave each other alone. As he quipped, a state with one dominant religion will lead to despotism; with two, vicious battles, but with many, peace and tranquility.[10]

These sentiments were echoed in America by Roger Williams, William Penn, James Madison, and Thomas Jefferson. Because of the innate pluralism of religious experience, they argued, repression inevitably produces grievance, instability, and violent cross-border strife. Extending toleration to diverse religious groups, on the other hand, would be conducive to greater peace and stability. In other words, religious freedom is the antidote of religious conflict.[11]

Those speculative insights find powerful corroboration today. In our global age, no society is religiously uniform. Saudi Arabia, for example, can deny this religious diversity, but that just marginalizes Shia Muslims and Christian guest workers who do not belong to the state-enforced Wahhabi-Sunni religion. Burma can claim that the Muslim Rohingya are not its citizens, but they have lived in that country for centuries. Repression is the seedbed of instability, strife, and ethnic cleansing.

Herein lies the crux of understanding the strong relationship between religious repression and international violence. Efforts to enforce religious uniformity inherently produce religious tension and often violence. Indeed, the repression of the innate religious diversity in society is one of the causes of the massive migration flows across the world. These days, from the smallest African village to rural American communities, we encounter religious others, and the prescription for religious strife appears to be the "live and let live" strategy of guarantees of religious freedom. Unfortunately, the third key trend is increasing global repression of religious rights. According to the Pew Research Center, government restrictions on religion, already widespread, increased globally between the fifteen years of reporting, 2007–2022.[12] These restrictions rose for all four categories studied: favoritism, laws and policies restricting religious freedom, limits on religious activities, and harassment of religious groups. This pattern provides evidence that governments are indeed attempting to clamp down on religion. Many political leaders apparently buy into a zero-sum logic that they need to restrict religion itself to curtail radicalism and terrorism. But multiple findings of global research suggest just the opposite. As government restrictions have grown, so have religious hostilities.[13]

Religious discrimination and persecution also represent some of the world's greatest human rights abuses. An especially shocking case is the systematic oppression of the ethnic Uyghurs by the Chinese government in the country's western province of Xinjiang. This ethno-religious minority of around eleven million is predominantly Muslim. Under the pretext of preventing a breakaway of the province, the Chinese Communist

Party launched an aggressive system of mass incarceration, rounding up over one million Uyghurs in a series of "re-education camps" that represent the "largest concentration camp system the world has seen since the Nazi regime." The Chinese authorities also employ pervasive surveillance technology to create a police state comparable to, if not more sophisticated than, the totalitarian regimes of Cold War-era East Germany and modern North Korea.[14] To prevent the perpetuation of Uyghur culture, the Chinese authorities separate children from parents for indoctrination and employ coercive population control policies, including widespread sterilization and forced abortions that have led to plummeting birth rates—policies that could "meet the legal criteria for genocide under international law."[15] Daniel Philpott shows that this campaign explicitly targeted the ability of Uyghurs to practice Islam by "preventing their minors from attending mosque, surveilling their mosques, punishing them for praying and worshipping, confiscating Qurans and other publications, forbidding men from growing beards and women from wearing veils, exercising control over the selection of clerics, preventing the celebration of religious holidays, and detaining Uyghurs who disobey."[16] In other words, Chinese repression targets Uyghur religion, not just ethnic identity. This subjugation—combined with continued repression of Buddhists in Tibet, persecution of Falun Gong meditation practitioners, and harsh regulation of Chinese Christians—earned China this execrable distinction: the highest ranking in the world on government restrictions of religion.[17]

Other global measures flesh out the diverse patterns of increasing government restrictions on religion around the world. The Religion and State (RAS) dataset demonstrates the vast array of government restrictions on religion. It is stunning how deeply governments are involved, often in meddlesome ways, in regulating religion, showing favoritism to dominant groups, and restricting the activities of religious minorities. In summarizing the consequences of this regulation, Johnathan Fox cites extensive documentation that oppressed religious minorities are often likely to lash out violently against their oppressors, which can spark reprisals by dominant groups in a continuing cycle of conflict.[18]

A devastating example concerns the Rohingya people in Myanmar. Long-standing discrimination against the predominantly Muslim minority in this Buddhist-majority nation sparked coordinated attacks on police stations by Rohingya militants in 2017. In response, the Burmese military launched a brutal campaign of ethnic cleansing—indiscriminately killing civilians and burning villages, forcing thousands of Rohingya to flee across the border to refugee camps in Bangladesh, where they remain.[19]

As this example illustrates, a fourth global trend is resistance by those persecuted. As Toft and her co-authors show, religious groups maintain considerable resources to push back against state restrictions or social repression.[20] But if pushed too far, they may lash out violently. This assertive religious response, in turn, can propel a cycle of further rounds of state repression and resistance, which helps to explain why the denial of religious freedom is uniquely destabilizing.[21]

But why *uniquely* destabilizing? After all, religious rights are logically linked with other liberties—such as freedom of expression, association, and property rights. Would people not equally resist infringements on other rights? Perhaps, but they often just endure such violations in the face of state power. Transcendent obligations and aspirations, on the other hand, go to the heart of human identity and dignity. So denying that which is "ultimate" to people, denying them the right to "be who you are," will likely produce the most vehement resistance. Weaponized identities, in turn, can produce cycles of violence that are hard to stop. Indeed, Pew documents a dramatic rise in religion-based social hostilities, mob violence, and terrorism since it began reporting in 2007.[22]

This points to the final global trend—the emergence of non-state actors as a source of repression and violence. Within countries, as the Pew Research Center documents, societal repression represents a major and distinct form of restriction on religious practice.[23] Powerful societal actors, normally representing the dominant or state-favored faith, can employ intimidation and violence to maintain their privileged position. This action is often triggered or invited by state favoritism and repression. Laws that privilege the majority religion or discriminate against minorities inevitably signal to society that certain groups are disfavored, inviting harassment, intimidation, and mob violence against them, often with impunity as authorities look the other way.

This blend of religious state repression, favoritism, and social hostilities also fuels transnational militant movements that destabilize societies and disrupt world order. The rise of the so-called Islamic State in Iraq and Syria

(ISIS), which committed genocidal atrocities against Christians and Yazidis, is a prime example.[24] Born out of the chaos of sectarian conflict in Iraq following the overthrow of Saddam Hussein, along with the subsequent civil war in Syria, ISIS was fueled by religious repression and grievances. In Iraq, Sunni Muslims, marginalized by the Shia-dominated government of Nouri al-Maliki and assaulted by Shia militias, were drawn to the ISIS movement, which promised a Sunni reign. That Shia dominance of post-Hussein Iraq, in turn, mimicked the repressive strategies previously employed by Hussein's *Sunni-dominated* regime against Shias. In Syria, Sunni militants flocked to the Islamic State banner as the Assad regime, dominated by the Alawite sect of Shia Islam, employed scorched-earth tactics against Sunni protesters and insurgents.[25]

In sum, we see how state religious repression and favoritism invite social hostilities, which can grow into regional insurgencies and transnational terrorism—major threats to global security and humanitarian tragedies. We now turn to scholarship that explores precisely how and why religious freedom matters so much to security and peace in the twenty-first century.

THE EMPIRICAL EVIDENCE

For centuries, even millennia, theologians, scholars, and thinkers have made arguments about why coercion in religion cannot work, why it produces strife, violence, and hypocrisy. Armed with unique global data, better methodologies, and more sophisticated theories, scholars now have the capacity to test propositions advanced by such classic thinkers to explain why the world works the way it does.

Let us begin with the pioneering work of sociologists Brian Grim and Roger Finke, who marshal prodigious evidence to test the links between religious freedom and peace. Based on innovative techniques to measure global restrictions on religion, they conducted sophisticated statistical analyses to test the relationships between repression of religion, religious persecution, and cross-national violence. Their empirical theory thus demonstrates the real-world dangers of state repression, favoritism, or complicity in sectarian assaults.[26]

The Price of Freedom Denied represents a rarely achieved aspiration in the social sciences. It addresses a vital concern, develops a universal theory to explain it, and draws upon global data to test the theory with sophisticated statistical methods and case studies. In other words, it is theory-driven, data-rich, timeless, and real-world in its applications. Because of the availability and transparency of their methods and data, others can replicate their findings with other approaches and different data sources, a hallmark of good science.

Great scientific theories, we learn from the history of science, achieve leverage by explaining more with less, often in a counterintuitive fashion. Grim and Finke attain this grail by anchoring their work in several propositions that they rigorously test:

- "to the extent that a religious group achieves a monopoly and holds access to the temporal power and privileges of the state, the ever-present temptation is to persecute religious competitors openly."
- "to the extent that governments deny religious freedoms, physical religious persecution and conflict will increase."
- "to the extent that social forces deny religious freedoms, physical persecution will increase."
- "to the extent that religious freedoms are granted to all religions, the state will have less authority and incentive to persecute religion."[27]

These propositions help explain a theoretical model that Brian Grim developed and then rigorously tested with Roger Finke (See figures 5.1 and 5.2). Backed by complex statistical analysis, figure 5.1 demonstrates the causal links that produce the "religious violence cycle."[28] Social hostilities or restrictions on religion induce governments to impose restrictions on religion, which triggers religious violence that can spill over borders, which in turn produces more social and government restrictions.

But as figure 5.2 shows, the religious violence cycle can be broken. Equal religious liberty and free competition produce broader religious participation in society, which spurs positive contributions to society that reinforce religious freedom. In other words, when governments ensure religious freedom and treat all groups equally, grievances lessen, and greater societal

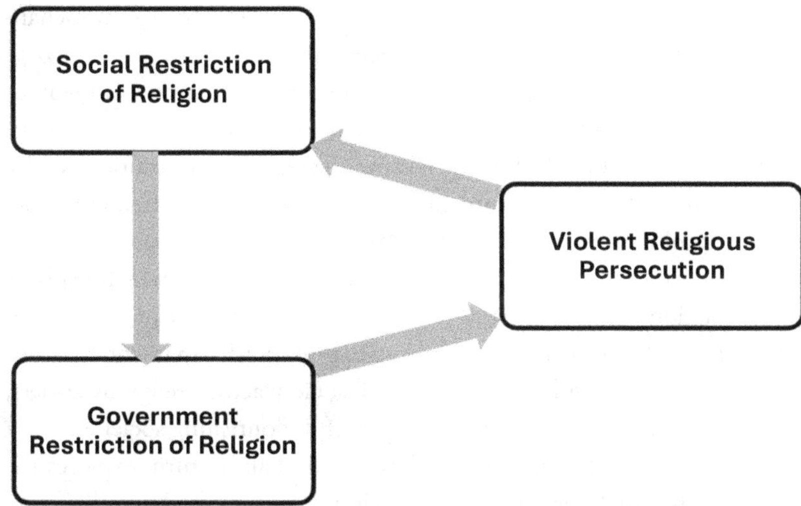

FIGURE 5.1. Religious Violence Cycle, provided with permission by Brian Grim and Roger Finke.

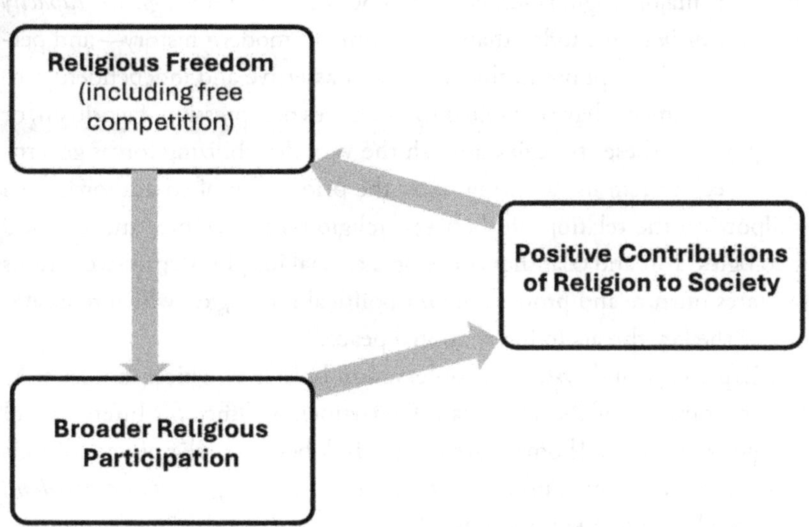

FIGURE 5.2. Religious Freedom Cycle, from Brian Grim, "The Social and Economic Impact of Religious Intolerance," Religious Freedom and Business Foundation, March 15, 2014.

tolerance and civility ensue, leading to positive cycles where groups channel energies and competition in civil society pursuits.

Why does religious liberty matter to peace? Their answer is theoretically elegant and empirically powerful: When religious freedoms increase, inter-religious conflict declines, grievances lessen, and persecution wanes. On the other hand, as government restrictions increase—often at the behest of dominant religious groups—so does violent persecution, inter-religious hostilities, regional strife, and war. This finding, which explains the interaction between societal pressures and government practices, provides real guidance to policymakers struggling with renascent religious tides. But it also provides wisdom to civil society actors, religious leaders, and citizens who wish to live in more peaceful, flourishing societies.

The scholarly team of Toft, Philpott, and Shah, in turn, explores the dynamics that make violations of religious freedom so destabilizing to global stability and peace. In *God's Century: Resurgent Religion and Global Politics*, they demonstrate that the resurgence of public religion across the globe has been driven by the very forces of modernization and globalization that formative thinkers expected would marginalize religion. Indeed, they find that "major religious actors throughout the world enjoy *greater capacity for political influence* today than at any time in modern history—and perhaps ever."[29] In response to this new era of assertive and independent religion, governments have defaulted to initiatives of repression, favoritism, or co-optation. These strategies unleash the very destabilizing forces governments seek to rein in. Drawing upon the prior work of co-author Daniel Philpott on the relationship between religion-state regimes and political theologies, Toft and coauthors develop a crucial insight: Repressive actions by states nurture and propel militant political theologies, which represent one of the key threats to international peace.[30]

Experience and systematic observation bolster statistical inquiries. As the first director of the U.S. State Department's Office on International Religious Freedom, Thomas Farr saw the link between religious conditions and security challenges up close. In his book, *World of Faith and Freedom*, bolstered by subsequent writings, Thomas Farr makes the case for promoting international religious freedom as a foreign policy objective precisely because it is in America's security interests to do so. During his time at the State Department, he was often frustrated at what he characterized as the "religion avoidance syndrome" by his colleagues, who viewed promotion of religious freedom either as a merely humanitarian gesture or, at worst, special pleading. But his experience illuminated how protecting religious pluralism and expanding religious freedom addressed the central security challenges of the twenty-first century—terrorism, fanaticism, religious conflict, and despotism. For example, he observes how virtually all the nations that present security challenges to the United States are also those where persecution and restrictions on religion are severe. The promotion of religion, he concluded, can help drain the swamps from which terror networks emerge; it can lessen regional tensions and international strife.[31]

These strategic dimensions of religious conflict serve as the focus of pivotal research by William Inboden. Having served in the U.S. State Department and National Security Council, Inboden, now at the University of Texas, has investigated the origins and ideological nature of threats to global peace and security.

Both during his work in government and now as a scholar, Inboden noticed (and then repeatedly corroborated) a powerful pattern first alluded to by Thomas Farr: "Those actors with the most egregious religious-freedom violations are remarkably consonant with those that pose a potential threat to the United States and its interests."[32] For example, every nation today that represents a security threat to the United States is an egregious violator of religious freedom. *Every single one.* Conversely, *not a single nation* in the world that respects religious freedom poses a security threat to the U.S. Remarkably, Inboden found that the same held true for the past century. "Every major war the United States fought over the last 70 years" featured an opponent that engaged in systematic religious persecution. This held for numerous smaller-scale military interventions.[33]

Moreover, the ideologies behind the nation's major security threats, from Communism and fascism in the twentieth century to transnational jihadist movements today, contain in their *core identity* a profound hostility to religious pluralism or religion itself. In sum, whether the security threat came from superpowers, global ideological movements, or theocratic states, the single characteristic they all shared "was an abiding hostility" toward religious freedom and pluralism.[34]

Inboden also focused his research on the self-professed ideology of violent Islamist movements. Taking seriously the self-proclaimed theology of the disparate groups—Al Qaeda, Al Shabab, Lashkar-e-Taiba, Boko Haram, the Taliban, and ISIS—he finds a common denominator in their hostility to religious pluralism. Indeed, religious intolerance and opposition to religious freedom are the "defining epistemic features of jihadism," central to their animating identity. Because jihadism regards religious pluralism as anathema, enforcing a single vision of right religion justifies its violence and repression, not only against non-Muslims but also against Muslims who refuse to embrace its monistic ideology. Inboden shows how the Islamic State's "orgy of violence emanates not just from bloodlust, but from its abiding theological commitment" to eradicating all other faiths or contrary interpretations of Islam. Moreover, the links between protections for religious freedom, religious pluralism, and democracy explain why "jihadism self-consciously posits itself as an ideological rival to liberal democracy." Democracy's protection of religious pluralism makes it anathema.[35]

One lesson Inboden draws from this analysis is that democracy advocates, both within Islamic societies and outside, should focus on the protection of religious freedom and pluralism as antidotes to jihadism. Indeed, the protection of religious exercise and pluralism can be seen "as the first seeds of democracy."

The relationship between the diffusion of religious liberty and American security is further explored by John Owen, professor of politics at the University of Virginia. Author of the magisterial book, *The Clash of Ideas in World Politics: Transnational Networks, States and Regime Change, 1510–2010*, Owen explores how and why states promote their domestic institutions abroad. Across the centuries, he finds that states of all sorts—liberal democratic, communist, fascist, monarchial, and theocratic—seek a congenial external environment by promoting abroad their domestic forms of governance.[36] For liberal democracies, the logic is compelling because, as Immanuel Kant famously posited, democracies do not make war with one another and thus conduce to a "democratic peace."

Owen explores the implications of this democratic peace by documenting how the expansion of religious liberty affects power relationships in the international system, especially how it enhances American influence. On the one hand, this emphasis on power suggests a congenial finding: We can do well by doing good; we can promote a moral aim *and* achieve gains in realpolitik. On the other hand, this claim seems to validate critics who see American promotion of religious freedom as a tainted cover for neo-imperialist foreign policies.

By exploring the actual mechanisms of this power enhancement, however, Owen answers the critics. He shows that devotees of religious liberty around the world—from human rights champions to aggrieved religious minorities—naturally form networks of mutual aid and ally with foreign countries that exemplify their quest. Thus, advocates of religious freedom, while far from uncritical of the United States, tend to favor better relations with it. As they gain influence within their own states, they press for more pro-American policies and more social contacts (such as trade, investment, and academic exchanges). Religious freedom, like political liberty, is a kind of carrier of American social power.[37] Ironically, as Farr observed, secular-minded U.S. officials not only fail to see the strategic interest implied in the diffusion of religious liberty but they sometimes promote or accept restrictive policies that poorly serve American interests.[38]

These patterns lead us to the pivotal recent work of Nilay Saiya, who is the world's leading scholar on the empirical relationships between religious repression and violence. In landmark research, he demonstrates how increasing religious repression over the past three decades has fueled religious carnage and violent religious extremism across the world.

Saiya begins by focusing on religious terrorism as a uniquely destabilizing force in the world. In his book, *Weapon of Peace: How Religious Liberty Combats Terrorism*, Saiya demonstrates how scholars today can capitalize on an unprecedented wealth of global data to reveal the deeper links between religious liberty and security.[39] He finds that religious violence, whether from Islamic, Christian, Hindu, Sikh, Buddhist, or Jewish actors, arises overwhelmingly from states and societies that repress religious exercise. "Where governments impede the expression of faith," he shows, "religious terrorism increases as does the likelihood that these states will export terrorism to other countries."[40] Moreover, because religious violence is more ruthless and resilient than other forms, it represents the most serious threat to peace within nations and internationally. In contrast, voluminous evidence reveals that "religiously free countries are far less likely to suffer from, or export," such destabilizing religious violence. This is a matter of enormous strategic importance.[41]

Let us begin with the striking statistical findings of this research. Looking first at the average number of yearly terrorist attacks each country experienced, Saiya finds that nations with high levels of religious restrictions experienced many times the attacks as countries with low levels of restrictions.[42] This relationship is remarkably linear: As the level of religious restrictions goes up, so, too, does the incidence of terrorism and violence. Over a two-decade period of analysis (1991–2013), religiously repressive states were the targets of 80 percent of all religious terrorist attacks, moderately restrictive states 12 percent, and religiously free states only 8 percent.[43] In other words, if state authorities wish to reduce the likelihood that their societies will suffer terrorist attacks, they should enact policies to protect religious free exercise.

Not only are repressing states the object of attacks but they are also the incubators of international terrorist groups. Indeed, nearly all international terrorist groups *originate* from religiously repressive settings: "91% emanated from highly restrictive countries; 8% from moderately restrictive countries; and only slightly more than 2% from religiously free settings."[44]

Figure 5.3 provides a visual depiction of these patterns. The three categories of government regulation of religion correspond to the *normatively neutral* terms employed by the Pew Research Center: low, moderate, and high restrictions. But as I showed in chapter 1, high restrictions reflect harshly repressive policies, while countries with low restrictions can accurately be described as religiously free. Those in the moderate category fall in between. The figure vividly shows the powerful link between increasing levels of government restrictions on religion and rising percentages of terrorist attacks, by origin or target.

Figure 5.3 also captures the dynamic nature of regimes and policies because it measures changing *settings* rather than some static categorization of *nations*. That is why the horizontal measure of religious regulation is registered in "country years," as restrictions change from year to year (sometimes markedly) for the 151 countries scored annually. The use of "country year" as the unit of observation enables Saiya to categorize over 3,500 observations as low, moderate, or high restrictions.[45] In this way, he uses the diverse and changing policies of governments over time to serve as a "natural" experiment. In experimental language, he demonstrates how

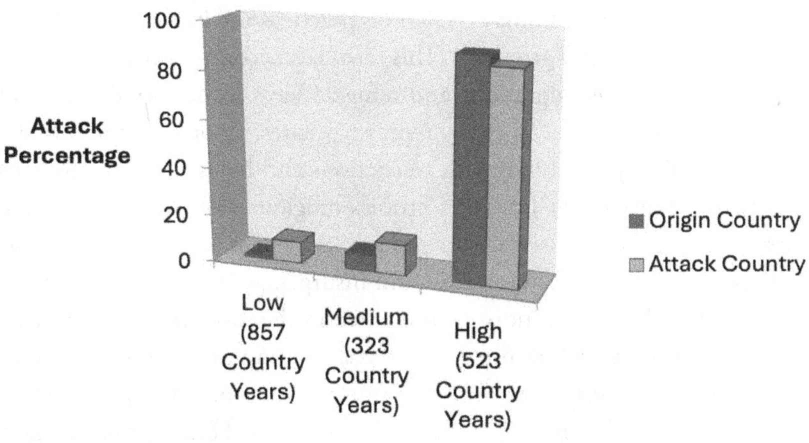

FIGURE 5.3. Government Religious Restrictions and International Religious Terrorist Attacks, 2001–2013, provided with permission by Nilay Saiya.

increases in his independent variable (religiously repressive policies) powerfully increase the outcomes of his dependent variable (terrorist attacks).[46]

The real world, in fact, provides abundant illustrations of the natural experiment of changing regimes and religious policies, and thus the value of measuring "country year" rather than country. In the early 1990s, the constitution of the new Russian Federation generally guaranteed religious freedom, but in the Putin era, the country has become increasingly repressive against religious minorities and, not surprisingly, more autocratic domestically and pernicious internationally. In contrast, for decades, Sudan was one of the most religiously repressive countries in the world, spawning multiple violent internal conflicts and harboring such international terrorist organizations as Al Qaeda. But with the toppling of its Islamist dictatorship in 2018 came reforms of repressive laws on apostasy and blasphemy and greater protections of religious minorities and women. Unfortunately, the outbreak of civil war between rival military factions in 2023 dashed the potential positive outcome of the short-lived secular government.

Saiya's research also probed the different forms of religious repression, which helps us see the specific pathways to violence. The most common and widespread practice, or pathway to violence, involves repression of religious minorities—"limits on religious practices and institutions that are not placed on majority groups."[47] This form has become more pronounced in our global age as migrations and refugees have made societies around the world more diverse. In many repressive states, favoritism towards the religious majority combines with restrictions and harassment of religious minorities. Saiya shows how this propels religious violence in two ways. First, and most obviously, it can produce violent resistance by religious minorities as well as militarization and insurgency. In India, centuries of repression of the Sikh minority culminated in the formation of a militant Sikh movement, which resulted in the assassination of a prime minister.[48] In Yemen, state enforcement of strict Sunni Islam sparked a violent rebellion by minority Shiites. The resulting civil war turned into a proxy struggle between two theocracies, Sunni-dominated Saudi Arabia and Shiite-led Iran, producing one of the worst humanitarian crises in the world. In the case of Sudan, the regime's campaign to enforce a militant form of Sharia upon its population of African Christians and tribal religionists sparked massive rebel resistance and a brutal two-decade civil war.[49] The recent war between Israel and Hamas in Gaza was sparked by the Islamist-justified atrocities of Hamas but made especially bloody by hardened Israeli attitudes toward Palestinians and the right-wing government's accession to Jewish settler encroachments on Palestinian property.

A second pathway that connects minority repression to terrorism takes the form of what Saiya calls "outbidding." Outbidding is where radicals of the favored majority attempt to outbid the state in maintaining the purity or militancy of the faith. If the regime is perceived as insufficiently strict, then fanatics may attempt to overthrow it with violence. In the case of Al-Qaeda, Osama Bin Laden saw the 9/11 attack on the United States as a means of ultimately bringing down the Saudi regime. In other cases, outbidding can lead to assassinations of state leaders seen as too accommodating of religious minorities, as happened in such diverse places as Sri Lanka, Israel, and Pakistan.[50]

Finally, by empowering religious majorities with favoritism, states encourage vigilante terrorism by majority militants against religious minorities. State codes against apostasy, blasphemy, defamation, and conversion embolden religious actors to inflict violence, property damage, and intimidation against vulnerable religious minorities or nonbelievers they accuse of such crimes. In India, Hindu Nationalists have orchestrated mob violence against Muslims, Christians, and Dalits (untouchables), often under the pretense that they are defending Hindus from untoward conversions.[51] In Pakistan, jihadis have waged a campaign of terrorism against those they accuse of committing blasphemy or apostasy, including assassinations of officials who seek to reform such laws. In the Muslim-majority states of Northern Nigeria, state-enforced Sharia emboldens Boko Haram and other jihadist militants to kill thousands of Christians, intensifying religious strife and sparking Christian reprisals against Muslims where they are the majority.[52]

The diverse demographic patterns of the three dozen Nigerian states also create a laboratory to test the role of diversity in stemming this religious strife. A careful study by Notre Dame political scientist Robert Dowd found that settings with the greatest mixing of Muslims and Christians produced the most inter-religious tolerance, while those with the greatest religious segregation produced the most intolerance and violence.[53] This is another confirmation of how forced religious uniformity incites violence.

A different type of pathway to violence involves restrictions on all religions, including majority faiths. In some cases, such as North Korea, this takes the form of violent repression of every form of religious expression. A far more common strategy is "religious co-optation," in which the government highly regulates government-sanctioned religions that must be subservient to the state. We see this in communist and former communist states, like China and Vietnam. But majority co-optation also operates in Turkey and the Muslim-majority nations of Central Asia. Often, the aim is to tame religion by making it dependent on the government. Yet by squelching independent religious expression, this strategy often sparks backlash and underground seditious movements.

Most terrorist attacks are domestic, with both perpetrator and victim from the same country. With the global revolution in communication and travel, however, terrorism increasingly crosses borders. But how, exactly, do *local* religious grievances lead to *transnational* terrorism? Saiya proposes three ways that happens: "(1) an outside-in strategy called *solicitation*, (2) an inside-out dynamic called *incubation*, and (3) direct *state support* of terrorism."[54]

Solicitation works because the repression of religious people within a country cannot be hidden in our globalized world. In their resistance to repressive states, insurgent religious groups find they can *solicit* support of co-religionists abroad—in the form of moral support, money, recruits, and even weapons. During the Chechen rebellion against Russian rule, for example, thousands of Muslims traveled to fight with their Islamic brothers against Moscow. The war against the Assad regime in Syria served as an even greater magnet, drawing Sunni fighters from more than ninety countries.[55]

Incubation, on the other hand, occurs when repression fosters extremism that propels beyond the borders where it originates. Often, this happens where dictatorships maintain such ruthless control that local resistance is crushed, leading militant ideologues to channel their energies elsewhere. Secular authoritarian (post-communist) regimes in Central Asia, for example, fearful of independent Muslim communities, have spawned and exported the very radical Islamist insurgents their harsh policies are putatively meant to crush.[56] Those Islamist insurgents have joined and fueled the Taliban, Al-Qaeda, and the Islamic State (ISIS). As Saiya documents, "a disproportionate number of foreign fighters involved in the Iraq and Syria conflicts hail from Uzbekistan," a regime that was especially repressive against Muslim civil society at the time.[57] As we will see in the concluding chapter, reforms in Uzbekistan dramatically liberalized that nation and propelled peaceful civil society initiatives. Since that transformation in 2018, we expect to see far less incubation of religious violence.

This analysis helps correct the common impression that religious persecution and violence in Muslim-majority countries must stem from inherent tenets of the Islamic faith. But Saiya's analysis, along with other scholarship, reveals wide variability in Muslim-majority settings, which undermines the idea that Islam itself is inherently antithetical to religious freedom. In sub-Saharan Africa, for example, Pew reports show low levels of religious restrictions in nearly all Muslim-Majority countries, with some even freer than their Christian counterparts.[58]

Violent persecution and terrorism in the Middle East, on the other hand, stem from historically driven patterns of government favoritism, repression, and co-optation. Moreover, one of the greatest sources of radicalism and insurgency, as noted above, arises from secular autocratic repression of Muslim communities, not from tenets of Islamic faith. Not surprisingly, the Muslim intellectuals who provide the underpinning for militant interpretations of Islam developed their violent ideologies while living under conditions of pervasive repression. Muslim-majority settings with generous religious freedom, in contrast, do not tend to produce or export religious terrorism and its ideologies.[59]

The most direct link between domestic religious repression and global security involves state-sponsored terrorism. This pathway operates similarly to religious outbidding. Political regimes that derive their very legitimacy and support from the dominant religion tend to harshly persecute religious minorities in their midst, which can create conflicts with other nations and foes among other religions. Supporting or sponsoring transnational terrorism and insurgencies, consequently, becomes a way "to wage war by proxy against their enemies."[60]

The prime example of this dynamic is the theocratic regime of Iran, in which Shiite clerics exercise complete political power. After seizing power in 1979, the regime sought to eliminate all competing sources of authority by violently repressing all religious minorities as well as Shiites who dissented from its melding of mosque and state. Such repression required a vast domestic security force. But the totalitarian character of the regime also propelled an aggressive operation to export its revolution and assault its perceived enemies, including Israel, the United States, and Saudi Arabia. This manifested in backing for Hamas and other Palestinian insurgents, Hezbollah in Lebanon, the Assad regime in Syria, Shiite militias in Iraq, and Houthi rebels in Yemen, where the intervention represented a dangerous and destructive proxy war with the Saudi regime.

RELIGIOUS REPRESSION AND THREATS TO INTERNATIONAL SECURITY: THE CANARY IN THE COAL MINE

As the above discussion suggests, violations of religious freedom produce strife and violence that can spill over borders and threaten regional or global peace. Persecuting nations become breeding grounds for religious extremism and violence. Keen observers of international security, therefore, suggest that religious conditions inside a nation can function like the proverbial "canary in the coal mine," providing an early warning of international danger.[61] In other words, what happens inside a nation, especially its treatment of vulnerable religious minorities, can be a strong predictor of its international posture.

Examples abound. Vladimir Putin's push for autocratic control of Russia began with a change in the religion law in 1997 that privileged the Orthodox Church and discriminated against religious minorities. This enabled Putin to co-opt the church to support his imperial designs, making Russia an increasing security threat. Emboldened by religious support, Putin launched his invasion of Ukraine, knowing he could count on supine Orthodox leaders, including Patriarch Kirill, to bless the war and parrot his justification.

Similarly, China became more belligerent internationally after Xi Jinping began a severe internal crackdown on religion, in contrast to the more relaxed policies of his predecessors. In addition to a general repression of all independent religious communities, using a vast surveillance infrastructure, the regime unleashed a brutal crackdown on the predominantly Muslim Uyghur population in Xinjiang province. This entailed mass detention, forced labor, "reeducation," suppression of Uyghur religious practices, political indoctrination of children, and forced sterilization. This should have signaled to outsiders a more aggressive international posture by the Xi regime.

Or take Saudi Arabia, which for decades enforced a severe Islamist (Wahhabi) doctrine inside the kingdom. Religious freedom advocates raised the alarm about the Kingdom's harsh treatment of its religious minorities, including Shia and Christian guest workers, and warned about how it exported militant theology by funding Wahhabi clerics and Islamic schools abroad. It took the attacks on September 11, 2001—in which the mastermind, Osama Bin Laden, and fifteen of the eighteen hijackers were Saudi-born—for the world to awaken to the global threat of the kingdom's religious regime.

An unheralded but potent example concerned the Islamist regime of Sudan. When Omar al-Bashir seized power in a coup in 1989, with the support of Muslim extremist Hasan al-Turabi, the regime systematically Islamized the society by enforcing rigid Sharia law. It also granted asylum to Osama Bin Laden. When African Christians and tribal religionists in southern Sudan resisted the Islamization of the nation, the regime launched a brutal campaign against them, using scorched earth tactics, indiscriminate killings, and abductions of women and children into slavery, which did not end until 2005.[62] Not only did this produce a huge refugee population, but it also signaled an early warning that something broader was brewing. One of the champions of the besieged African Christians, the late Catholic Bishop Macram Gassis, gave a speech in Washington, DC, in February 2000. He said that "the jihad that has been unleashed by these militants against my people will come to the United States." I attended this lecture. At the time, I thought he used this trope for dramatic effect, but he was, of course, prophetic, as we learned only a year and a half later, on September 11, 2001.[63]

Turning to the Iranian case again, the harsh treatment of its small Baha'i population provided a crucial predictor of its bellicose international posture. A benign government would have viewed Baha'is—accurately—as a decent, peaceful, enterprising, and entirely unthreatening minority. But the Iranian clerics treated Baha'is as apostates, as a threat to religious purity, as a source of pollution that needed to be eradicated. From 1979 onward, the regime shuttered Baha'i houses of worship, dissolved its spiritual assembly, expelled Baha'is from universities, fired thousands from their jobs, arrested many others, and executed some two hundred Baha'i civil and religious leaders.[64] The Baha'i International Community produced a booklet documenting this "cultural cleansing in Iran," a heartbreaking account complete with photographs of property destruction and men and women executed by the regime. In one shocking case, authorities arrested ten women (ages 17 to 57), the equivalent of Sunday school teachers in the West, for teaching religious classes to Baha'i youth, and in succession led them to the gallows to be hanged.[65] It should come as no surprise that a regime animated by such a virulent theology would become the world's leading backer of violent militia movements in Iraq, Yemen, Lebanon, Syria, and Gaza. In the global era, what happens inside a country religiously does not stay within that country.

WOMEN'S STATUS AND TERRORISM

As we saw in chapter 4, religious freedom and agency can empower women, especially in traditional societies. A growing body of empirical scholarship also finds that enhancement in women's status significantly reduces terrorism, both within nations and transnationally.[66] In other words, religious freedom and empowerment of women work in complementary fashion to reduce the global scourge of religious militancy and violence.

Hillary Clinton, throughout her public career but especially as Secretary of State in the Obama administration, advanced the argument that the subordination of women represented a national security threat. In what came to be called the Hillary Doctrine, she argued that nations that provide women equal rights are more stable, secure, and peaceful. Conversely, the places in the world most plagued by extremism and conflict were also places where "women's lives were most undervalued." Thus, to reduce terrorism, the United States must stand up for women and girls.[67]

With diverse societies around the world providing a vast laboratory, sophisticated statistical studies provide strong support for the Hillary Doctrine. As measures of women's political, social, and economic statuses rise, the incidents of terrorism against Americans decline.[68] The same holds true for violence within states and transnational terrorism more generally.[69]

A host of interrelated factors explains these robust relationships. Women represent mitigating or moderating voices; thus, the subordination of women, from the household level on, mutes those voices.[70] Indeed, empowered women may possess a veto over the violent designs of men.[71] The absence of women in teaching, in turn, reinforces hyper-masculine ideas about men, domination, and violence.[72] Societies that subordinate women also maintain traditions, such as bride price, that keep many men out of the marriage market, making them ready recruits of militant terror groups.[73]

In addition, militant religious groups preach the subordination of women and actively recruit alienated men into their ranks. Especially in Islamic societies where such militants represent a threat to the state, governments may make concessions to subordinate women, hoping to buy off their militancy. But that tends to embolden the militants, who use terrorism as a tool of subordinating women.[74] Unfortunately, the misogyny inherent in the ideology of ethnonationalist, right-wing, and religious terror groups means that they may react with violence to government efforts to enhance the status of women.[75] Thus, despite the strong relationships between women's empowerment and reduced terrorism, short-term spikes in violence may result from efforts to open opportunities for women, indicating the need for state capacity to enforce those policies.

This discussion provides a valuable qualification of the findings of this chapter. As powerful as religious repression and privilege are in producing violence and global terrorism, other factors, especially the poor status of women, contribute to that scourge. Thus, educating girls, expanding professional opportunities for women, and ensuring their legal protection represent crucial tools to stabilize societies and reduce violence. But as we learned in chapter 4, privileging dominant religious majorities tends to lock women in subordinate status. Religious freedom and women's empowerment work in tandem to produce more peaceful, flourishing societies.

CLASHES AMONG NATIONS

Interstate war represents the most dangerous potential impact of religious repression. While Saiya's initial research focused on terrorism, his broader work, along with other scholarship, connects to the potential of momentous *clashes between nations* arising from religious persecution. In a major examination of comparative religious policies, scholars find that states that discriminate against ethnoreligious minorities were more likely to initiate or become involved in crises and wars with other states. Indeed, as the degree of discrimination intensifies, the likelihood of involvement in interstate conflict increases.[76] The logic of this relationship flows from the character of regimes that create an environment of "inequality and violence" against unfavored minorities. Such regimes are more likely to "exhibit violence in their foreign policies as they externalize a worldview centered on their own sense of superiority."[77]

Examples abound of this relationship. The clerical regime in Iran, which harshly persecuted religious minorities, sparked a long and bloody war with Iraq. When Pakistan enacted harsh blasphemy and apostasy laws that created a domestic environment of hostility toward religious minorities, its foreign policies entailed support for Islamist insurgencies abroad and more truculent postures toward neighbors. The relationship holds, even controlling for democracy. When Hindu nationalists won control of Indian democracy, the country took a more aggressive posture toward Kashmir, sparking greater tensions with Pakistan. A domestic environment of general religious hostility, in short, fosters greater tendencies to use force in international disputes and sparks crises with other countries.

On the other hand, religiously free states are far less war-prone than repressive counterparts. Indeed, Saiya's exploration of modern history found that no pair of "religiously-free states has ever fought on opposing sides during an interstate war."[78] Other scholars document that religiously free societies do not make war on each other.[79]

MAJORITY VERSUS MINORITY VIOLENCE

The scholarship on the link between a regime's repression of minority religious groups and its bellicose international posture suggests a profound question about religion-state patterns. Does religious violence flow mostly from radicalized minorities or militant majorities? In *Weapon of Peace*, Saiya did not attempt to distinguish between violence carried out by minorities and majorities, due to limits on measuring available data. So he settled for overall statistical relationships. In subsequent research, however, he capitalizes on a new measure to address that pivotal question.[80] The answer is surprising and stunning. In *God's Warriors: Religious Violence and the Global Crisis of Secularism*, Saiya finds that, over a two-decade period (1998–2018), 90 percent of all identifiable cases of religious violence around the world can be attributed to *religious majorities.* Moreover, in statistical analysis and case studies, he shows that this violence stems overwhelmingly from majorities *privileged* by the state, not those treated equally in law.[81]

This leads Saiya to propose a novel explanation for the problem of religious violence in the world today. He terms it "the paradox of privilege."[82] Modern religious violence stems not from embattled, oppressed, and marginalized religious minorities, as most prior scholarship suggested, but from dominant and privileged religious majorities.[83] This finding of real-world import indicates how current global research on religious freedom represents a model of the scientific enterprise.[84]

Saiya provides robust evidence of the paradox of privilege through systematic statistical analysis.[85] He finds that "religious privilege is positively, consistently, and significantly associated with majoritarian violence."[86] Indeed, "the more states favor dominant majorities and discriminate against minority ones, the more majoritarian violence they produce."[87] These findings hold with alternative specifications and controls for diverse other variables. This leads Saiya to conclude that the paradox of privilege "lies at the heart of contemporary religious violence."[88] Saiya corroborates this explanation with detailed accounts of religious violence in contemporary Christianity, Islam, Hinduism, Buddhism, and Judaism. These chapters show that all religions are multivocal and can, and likely will, become violent if privileged by the state.

One of the most vivid illustrations of this pattern is the paradox of Buddhist violence, of "monks behaving badly." Among the world's religions, Buddhism is most associated with peace, tolerance, compassion, and nonviolence. Yet, both in the past and in several Asian societies today, we see graphic instances in which Buddhists, including monks, participate in violent and systematic attacks on non-Buddhists. What explains this puzzle? According to an article by Nilay Saiya and Stuti Manchanda, the answer lies in the privileged relationship of Buddhism with the state. Simply put, "Buddhist violence tends to occur in countries where Buddhism and the state are closely intertwined but not in countries that maintain an institutional separation between religion and government." This finding is powerfully corroborated by sophisticated statistical analysis of global data, along with vivid case studies of Buddhist violence in Sri Lanka, Myanmar, and Thailand. As this article shows, favoritism by the state weaponizes religious identity and radicalizes elements of the Buddhist majority, creating a climate of impunity for vigilante violence and support for military assaults on non-Buddhists.[89]

In Myanmar, for example, the depth of state favoritism and the integration of Buddhism help explain the systematic campaign of ethnic cleansing against Rohingya Muslims that produced a million stateless refugees. In that nation, a ministry of religious affairs is charged with purifying and propagating Theravada Buddhism. In addition, a 2010 law prohibiting interfaith marriage—tellingly known as "Safeguarding the National Identity"—inflamed Buddhist calls for expelling Rohingya and invited vigilante action against Muslims as a threat to the purity of Buddhist culture. Nothing of this sort occurs where Buddhism and the state are institutionally separated. While not systematically delving deeply into Buddhist theology, this article conveys that when monks behave violently, they are directly violating the teachings of their founder.[90]

Saiya anchors his broader analysis of majoritarian violence in what he calls the crisis of secularism. Since the 1970s, religious organizations around the world have pushed back at repressive secular states that tended to restrict their independent functioning. Governments responded with measures to control religion, often by extending privileges to religious majorities and discriminating against religious minorities. This attempt to co-opt majorities backfired because it emboldened majorities to enact intimidation and violence against disfavored religious minorities, often with impunity, which hardened religious identities. Saiya proposes an alternative vision for governments, which he calls "political secularism."[91] In contrast to "philosophical secularism," which seeks to marginalize religion, political secularism provides a neutral and level playing field for all religious groups to operate in society.

In a sense, political secularism to Saiya conforms to the broad definition of religious freedom. It entails four core components: separation, neutrality, equality, and freedom. *Separation* recognizes that religion and state constitute different realms of authority that function ideally when they operate independently within their own realms. Religious authorities do not wield the sword of the state, and government authorities do not interfere with religious civil society. State *neutrality* requires impartial treatment of all religions. This is closely related to *equality*, which "protects minorities—both religious and nonreligious"—from the tyranny of the majority. Finally, *freedom* ensures that the other core components—separation, neutrality, and equality—are not practiced in a pinched way that allows government bureaucrats to restrict religious exercise or trample on transcendent duties. As I will develop more in the concluding chapter, Saiya concludes his book by proposing a positive vision of "covenantal pluralism" for how diverse religious groups, majorities and minorities alike, can coexist amicably for the good of society.

WEAPON OF PEACE?

Thus far, we have seen that religious persecution, whether by governments or social actors, propels religious violence. But this makes only a negative case. To what extent, or how, does religious freedom actively promote peaceful and flourishing societies? Saiya offers several "pathways to peace" paved by religious liberty, all of which are corroborated by numerous studies.

First, religious freedom fosters an open marketplace of ideas that promotes diversity of views within and between religions. Restrictive environments facilitate radical theologies. Religiously free societies, in contrast, enable people to question and reform their faith, preventing extremist voices from dominating the discourse. Religiously free settings also expose "the logical inconsistencies and incorrect construal of religious dogma by radicals," thus diminishing the appeal of extremism that breeds violence and repression. Societies in which the natural religious pluralism is not squelched tend to be more peaceful.[92]

Second, religious freedom encourages religious actors to channel their ideas and grievances through legitimate political channels. According to international law, religious freedom includes the right of religious citizens and groups to participate in political and civic affairs on an equal basis with others. This makes them stakeholders in democratic governance and tends to moderate messages and demands. They must compete for votes and play by the rules, which prevents them from using the sword of the state to restrict the freedom of competitors.

Third, religious liberty "unlocks the 'spiritual capital' of faith-based actors, enabling them to make positive contributions to society." Through a host of social services, educational programs, development initiatives, and health clinics in many parts of the world, religious institutions "have been instrumental in increasing literacy, reducing poverty, providing access to potable water, administering health care, running counseling centers and leading peace and reconciliation processes." Such civil society contributions reduce grievances that spark violence and cultivate more peaceful and stable countries.[93] Religious freedom, as we saw in previous chapters, is in fact "associated with better health outcomes, higher levels of earned income, and better educational opportunities for women."[94]

Fourth, free exercise of religion works against authoritarianism and tyranny by limiting the reach of state power. When states grant religious freedom, they put limits on their own authority, eschewing the domain of religion and belief. This limitation lowers the stakes of seizing political power, since electoral majorities cannot use that power to restrict the fundamental rights of others, whether religious minorities, dissidents, skeptics, or nonbelievers. As the American founders believed, securing the transcendent rights of citizens helps foster limited government.[95]

In addition to these domestic contributions, religious freedom cultivates and empowers *international* peacemakers. Theological teachings on justice and peacemaking found in diverse religious traditions are far more likely to manifest and blossom under conditions of religious independence from state repression or co-optation. Systematic research on religious peacemaking shows this. Drawing upon global data, Toft, Philpott, and Shah document the extent to which religious actors have played a major or supporting role in mediating an end to civil wars and other conflicts. They find that, in a fifteen-year period starting in 1989, of the twenty-five mediations, religious actors played a strong role in eleven and a supporting role in an additional ten. In other words, transnational religious actors were significant players in the successful end to conflicts and civil wars. [96] Other studies show how religious communities and leaders dramatically facilitated numerous peaceful transitions from authoritarian rule to democratic societies, in such diverse settings as South Africa, the Philippines, and East Germany.[97] Finally, religious actors have played prominent roles in numerous post-conflict reconciliation initiatives, such as truth and reconciliation commissions. Applying the theological practices of truth-telling, apology, and forgiveness, rather than retribution, these initiatives help reconcile societies wounded by past atrocities. In addition, they have been more successful than legal or secular approaches in consolidating post-conflict societies and thus preventing further violence.[98] This success has sparked a profound rethinking about the nature of justice itself and its link to peace. Daniel Philpott shows how theological conceptions of justice as the "restoration of right relationships" in society appear to foster enduring grounds for stable peace.[99]

As this broad discussion suggests, religious freedom works on multiple levels. It moderates majority communities and allows multivocal expressions of the majority faith. It provides peaceful avenues for participation by minorities and undercuts that source of militancy. By giving all a stake in the pluralist fabric of society, it cultivates interreligious interactions and amity. It empowers global peacemakers. It is a weapon of peace.

SUMMARY LESSON—THE RELIGIOUS FREEDOM PEACE

Mounting scholarship demonstrates that religiously repressive governments and societies, along with fragile states that cannot protect religious rights, are incubators of radical theologies and militant movements that produce national and transnational violence. Such environments embolden majority communities to repress minorities and harass dissenters, which undercuts democratic systems. They produce insurgent groups. And they weaponize religious identities that make religious conflicts difficult to end.

Religiously free countries, on the other hand, have far lower levels of religious violence at home, less propensity to export violence abroad, and more peaceful relations with other nations. Strikingly, studies find that the powerful relationship between religious freedom and peace remains even when *controlling for democracy*. In other words, because not all electoral democracies guarantee equal religious rights—and too many engage in favoritism and repression—religious freedom uniquely lowers terrorism and interstate conflict by undercutting the militancy and grievances that propel such intractable violence. Thus, while Immanuel Kant posited a "democratic peace," it appears that in the twenty-first century, hope lies even more in "*the religious freedom peace*."[100]

CHAPTER SIX

CHARTING THE WAY FORWARD

This book presents cogent evidence for the powerful role of religious freedom in promoting and sustaining human rights, democracy, flourishing economics, uplift for the poor, access for the marginalized, empowerment of women, interreligious amity, and peace. In turn, we have seen how violations of religious liberty spark violence and strife, undermine democratic norms, sap economic vitality, and lock the poor, vulnerable women, and cultural minorities in rigid socioeconomic straitjackets. Momentously, religious persecution, violence, and sectarian civil wars have propelled massive waves of refugees, which in turn have destabilized other societies and provoked bigotry and discrimination against religious "others."

The full weight of why religious freedom matters, however, emerges in the interactions of its different dimensions. Religious equality supports the rule of law and democracy, which provides avenues of uplift for the poor. Protecting equal religious rights gives all a stake in the system and generates citizen loyalty and trust, which drastically reduces interreligious strife and violence. Healthy religious competition promotes vigorous civil society and social capital, which buoy flourishing economies. Generous legal protection for diverse religious practices and beliefs provides leverage for outcasts and women to challenge the dominant views of caste or gender roles. Religiously free societies are both better trading partners *and* security allies. Securing global peace and security depends on protecting religious freedom, which also propels equitable economic growth.

In other words, the different dimensions of religious freedom reinforce each other and corroborate this book's central theme: *Because religious freedom goes to the heart of human experience and personhood, it is crucial to the kind of flourishing future most of us seek.* Backed by sophisticated causal theories, this theme has been rigorously tested against alternative explanations, corroborated by diverse methods, and replicated across the vast laboratory of time and the globe. It illustrates—in elegant, parsimonious, and encompassing ways—the very attributes of great scientific theories.

To be sure, all the research presented in this volume must be properly qualified. While religious freedom remains a vital underpinning to flourishing societies, it operates in concert with other factors, even when its impact is transformational.[1] Global forces, moreover, will impinge on the positive impact of religious freedom. Religious agency promotes uplift for the poor, but that does not remedy the vast inequalities of wealth and opportunity afflicting the globe. Ethnic or nationalist conflicts often have roots in state religious privilege, but tribal clashes independent of religion continue to destabilize parts of the world.[2] And the climate crisis poses a unique challenge to humanity that could exacerbate international and societal divisions.

Nonetheless, the singular and compelling findings presented in this book should transform how we understand the challenge of religion in the twenty-first century. With the collapse of the secularization prospect, many governments today treat resurgent religion as a problem to be controlled or co-opted. This book suggests that great advances in human flourishing can only happen if that default position is replaced by the paradigm of global religious freedom.[3]

What remains to elaborate? Where do we go from here? In this conclusion, I will elaborate on key themes, probe broader implications, explore challenges, and offer a vision for the way forward.

CLARIFYING SECULARISM AND THE BEST REGIMES FOR PROTECTING RELIGIOUS FREEDOM

One of the most confused of modern discourses relates to "secularism" or the "secular state"—terms often used pejoratively by religious believers. In assessing this terrain, Daniel Philpott discovered nine different concepts or definitions of the secular, "four of which are neutral or positive and five are negative."[4] Because protecting religious freedom is inextricably linked with various manifestations of the secular, this landscape needs charting.

Some advocates for religious freedom speak of the secular state positively, because it suggests neutrality between diverse religions and keeps government out of the business of defining what is religiously orthodox.[5]

In other cases, scholars or advocates draw distinctions between different types of secularism. The late Pope Benedict lauded the "positive" secularism in the United States, which protects religion from the state and ensures its healthy role in public life, versus the anticlerical or "hostile" secularism found in Europe.[6] In a fuller scholarly analysis, Ahmet Kuru uses the terms "passive" versus "aggressive" secularism to capture what Benedict was alluding to.[7] China, which enforces atheism as official policy, would be an extreme example of aggressive secularism, though a better term might be authoritarian secularism. Jonathan Fox provides actual measures of how much states ruled by aggressive or "jealous secular gods" restrict religion.[8] Finally, Nilay Saiya positively depicts "political secularism" as a legal system of liberty and equality most congenial to religious freedom and interreligious amity. He contrasts this system with a "philosophical secularism" that seeks to limit the role of religion in public life or society.[9]

Given this confusing terrain, and the negative connotations of secularism, I wonder if better terms might be employed to depict the best regimes for protecting maximum religious freedom. The "religiously neutral state" captures something of the concept here. But neutrality can be practiced in a pinched way toward religious communities and allow government bureaucracies to trample legitimate free exercise rights, as I have documented for the United States.[10]

The legal concept of "benevolent neutrality," which provides generous accommodations for religious practice, better captures the constitutional philosophy I have in mind. It combines neutrality among different faiths with robust protections for religious free exercise, conscience rights, institutional autonomy, and societal havens for diverse ways of life. As a legal principle, benevolent neutrality imposes an exacting standard on states to justify inroads on religious practice.[11] Benevolence also contains rich religious connotations. The Latin term *benevolentia*, in Catholic social teaching, suggests an attitude that "wills the good" of others.[12] Benevolent neutrality thus reflects the idea that when all religions enjoy equal and generous free exercise, they tend to defend each other's rights as well.

THE PARADOX OF PRIVILEGE

One of the central findings of this book concerns the fraught relationship between religion and the state. Like a law of physics, the fusion of religion and government is bad for both governance and religion.

For governance, the political melding of faith with nation, regime, or tribe contributes to corruption, repression, autocracy, and even violence. Across the world, we see movements by religious nationalists to link the dominant faith with national identity. With Islamist movements in the Middle East, Hindu nationalists in India, Christian nationalists in the United States, and Buddhist chauvinists in Asia, we see this trend. The impulse is understandable when once-dominant religious communities see their cultural influence eroded by growing religious pluralism or aggressive secular ideologies.[13] But often, the attempt to reassert cultural prominence by capturing state organs sparks repression against religious minorities and stifles dissent. In turn, would-be autocrats cunningly co-opt majority faith leaders for their own ends, undermining democracy and rule of law.

Consequently, while government persecution against all religions represents an obvious threat to religious communities, as we see in North Korea and China, so does majority favoritism, which contributes to minority discrimination in far more countries.[14]

The broader dynamic at play in the melding of religion and state is captured by the idea of the "paradox of privilege," a rich concept with profound implications for politics, peaceful societies, economics, and religion itself.[15]

As discussed in Chapter 5, a vast majority of religious violence in the world today is generated not by repressed religious minorities but by religious majorities emboldened and radicalized by the privileges they enjoy from governments.[16] Perhaps the most vivid illustration of this phenomenon is the case of Buddhist monks "behaving badly," participating in violent attacks against religious others. In other words, even Buddhism, a faith deeply associated with peace and compassion, can be drawn into violence when fused with the state.[17]

Majority privilege usually goes hand in hand with discrimination against religious minorities and repression of dissenters, which Jonathan Fox shows is the dominant pattern across the globe.[18] In turn, religious independence and equality in law, for majorities and minorities alike, is the antidote to religious strife and an underpinning of democratic ethos. As discussed in Chapter 2, when the Catholic Church officially renounced state privilege and endorsed religious liberty at Vatican II, it became the engine of the last great wave of democratization on Earth.[19]

So the paradox is clearly political, that when governments grant privileges to dominant religions, thinking that will stabilize society, they make majorities more aggressive and less civil. Privileged religious majorities tend to engage in intimidation or even violence against religious minorities, often with impunity. Majority privilege undermines flourishing civil society, civil liberties, and democratic norms, as documented in Chapter 2. Moreover, even though governments patronize religions to gain greater legitimacy, recent research shows that state support for religion is associated with lower levels of public confidence in government.[20]

The paradox of privilege also extends to economics. As we learned in Chapter 3, the ulama-state alliance that emerged in Muslim empires and the subsequent enforcement of rigid sharia law stunted economic enterprise in Mideast societies. In a telling example of the paradox, Muslim businessmen in the Ottoman Empire were charged higher interest on loans than Christians and Jews, because their preferential treatment in credit courts made them high-risk borrowers. This redounded over the generations to inhibit the development of modern economic institutions in Muslim majority countries. Moreover, as shown in Chapter 4, majority privilege reinforces economic straitjackets that prevent uplift for the poor and empowerment for women.

But perhaps the most profound implication is that privilege can undermine the religious essence itself. All great religious traditions contain wellsprings of moral guidance and ethical teachings that can contribute to healthy families, communities, and flourishing societies. A wide array of scholarship in sociology, political science, religious studies, and even theology suggests that state sponsorship can compromise or warp those religious principles. Over time, the fusion of faith with political power traduces the credibility of co-opted religious leaders and saps the vitality of religious commitments.[21] Evidence comes from modern Iran, where repressive and corrupt clerical rule has dramatically weakened allegiance to Shia Islam and increased the nonreligious population. Shockingly, in one survey more Iranian respondents claimed *no religion* than pledged fealty to Shia Islam.[22]

On the other hand, when majorities renounce privilege and agree to enjoy equal liberty under law—accepting pluralism—they tend to flourish more authentically.

The most systematic and global examination of the paradox of privilege is provided by Nilay Saiya in his landmark work, *The Global Politics of Jesus: A Christian Case for Church-State Separation.* In this book and subsequent analysis, Saiya marshals global data and case studies to document the impact on Christianity, the world's largest religion, when it becomes enmeshed with the state. To the degree that Christianity is backed by political power or granted privileges by governments, it becomes fundamentally unchristian and loses its vitality.[23]

As a political scientist, Saiya provides an unusual *theological* analysis to make this case.[24] Distinct among religious traditions, he argues, Christian doctrine sharply distinguishes the kingdom of God, or what Saiya calls "The Kingdom of the Cross," from the kingdom of the world—of principalities and powers. The kingdom of the world tends to be tribal, exclusivist, coercive, and violent. On the other hand, the Kingdom of God as proclaimed by Jesus entails uncompromising love instead of coercion, universal dignity instead of exclusion, forgiveness instead of retribution, and peace instead of violence. As Saiya argues, deploying the sword of the state to promote the faith inevitably contradicts these essential teachings.[25] Or, as one author underscored the point, "The best way to get people to lay down the cross is to hand them the sword of the state."[26]

On the other hand, Christianity is most authentic when it depends on the voluntary support of its followers, not the state. Obviously, this occurs in religiously free and pluralist societies. But it can even function where the faith confronts political repression, just not where it is privileged.[27]

Remarkably, Saiya demonstrates that state favoritism represents *the greatest threat* to the growth of Christianity in the world today. Based on a decade of demographic trends (2010–2020), Saiya and his co-author trace patterns of growth or decline of Christianity in a large sample of nations.

Employing measurable indicators, such as church attendance, participation in youth programs, and faith-based charities, they show that when Christianity is privileged by the state, it tends to lose its vitality and membership. In fact, statistical tests demonstrate that as Christian privilege goes up, its percentage of the national population declines over time.[28] Thus, Christian privilege leads to the secularization of societies—a statistical confirmation of sociological theories.[29] On the other hand, in places where Christianity operates on equal terms with other faiths, or even under some conditions of persecution, it tends to grow. In other words, political patronage undermines evangelization, the *great commission* of spreading the gospel, of making disciples.[30]

A vivid illustration of this pattern concerns the Catholic Church, the largest Christian denomination in the world. Even though religious restrictions are low overall for Catholic majority nations, enough variation exists to measure the impact of state privilege. Saiya found that Catholic majority countries where privilege is highest saw Catholic membership *decrease* as a share of the population over the recent decade, while Catholic majority countries where privilege is lowest saw Catholic membership *increase*. Projecting into 2050, none of the ten countries expected to see the largest gains in Catholic population have high levels of privilege.[31]

Perhaps the "curse of privilege" is a more accurate depiction of the phenomenon than the paradox of privilege.

This curse of privilege extends to religious communities that receive support from political movements or parties. In the United States, recent studies suggest that the association of evangelical Christianity with the Christian Right and the Republican Party has helped propel the growth in the percentage of Americans who express no religious affiliation. In other words, the politicization of the evangelical church has undermined its growth and spurred secularization.[32]

This finding should offer a cautionary note for the American Catholic Church, the next largest religious community in the nation. While Catholic leaders welcomed GOP support for the pro-life cause and their institutional autonomy,[33] the nativism of the Republican MAGA movement clearly violates Catholic social teaching, as Pope Leo XIV has intimated.[34] In spite of this, prominent Republican Catholics seek an unprecedented privileging of their conservative brand of Catholicism by the state.[35] One aim is to gain public tax support for Catholic parochial schools, an outcome that would propel deeper entanglement of the Catholic Church with government and tempt Church leaders to mute their prophetic voices for potential tax dollars.[36] The "curse of privilege" suggests that church leaders would be wise to resist succumbing to the temptation of state privilege, lest they risk undermining church credibility and vitality, as happened with their evangelical counterparts.

A crucial challenge facing the world is the rise of Christian nationalism, a global ideology that seeks to integrate national identity with Christianity. Saiya shows that this ideology is a distortion—theologians might say heresy—of authentic Christianity and the teachings of Jesus. Because Christian nationalism rests on exclusivity and jettisons the principle of citizen equality, it is fundamentally anti-democratic and tends to fuel strife and even violence.[37]

In the United States, Christian nationalists have emerged as a growing threat to democracy, civil tolerance, and religious equality. Skeptics wonder if the term is merely a construct of scholars hostile to policies Christians might support. After all, what is wrong with Christians engaging in politics to back policies that reflect their values?[38] Nothing, of course! But as voluminous empirical research shows, Christian nationalists depart from this kind of advocacy and embrace autocratic aims.[39] Spearheaded by a growing movement that strives to seize power over all sectors of society, Christian nationalists overwhelmingly backed Donald Trump in his 2024 election and provided the strongest support for his autocratic moves to gain unchecked presidential power. Because of their aggressive posture, some Christian nationalists even criticize the Christian virtue of empathy.[40]

While ostensibly defending religious liberty, this movement represents a threat to that cause, not only domestically but on the global stage, because it undermines America's enlightened international leadership. Born of its constitutional heritage on religious liberty, the United States has played a leading role in promoting international religious freedom, both by its example and its global leadership.[41] Indeed, some eighteen nations have developed or strengthened international religious freedom initiatives, often following the lead of the United States.[42] This legacy may be in peril. The "American First" agenda of the MAGA movement, its assaults on democratic norms and institutions, and nativist cruelty toward refugees threaten to undermine the nation's credibility, goodwill, and capacity to play its leadership role going forward.[43] If this trend continues, it would represent a tragedy for the cause of global religious freedom.

In contrast to this picture, a formidable scholarship demonstrates that authentic Christianity, fueled by voluntary support, strongly promotes democracy, human rights, civil society, and uplift for the poor around the world.[44] Christian human rights champions have become global "Holy Humanitarians" and "militants for peace and justice."[45] They can only perform this role if they resist the siren's song of privileged Christian nationalism.

GOOD RELIGION, BAD RELIGION?

As the sociology of religion teaches us, every religious tradition is pluralistic.[46] Each can be interpreted or practiced in a variety of ways under different conditions. As we see in the paradox of privilege, religion-state patterns profoundly shape the trajectories of religious communities. *This leads to the stunning possibility that we now possess insight into what makes religion good or bad, compassionate or cruel, peaceful or violent.* To be sure, the tenets, cosmology, or political theology of religions play a role as well.[47] Human sacrifice was practiced in some religious societies, and militant theologies give sanction to terrorism. But emerging patterns strongly suggest that state privilege is the *key factor* in shaping, or rather *warping*, faith in the twenty-first century,[48] a finding of enormous import for religious believers, political leaders, and people everywhere.

EQUALITY AND INEQUALITY

As noted above, religious privilege, particularly extended to dominant religions, is a pervasive and pernicious phenomenon around the globe today. It not only leads to discrimination against minorities but also to the cooptation of majorities.

What can give advocacy for religious freedom a bad name is when some groups seek privilege under the guise of fighting for their religious rights.[49] This goes to a crucial dimension of the very idea of religious freedom: It is not only about *liberty*; it is also about *equality*. This is one of the most important lessons that I learned in writing this book, and one that needs exploring.

International law and advocacy primarily focus on the right to "Freedom of Religion or Belief" (which, in international parlance, is abbreviated as FoRB). This emphasis is not surprising. Recall the foundational document on international religious freedom, Article 18 of the *Universal Declaration of Human Rights*, adopted by the UN in 1948 in the wake of the Holocaust. It emphasized freedom and rights, but with no explicit mention of equality. One might contend that equality is implied in this document, because without legal equality, the right to religious freedom is imperiled. And the language of equality does arise in discussions about rule of law, as in promoting legal equality for religious minorities. But this dimension has been undeveloped. Thankfully, scholars have begun exploring the need to redress religious inequalities around the globe, leading to fresh insights and applications.

Several lessons emerge from this enterprise. First, religious equality entails protecting *religious agency*, "the right to mix and match different beliefs," to interpret faith for oneself. As Mariz Tadros notes, "millions of people around the world exercise religious agency in a dynamic and fluid way." Thus, religious practice is far more diverse than even the most detailed enumeration of the world's religions suggests. Religious freedom, moreover, entails the freedom to challenge one's own religion from within, or to interpret and practice it in ways that differ from religious purists. Hence, the term "religious minority" is inadequate to capture this dimension, because a member of the majority faith can suffer from discrimination just as much as religious "others."[50] A Hindu woman who finds multiple faith practices empowering can suffer harassment by ultra-right Hindus who strive to enforce their view of Hindu purity.[51] Ditto for being the wrong kind of Muslim in many Muslim-majority nations.

Second, focusing on inequalities helps us see the intersections of religious marginalization with persistent poverty or the repression of women. As we learned in Chapter 4, religious freedom unleashes agency in other arenas of life and contributes to uplift for the poor and empowerment for women. International development initiatives that slight religious inequalities, therefore, will fail to achieve their potential.

Third, understanding religious inequalities challenges us to broaden our understanding of religious freedom, to expand the horizons of how to create more inclusive societies. FoRB is not only an awkward acronym but seems terribly limited considering the vast and sometimes hidden inequalities around the world. Fully incorporating equality into our conception of religious freedom remains the unfinished business of constitutionalism and international law.

Finally, redressing religious inequalities must incorporate indigenous peoples, whose marginalization can be invisible to governments and international development agencies, but whose way of life is infused with spiritual meaning. Ancestral lands, revered forests, and sacred burial grounds anchor the ways of life of indigenous peoples. Therefore, the encroachment or destruction of such places represents a fundamental violation of religious freedom. This dimension deserves elaboration.

THE INDIGENOUS DIMENSION

Critics of the promotion of religious freedom by the United States or other Western powers contend that they often slight indigenous religious practices.[52] There is truth in this claim. Indigenous, tribal, or folk religions—in which the natural world is infused with spirits and religious beliefs are interwoven with ways of life—can be invisible to outsiders. Elizabeth Shakman Hurd provides several vivid illustrations of this blindness. In the Central African Republic (CAR), for example, a U.S. State Department report on religious freedom acknowledged that 60% of the women imprisoned in the country were charged with "witchcraft," which to the practitioners represented a traditional African religious practice. Yet the U.S. gave the CAR a positive ranking on religious freedom, apparently because it, like the CAR government, did not consider such practices religious. Another example concerned the threats to the way of life of the K'iche' people, a Mayan ethnic group living in the western highlands of Guatemala. Their representatives rejected the proposed mining and hydroelectric projects that would destroy their ancestral lands and their way of life. The Guatemalan government and outside corporations proceeded anyway, resulting in massive violations of the cultural heritage of the K'iche'. Ignoring this record, the State Department wrote that "no reports of abuses of religion" occurred that year.[53]

Similarly, Katherine Marshall, an international development scholar and advisor to the World Bank, lamented the "vulnerability and invisibility of indigenous belief systems and religions that are being decimated by the loss of territories and land." These include "natural features or ancestral burial sites that are critical to their worldview and spiritual systems and beliefs." She concluded, "It is tragic and wrong that indigenous peoples feature so little in debates" about freedom of religion and belief.[54]

One lesson, perhaps, is that the U.S. State Department needs to solicit and incorporate the insights of anthropologists and ethnographers in its country reports on religion. The same can be said of the work of international development agencies. This would address the complaint that religious freedom advocacy by the United States or European nations shields only "Western" notions of religion.

But beyond soliciting such insights, advocates and governments must take far more seriously the ways that mining, logging, agribusiness, hydroelectric projects, and highways can shatter the spiritual lives of indigenous peoples. As we saw in Chapter 4, this case is being pressed by scholars and advocates who understand the enormous stakes involved.

Even in the cradle of religious liberty, the contemporary United States, constitutional protections for free exercise have failed to shield native peoples from encroachments on sacred lands, not only in the shameless past but also today. In one case, the Supreme Court ruled against a California tribe that showed a planned forest road through Chimney Rock would destroy their spiritual heritage.[55] More recently, a sacred site for the Apache tribe from time immemorial, Oak Flat in the Tonto National Forest of Arizona, had for years been protected by the federal government to allow members to worship, pray, and conduct religious ceremonies central to the tribe's existence.[56] But in 2014, powerful lobbyists attached a rider to a must-pass defense bill that transferred the site to a foreign-owned copper mining operation, which would obliterate the sacred ground with a vast mining pit. Despite the protections of religious free exercise in the First Amendment and federal legislation, the Supreme Court refused to hear the appeal by the tribe, in effect saying the government could do with "its land" as it wished. In dissenting from this judgment, Justice Gorsuch likened the obliteration of Apache sacred ground to the destruction of a historical cathedral.[57]

ADDRESSING THE CRITICS

As introduced in Chapter 1, a chorus of intellectuals criticizes the very idea of religious freedom as a coherent and universal set of rights. Or they see it as a Western Christian construct imposed on other societies and thus a projection of imperialist power.[58] These critics can provide a corrective to the blinders of Western political leaders or advocates, as we see above in Hurd's investigation of the slighting of indigenous practices by the U.S. State Department.

But the critics go much further, reflecting a profound skepticism about universal claims, especially regarding religion.[59]

Their critique has several lines. One claim is that "religious freedom is so variable and contingent across historical time and cultural context that it lacks any universal normative force."[60] The freedom of religion cannot, therefore, represent a universal principle. Nonetheless, declarations of the right to unmolested faith ripple throughout millennia, belying this depiction, as does the body of international law.[61] Even more compelling, the vast empirical findings presented in this book testify to the reality of religious freedom as a coherent normative ideal with real-world impact.

A second line of criticism sees only power and self-interest in the West's invention and promotion of its *constructs* of religion or religious freedom. Explicit in this line of critique is that powerful Western nations, such as the United States, back favored and even dominant religious groups. Nonetheless, those clamoring for religious freedom often represent tiny, heterodox, and dissenting sects, such as Ahmadis, Baha'is, Yazidis, and Chaldean Christians, who in recent times have suffered some of the most horrific persecution in the world.[62] These minorities seek international allies who magnify their voices. In other words, religious freedom is a weapon of the weak.

Finally, critics see any Western intervention in conflict areas, such as Syria, in the name of religious freedom, as hardening religious identities of people who have multiple allegiances and mix religious practices. Such political intervention funnels people into sectarian groups and empowers established religious authorities.[63] Skepticism about the motives of Western leaders, or their ignorance of local religious conditions, is always warranted. But as we have seen, religious freedom advocates champion the right of all persons to criticize, reform, or exit religious communities, the opposite of empowering religious authorities.

Much of the critique, then, focuses on the *promotion* of religious freedom by governments, which can become entangled with power interests. Again, this is a useful caution, but enlightened governmental leaders, working with local stakeholders and NGO advocates, can play a valuable role, as we will see later in the case of Uzbekistan. Moreover, in assessing Western religious freedom initiatives, critics describe what appears to result from "an *insufficient* rather than an *overzealous* commitment to religious freedom," as indicated by the slighting of indigenous ways of life (emphasis mine).[64]

EMERGING CHALLENGES: CLASHES OVER SEXUAL IDENTITY, MARRIAGE, AND ABORTION

Dramatic changes in public policy and opinion on abortion, homosexual behavior, gender identity, and same-sex marriage represent new flash points of polarizing cultural conflict. Religious traditionalists often find themselves defending their conscience rights to act on religious understandings of marriage or refusing to participate in abortion or contraceptive services. Religious institutions, in turn, struggle to maintain their autonomy in the face of antidiscrimination laws or court interpretations that would force them to violate their understandings of sacred duty. Feeling themselves under siege, religious traditionalists can respond aggressively, sometimes backing autocratic populists who speak to their sense of threat. Cultural progressives, on the other hand, see religious bigotry standing in the way of greater inclusion and fairness for women and sexual minorities. This is not a recipe for civility and partnership in promoting religious freedom, at home or abroad.

Let us look at these emerging clashes.[65] One arena entails *rights of conscience* for medical professionals whose religious duties prevent them from performing or supporting abortion or assisted suicide. In Sweden, doctors, nurses, and midwives with religious objections to abortion or assisted dying are effectively excluded from medical professions because the law provides no conscience objection.[66] Before *Roe v. Wade* was overturned in the United States, Catholic and evangelical doctors and nurses often found themselves under pressure or required to perform or assist in abortions. Similarly, Catholic institutions, even orders of nuns, were required to provide contraceptive services in their health plans. A particularly vivid case involved a multi-year legal struggle by Little Sisters of the Poor, a mendicant order of nuns that served the elderly poor. They faced heavy fines during the Obama administration because the federal government mandated that the nuns violate their vows and provide contraceptives and abortifacients in their health plans. It took nine years of litigation before the Little Sisters were granted a religious exemption to the mandate.[67] Family businesses with objections to what they see as abortifacients in health care plans have also run into federal mandates, igniting extensive litigation.[68]

Once Roe was overturned and draconian laws against abortion were enacted in conservative states, the tables switched, and pregnant women in dire medical crisis were turned away from hospitals that feared prosecution for violating abortion bans. Both extremes undermine public confidence in religious freedom as a bipartisan cause.

Another arena of conflict involves same-sex marriage and laws against discrimination based on sexual orientation and gender identity (SOGI), which blossomed in recent years. As gender and sexual minorities gain victories in legislation and in the courts, particularly the right to have same sex marriages guaranteed in law, traditional religious persons and institutions find themselves treated or depicted as bigots who favor discrimination. In countries without the strong free speech protections found in the American First Amendment, citing Bible verses against homosexual behavior or affirming traditional teachings on marriage has led to hate crimes prosecutions.[69]

The legalization of same-sex marriage also collides with religious institutions that insist on adhering to traditional teachings on marriage as divinely ordained between one man and one woman. Religious nonprofit charities have been mandated by governments to include same-sex couples in their ministries. As a result, in the United States, long-standing Catholic adoption and foster care programs had to shutter services in states that provided no religious exemptions for mandates that they place children with same-sex couples. This happened, even when children's advocates saw the church as serving an important niche in this arena.[70]

Religious educational institutions have also been under pressure from state bureaucracies for only hiring those who adhere to the tenets of their faith. U.S. parochial schools have faced lawsuits for suspending employees who departed from church teachings. In other words, state education authorities sometimes treat private religious schools like public schools.[71]

Religious freedom defenders see a pattern of pressure on religious institutions to exit the public square. This has elevated the importance of preserving religious institutional autonomy for flourishing and diverse civil societies around the world, which will also preserve the religious freedom of individuals whose faith is embedded in communal practices and institutions.[72]

Private businesses owned by devout religionists have also collided with SOGI laws. Christian vendors of marriage services, such as photographers, florists, and cake designers, often see their art as being in the service of the traditional vision of marriage as divinely ordained. While selling ready-made items to all customers, they have been sued for refusing to offer their artistic services to same-sex couples, and in some cases have lost or closed their businesses. In this climate, efforts by Congress to pass a sweeping Equality Act to prevent discrimination based on sexual orientation and gender identity, without religious exemptions, have ignited a storm of alarm in religious circles.[73]

One problem with these new clashes is that citizens become polarized into camps that see each other not as fellow citizens to be persuaded but as mortal enemies to their way of life, their identity. In culture wars, culture loses. Compromise and civility vanish. The other problem is that religious liberty gets transformed into a conservative or partisan cause, which gives it a bad name in progressive circles. In media reports and partisan outlets, we see "religious liberty" or "religious freedom" put in "scare quotes" as code words for intolerance.[74]

Complexity and nuance, moreover, get lost in culture wars. In the United States, some of the strongest defenders of conscience exemptions in contraceptive mandates or marriage services have also championed the cause of Sikhs in the military, the right of Muslims to build mosques, and the preservation of access for native tribes to ancestral lands. That goes for defending religious institutions from intrusive state or local governments.[75]

Moreover, when we shift attention beyond North America and Europe, the picture changes. Religiously repressive regimes around the world are also the ones likely to criminalize homosexuality and transgender identity. As we learned in Chapter 4, regimes of religious freedom are far less perilous for sexual minorities than religiously repressive ones.[76]

In the West, however, the cultural clash renders only winners and losers, especially through litigation, elevating the stakes. Is compromise or common ground possible?

What has come to be called the "Utah Compromise" provides a model. In 2015, the Supreme Court was on the verge of declaring same-sex marriage a right, which signaled to Utah lawmakers and Mormon leaders that such a judicial fiat would leave little room for preserving the autonomy of their religious institutions. On the other hand, even if granted the right to marry, LGBT persons in Utah would still lack secure protections against discrimination in housing and employment. So both sides engaged in intense negotiations aimed at securing a win-win legislative compromise. Gender and sexual minorities gained protection against discrimination in housing and employment, often better than in more liberal states, while religious institutions retained the autonomy to operate according to their religious tenets, particularly regarding marriage. Faith communities retained the right to affirm traditional teachings on marriage and to operate their counseling services consistent with that vision.[77]

An intriguing feature of the legislative package appealed to both sides—protection from losing jobs or professional licenses for speech and actions in the public square. As Stuart Adams, the principal author of the legislation, put it, "In Utah there can be no workplace retaliation for either marching in a gay pride parade or speaking at a pro-life event." A journalist observed that this principle makes "it easier for residents who disagreed on fundamental issues to live and work together in peace."[78]

The Utah compromise sparked initiatives aimed at replicating this achievement. One coalition of religious organizations and LGBT advocates, Alliance for Lasting Liberty, articulated its vision with two goals:

> LGBT Americans should have civil rights protections when it comes to employment, housing, and publicly available services; and religious Americans—and their faith-based institutions—should be able to live, work, and serve their community in ways that are consistent with the teachings and tenets of their faith.[79]

While some conservative critics see such compromises as one-sided or even impossible,[80] the aim itself is admirable. It seeks a "commitment to civic pluralism" that "allows Americans to remain true to their beliefs and live peacefully with one another while having real differences."[81] Intriguingly, this commitment to civic pluralism foreshadows a broader vision of the way forward, a vision of how religious communities can embrace the reality of pluralism without giving up their spiritual convictions.[82]

COVENANTAL PLURALISM

Religious pluralism is the key reality and challenge of the modern era. Growing religious diversity in societies around the world can be resisted or denied, but only with state repression and societal strife. Countries can protect religious freedom by changing constitutional provisions and laws to ensure the generous and equal rights of different religious groups, which, as suggested earlier, may be optimally achieved through systems of benevolent neutrality. But that is unlikely to happen unless religious communities and their leaders buy into that change and live it out. This brings us to an emerging vision for how diverse religious people can accept the reality of pluralism—live and work together—without giving up their religious truths or commitments. It is called *Covenantal Pluralism*, a vital companion to legal protections.

Covenantal pluralism has been embraced by some of the most astute scholars and diverse advocates of religious freedom.[83] The term was first conceived by Chris Seiple, founder of the Institute for Global Engagement (IGE), a "think and do tank" that promotes religious freedom by working with diverse religious stakeholders in highly charged environments.[84] The concept was fleshed out by Seiple and his colleagues in an evocative article: "Toward a Global Covenant of Peaceable Neighborhood."[85] That vision ultimately blossomed into a major initiative of the Templeton Religion Trust.[86]

Covenantal pluralism rests on several core principles. It emphasizes *respect* over mere *tolerance*, especially the pledge of mutual respect to protect each other's liberty of conscience. It stresses a *multi-faith* approach, which recognizes real religious differences, instead of an *interfaith* approach that suggests a blending of theologies. It emphasizes patriotism over nationalism, especially the scourge of religious nationalism. It celebrates the healthy competition of religiously free societies, as opposed to religious monopolies. It cultivates the capacity for deep listening, which requires a healthy dose of humility. To Chris Seiple, these attributes help us become "more fully human," more trustworthy.[87]

To elaborate, "a world of covenantal pluralism is characterized both by a constitutional order of equal rights and responsibilities and by a culture of reciprocal commitment to engaging, respecting, and protecting the other."[88] Moving beyond banal calls for tolerance, it instead promotes the hard work of forging "real relationships, collaboration, and understanding." It rejects relativism by promoting character virtues, "such as humility, empathy, patience, and courage," that enable these interfaith relationships.[89]

Covenant evokes something deeper and more enduring than a mere contract, something solemn and binding. The language of covenant, of course, is central to the Abrahamic faiths, to the theological idea of God's enduring commitment to his people. But as UK Rabbi Jonathan Sacks shows, the trust and reciprocity entailed in covenant can apply to all faiths or none.[90]

Indeed, key documents of international law incorporate the language of covenant: the *International Covenant on Civil and Political Rights* and the *International Covenant on Economic, Social, and Cultural Rights*. The UN committee that produced the *Universal Declaration of Human Rights* also represents a model of covenantal pluralism in action.[91]

In a sense, covenantal pluralism represents a positive vision for how religious communities can embrace religious freedom, not as secularism but as a reciprocal duty to respect each other in society. In the place of fear and hostility, it offers hope. It also recognizes the global reality that every religious tradition is a minority somewhere, suggesting a broader need for reciprocity beyond national borders. It thus represents an eloquent challenge to religious nationalism and weaponized religion.[92]

Covenantal partnerships require literacy, both of one's own faith and of central tenets of other faiths. This suggests the need to incorporate greater knowledge of global religions in schools, colleges, and even in religious communities. Interfaith understanding and collaboration are impossible without that literacy. Moreover, interfaith engagement cultivates the competencies and skills that enable deeper engagement. Religious leaders will defend each other's rights when they know each other.[93]

The vision of covenantal pluralism is not utopian, and examples abound of genuine interfaith collaborations. Seiple and Hoover, for example, assembled a wide range of scholars and practitioners, from diverse religions and nations, who document vivid models of covenantal pluralism in action.[94]

A telling example from the United States involved the effort by American Sikhs to eliminate a bigoted 1923 Oregon law preventing teachers from wearing any religious attire in public schools. A legacy of the Ku Klux Klan, the law originally targeted Catholic nuns, but its tentacles extended over time to prevent Orthodox Jews, Muslim women of cover, and Sikhs from teaching in Oregon public schools, showing how efforts to curb religious freedom for one community inevitably redound to others. Drawing upon the nation's rich heritage of religious liberty, Sikhs spearheaded a broad coalition of Baptists, Adventists, Catholics, Jews, and Muslims that overturned the law.[95] Signifying the common ground of the campaign, a Seventh-day Adventist organization subsequently gave its annual religious freedom award to the Baptist legislator who sponsored the law sought by Sikhs.[96]

Also in the United States, an intentional initiative to build cross-religion relationships and literacy is led by Muslim activist Eboo Patel. Rather than focusing on interfaith dialogue, which can devolve into bland platitudes, Patel began by emphasizing service learning among young people. Inspired by his own experiences, he established an interfaith youth corps that brings together religiously diverse high school students to perform service projects in their communities. After building bonds by working together to improve their neighborhoods, participants are encouraged to share how their respective faiths teach about service or hospitality and ask questions of religious others. From that foundation, he established *Interfaith America* to equip leaders across society for the hard but momentous task of creating "the world's first truly interfaith nation."[97]

An outstanding example from abroad is the Nahdlatul Ulama movement in Indonesia. The largest Muslim organization in the world, it upholds a commitment to the separation of religious and political authority and promotes pluralism and interfaith cooperation. It supports research projects on Islam and pluralism and cosponsors high-level interfaith conferences. It embodies the ideals of covenantal pluralism, as it seeks "to preserve and strengthen a rules-based international order founded upon universal ethics and humanitarian values."[98] It has played a crucial role in reestablishing and maintaining democracy in the nation, and it pushes back against "political weaponization of identity" by militant Islamists often funded by the Gulf states.[99]

Another fascinating example is the case of Uzbekistan. It was designated by the U.S. State Department as a "Country of Particular Concern" (CPC) for its egregious violations of religious freedom. But as its leaders began to enact economic and political reforms, they became more open to dialogue on religion. In a model of covenantal pluralism, cabinet ministers and parliament leaders engaged with State Department officials at the governmental level, while religious leaders and civil society actors engaged with non-state actors, including Chris Seiple of IGE. Indeed, IGE sent a delegation to Uzbekistan to meet with local religious leaders, academics, and governmental officials. This resulted in the signing of a "Memorandum of Understanding" between IGE and the "Uzbekistan president's think tank and a local NGO to partner on research, conferences, workshops, and delegation visits to build religious freedom in the country." The nation made so much tangible progress on religious freedom that it was removed from the CPC list.[100] Progress can happen.

We also see the spirit of covenantal pluralism when diverse religious groups forge alliances for human rights. As I observed myself, American religious leaders who fought like cats and dogs over domestic issues formed powerful alliances against global religious persecution, human trafficking, and other violations of human dignity. In the process, they came to a deep respect for each other.[101]

Internationally, human trafficking and the climate crisis serve as catalysts for historic collaborations. In 2014, the Vatican convened major leaders from Catholic, Anglican, Orthodox, Jewish, Muslim, Hindu, and Buddhist traditions to pledge common efforts against modern forms of slave labor and trafficking of women and children into sexual exploitation.[102] In 2021, Pope Francis joined with Orthodox Ecumenical Patriarch Bartholomew and Archbishop of Canterbury Justin Welby of the Anglican Church to issue a joint environmental message on the care of creation.[103]

If there is a common bond that can unite diverse religious traditions, it is *reverence.* In an elegant historical excavation, Paul Woodruff describes reverence as the "forgotten virtue," one that people from diverse cultures can recognize in others, in their prayers and rituals, in their sense of awe and mystery, in their search for the divine. Even nonreligious people experience reverence—in nature, in the birth of a child, in the face of death, in community, and in the mystery of life itself. And all can show respect for the ultimate or transcendent obligations that put claims on people, for the reverence they experience in their faith or ultimate commitments.[104]

"VIE ONE WITH ANOTHER IN VIRTUE"

One of the most eloquent models of the spirit of covenantal pluralism is found in the Muslim Koran, Sura 5:48:

> For each We have appointed a law and a way. And had God willed, he would have made you one community [with one religion]. But He made you as you are so that he might test you by means of that which he has given you. So vie one with another in virtue.

Reza Shah-Kazemi observes:

> This remarkable verse—furnishing us with the clearest possible scriptural explanation of the reason for religious diversity—teaches us that each of the religions is rooted in divine revelation and is thus to be revered and not just tolerated. Peaceful coexistence with adherents of other faiths, based on authentic respect, is the natural consequence of this fundamental teaching of the Koran.[105]

To "vie one with another in virtue" evokes the healthy competition of a religiously free society, where religious groups act on their humanitarian impulses and respond to each other's initiatives. As we have seen, such competition often spurs complacent religions to better serve their communities.

A FINAL REPRISE

Historic opportunity and unique peril mark our era, and the quest for religious freedom lies at the center of this strategic moment. Religious freedom matters but is imperiled. The idea of religious liberty is one of the great innovations in global history. Yet it needs reaffirmation and rearticulation in each age and culture. Today, this task could not be more pressing. In a world of resurgent religion, cultivating and protecting freedom of conscience, belief, and exercise represent the best means of enabling societies to live with religious differences civilly instead of violently.

Central to the core identities of a vast majority of people on Earth, religion will endure as such into the foreseeable future. Denying the right to live by transcendent obligations, "to be who we are," represents a fundamental violation of human dignity. Similarly, government favoritism toward a dominant faith and widespread harassment of religious minorities are transgressions against equality in law. Thus, the key justification for religious freedom is justice—simple, profound justice.

Without clarity about the universal human aspiration for meaning and belonging at the heart of religion, we will see counterproductive cycles of repression, conflict, violence, and further repression.

This suggests a profound paradox of our age: At the very moment when the wisdom of religious freedom becomes manifest, it is under siege—assaulted by autocratic regimes, pressured by religious nationalists, undermined by theocratic movements, violated by aggressive secular policies, sapped by inertial bureaucracies, and shunned by elite hostility or ignorance. Comfortable religious communities take it for granted; dominant faiths sacrifice it for the corrupting sword of the state. Not only do we see widespread violations around the world, but looming threats in the West also jeopardize previous gains.

Behind this sobering picture, however, lies promise. We are witnessing a historic convergence of empirical evidence and events on the ground that corroborate a key ontological reality: Humans are spiritual creatures who thrive best and most harmoniously when they enjoy the freedom to express their fundamental dignity. Religious liberty is crucial to thriving societies and peace.

This reality produces a strategic opportunity for policymakers and civil society leaders groping for remedies to the destabilizing religious strife afflicting the globe.[106] Initiatives to defend religious liberty can model a way to break this cycle. Through enhanced thinking and creative action, political leaders, religious authorities, academics, and citizens can discover the self-reinforcing positive dynamics of greater religious free exercise, mutual respect, and peace. In the place of counterproductive measures of repression or co-optation—often the default impulses—enlightened strategies that protect the freedom of conscience and religious practice offer the best means of navigating the crucible of the twenty-first century: *living with our differences in a shrinking world.*

NOTES

Chapter One

1. Emily Bazelon, "In Defense of Religious Freedom," *Slate* (March 14, 2014), https://slate.com/news-and-politics/2014/03/religious-liberty-the-owners-of-hobby-lobby-have-it-wrong-but-religious-rights-are-worth-defending.html. In the article, Bazelon mused that "religious freedom looks like a shield fundamentalists are throwing up against, well, sexual modernity."

2. Nilay Saiya, "Christian Nationalism's Threat to Global Democracy," *The Review of Faith & International Affairs* 22, no. 1 (2024), https://www-tandfonline-com.ezproxy.lib.ou.edu/doi/full/10.1080/15570274.2023.2204679; Nilay Saiya, "The Rise of Theocratic Democracy," *Journal of Democracy* 4, no. 4 (October 2023): 66–79; Philip S. Gorsky and Samuel L. Perry, *The Flag + The Cross: White Christian Nationalism and the Threat to American Democracy* (Oxford: Oxford University Press, 2022). Gorski and Perry document how cries for religious freedom by Christian Nationalists in the United States really mean "freedom for us," a privileging of their place in American society, on pages 90–93.

3. See Winnifred Fallers Sullivan, Elizabeth Shakman Hurd, Saba Mahmood, and Peter G. Danchin, eds. *Politics of Religious Freedom* (Chicago: University of Chicago Press, 2015); Winnifred Fallers Sullivan, *The Impossibility of Religious Freedom* (Princeton, NJ: Princeton University Press, 2005); Elizabeth Shakman Hurd, *Beyond Religious Freedom: The New Global Politics of Religion* (Princeton, NJ: Princeton University Press, 2015); Saba Mahmood, *Religious Difference in a Secular Age: A Minority Report* (Princeton, NJ: Princeton University Press, 2015). For a systematic critique of this scholarship skeptical of religious freedom, see Daniel Philpott and Timothy Samuel Shah, "In Defense of Religious

Freedom: New Critics of a Beleaguered Human Right," *Journal of Law and Religion* 31, no. 3 (2016): 380–95.

4. On the public impact of resurgent religion, see Jose Casanova, *Public Religions in the Modern World* (Chicago: University of Chicago Press, 2011).

5. Gilles Kepel, *The Revenge of God: The Resurgence of Islam, Christianity, and Judaism in the Modern World* (University Park: The Pennsylvania State University Press, 1994), translation of *La Revanche de Dieu* (Points-Actuels, 1991).

6. See Samuel P. Huntington, *The Clash of Civilizations and the Remaking of World Order* (New York: Touchstone, 1996), 95–101.

7. Demographic trends indicate that Christianity and Islam will remain the top two global faiths, together taking up an increasing greater share of the world's population, from around 55 percent in 2010 to over 60 percent in 2050, though that increase will come entirely from the growth of Islam, nearly catching up to Christianity by mid-century. See Pew Research Center, "Key Findings from the Global Religious Futures Project," December 21, 2022: https://www.pewresearch.org/religion/2022/12/21/key-findings-from-the-global-religious-futures-project/, accessed May 14, 2025. In *Clash of Civilizations* (1996), Huntington underscores the dramatic growth of Islam, as documented by Pew, which he sees as eventually overtaking Christianity, though that assessment probably underestimates Christian growth in Africa and Asia. For systematic treatments of why Christianity grew into the world's largest religion, and why it will continue to grow in the global South, see Rodney Stark, *The Triumph of Christianity: How the Jesus Movement Became the World's Largest Religion* (New York: HarperOne, 2011); and Philip Jenkins, *The Next Christendom: The Coming of Global Christianity*, Revised and Expanded Edition (New York: Oxford University Press, 2007). On the general triumph of religion, including a critique of Pew's projections as too cautious on religious growth, see Rodney Stark, *The Triumph of Faith: Why the World is More Religious Than Ever* (Wilmington, DE, ISI Books, 2015); later (New York: Regnery Gateway, 2023).

8. While Ronald Ingelhart claims that the world is becoming less religious, his actual data show that "religion's sudden decline" is heavily concentrated in the most advanced societies, which happen to have far less of the world's population. See Ronald F. Ingelhart, *Religion's Sudden Decline: What's Causing It, and What Comes Next* (New York: Oxford University Press, 2021). Similarly, Charles Taylor's magisterial depiction of "a secular age," by his own acknowledgment, is primarily a Western phenomenon. In turn, his description of traditional societies of the past, in which the transcendent suffused all aspects of life, could apply in some respects to many traditional societies today. See Charles Taylor, *A Secular Age* (Cambridge, MA: Harvard University Press, 2007).

9. In chapter 5, we will see how state repression and majority favoritism nurture violent religious movements. On the idea of building enclaves of faith, see Rod Dreher, *The Benedict Option: A Strategy for Christians in a Post-Christian Nation* (New York: Sentinel, 2017). Religiously free states enable the creation of such enclaves of faith.

10. Monica Duffy Toft, Daniel Philpott, and Timothy Samuel Shah, *God's Century: Resurgent Religion and Global Politics* (New York: W.W. Norton, 2011).

11. Pew Research Center, "The Global Religious Landscape," December 18, 2012: https://www.pewresearch.org/religion/2012/12/18/global-religious-landscape-exec/.

12. Michael Lipka, "Why People with No Religion Are Projected to Decline as a Share of the World's Population," Pew Research Center, April 7, 2017, http://www.pewresearch.org/fact-tank/2017/04/07/why-people-with-no-religion-are-projected-to-decline-as-a-share-of-the-worlds-population/.

13. The term "unaffiliated" refers to people who express no affiliation with a particular religion or religious group. Because it can include some people who have spiritual beliefs or practices, it contains more than just atheists and agnostics, thus overstating the actual share of the population with no religion.

14. Brian J. Grim and Philip Connor, "Changing Religion, Changing Economics: Future Global Religious and Economic Growth," *Religious Freedom & Business Foundation*, October 21, 2015, p. 14, https://religiousfreedomandbusiness.org/wp-content/uploads/2015/10/Changing-religion-Changing-economies-Religious-Freedom-Business-Foundation-October-21-2015.pdf. For the 1970 figure of the unaffiliated, Grim and Connor use the World Religion Database, sponsored by the Institute on Culture, Religion, and World Affairs at Boston University: https://worldreligiondatabase.org/. For the 2010 and 2050 figures, they use the Pew Research Center, "The Future of World Religions: Population Growth Projections: 2010-2050," April 2, 2015, http://www.pewforum.org/2015/04/02/religious-projections-2010-2050/.

15. Fenggang Yang, "The Growth and Dynamism of Chinese Christianity," in *Christianity and Freedom, Vol. 2: Contemporary Perspectives*, eds. Allen D. Hertzke and Timothy Samuel Shah (New York: Cambridge University Press, 2016). Since Yang provided his predictions, Xi Jinping has launched a severe crackdown on religion in China, introducing vast surveillance technology to make it even more difficult for believers to meet for worship and fellowship. It remains to be seen if this effort will stem the growth of Christianity in China.

16. Pew Research Center, "The Gender Gap in Religion Around the World: Women Are Generally More Religious than Men, Particularly Among Christians,"

March 22, 2016: https://www.pewresearch.org/religion/2016/03/22/the-gender-gap-in-religion-around-the-world/.

17. Timothy Samuel Shah, *Religious Freedom: Why Now?* (Princeton: The Witherspoon Institute, 2012), vi. Timothy Shah and Jack Friedman co-edited a volume that brought together scholars from diverse fields who elaborated on the naturalness and innateness of religion in human experience, as corroborated by cognitive and evolutionary sciences. *Homo Religiosus? Exploring the Roots of Religion and Religious Freedom in Human Experience*, eds. Timothy Samuel Shah and Jack Friedman (Cambridge and New York: Cambridge University Press, 2018).

18. Brian Grim and Roger Finke, *The Price of Freedom Denied: Religious Persecution and Conflict in the Twenty-First Century* (New York: Cambridge University Press, 2011).

19. This is how Peter Berger described our era at a conference I organized for the John Templeton Foundation in Istanbul in April of 2009. See Peter Berger, *The Many Altars of Modernity: Towards a Paradigm for Religion in a Pluralist Age* (Berlin: De Gruyter, 2014).

20. United National General Assembly, *Universal Declaration of Human Rights*, A/RES/217(3), 1948: https://www.un.org/en/about-us/universal-declaration-of-human-rights, Article 18.

21. As of 2019, 173 nations have become official parties to the *International Covenant on Civil and Political Rights*, with an additional six signatories, including China, and eighteen countries taking no action. See United Nations General Assembly, *International Covenant on Civil and Political Rights*, Resolution 2200A (21), 1966, https://www.un.org/en/development/desa/population/migration/general assembly/docs/globalcompact/A_RES_2200A(XXI)_civil.pdf.

22. Sandra L. Bunn-Livingstone, "A Historical Analysis: International Religious Freedom 1998–2008," a paper presented at the Pew Charitable Trusts Conference, April 30–May 2, 2008. Daniel Philpott and Timothy Shah provide a summary of these ancient examples: "In Defense of Religious Freedom: New Critics of a Beleaguered Human Right," *Journal of Law and Religion* 31, no. 3 (2016): 391–92.

23. Qur'an 2:256. The Qur'an continues to note that, under freedom, truth will eventually prevail, which conveys a supreme confidence in one's faith. See *My Mercy Encompasses All: The Koran's Teachings on Compassion, Peace & Love*, Gathered & Introduced by Reza Shah-Kazemi (Emeryville, CA: Shoemaker & Hoard, 2007).

24. Pew Global Attitudes Project, October 4, 2007, http:// pewglobal.org/reports/pdf/258topline.pdf.

25. Kevin Hassan, *The Right to Be Wrong* (San Francisco: Encounter Books, 2005).

26. Pew Research Center, "Government Restrictions on Religion Stayed at Peak Levels Globally in 2022," December 18, 2024: https://www.pewresearch.org/religion/2024/12/18/government-restrictions-on-religion-stayed-at-peak-levels-globally-in-2022/. An analysis by Brian Grim of a previous Pew report found that 85 percent of the world's population lives in societies with high government restrictions or social hostilities. This is because some of the world's most populous nations, such as China and India, fall into that category. Brian J. Grim, "Economic Growth Slowed by Decline in Religious Freedom," Religious Freedom and Business Foundation, 2019, https://religiousfreedomandbusiness.org/economic-growth-slowed-by-decline-in-religious-freedom#:~:text=RFBF's%20analysis%20of%20Pew's%20study,7.7%20billion%20%E2%80%94%20live%20today%20in.

27. Religion and State (RAS) Project, Bar-Ilan University, Israel: https://ras.thearda.com/. Jonathan Fox, director of the RAS Project, presents and analyzes that data in *The Unfree Exercise of Religion: A World Survey of Discrimination Against Religious Minorities* (New York: Cambridge University Press, 2016); and *Political Secularism, Religion, and the State* (New York: Cambridge University Press, 2015).

28. Pew Research Center, "Government Restrictions on Religion Stayed at Peak Levels Globally in 2022." This is the fifteenth annual Pew report, and it shows significant increases of both government restrictions and social hostilities since 2007.

29. Grim, "Economic Growth Slowed by Decline in Religious Freedom," 2019.

30. Roger Finke, "Origins and Consequences of Religious Freedoms: A Global Overview," *Sociology of Religion* 43, no. 3 (2013): 299.

31. Grim and Finke, *The Price of Freedom Denied*, 18, emphasis in original.

32. Philpott and Shah, "In Defense of Religious Freedom."

33. Paul Marshall provides a kind of taxonomy of nations with the greatest levels of persecution. While his taxonomy concerns persecution against Christians, it is pertinent to more general categories of religious persecution. Here is his taxonomy: self-professed Communist countries; religious nationalist states, especially in South Asia; Muslim-majority nations ruled by Islamists; and post-Communist, national security, and other authoritarian states. Marshall also warns that Western secularist states, while not rising to the level of persecution, are moving in the wrong direction. See Paul Marshall, "Patterns and Purposes of Contemporary Anti-Christian Persecution," in *Christianity and Freedom, Volume 2: Contemporary Perspectives*, edited by Allen D. Hertzke and Timothy Samuel Shah (New York: Cambridge University Press, 2016).

34. Freedom House, "The Uphill Battle to Safeguard Rights," *Freedom in the World 2025*, February, 2025: https://freedomhouse.org/report/freedom-world/2025/uphill-battle-to-safeguard-rights.

35. The centrality of religion to human culture is corroborated and elaborated in Shah and Friedman, *Homo Religiosus?*

36. Shah and Friedman, *Homo Religiosus?*, 1.

37. Paul Bloom, "Religion is Natural," *Development Science* 10.1 (2007), 150, as quoted in *Homo Religiosus?*, 1.

38. Timothy Samuel Shah, *Religious Freedom: Why Now?*, vi.

39. Shah and Friedman, *Homo Religiosus?*, 186.

40. Daniel Philpott, "Why Religious Freedom is a Human Right," *The American Journal of Jurisprudence* 68, no. 3 (December 2023): 177–94.

41. Philpott, "Why Religious Freedom is a Human Right," 190.

42. Philpott, "Why Religious Freedom is a Human Right," 186.

43. This is Philpott's fuller definition of religion: "an interconnected set of practices through which people seek right relationship with a superhuman power. Through the superhuman power, people find answers to ultimate questions and help in the real circumstances of their lives, including everyday matters. Religious practices are premised upon and connected to a set of beliefs. Religion involves rituals of worship, a community, a corps of specialists, and a variety of norm-governed practices, including discursive practices, behavior-regulating practices, and a moral code, all of which reflect right relationship with a superhuman power." Philpott, "Why Religious Freedom is a Human Right," 188.

44. Paul Tillich, *The Courage to Be* (New Haven: Yale University Press, 1970). Tillich famously defined religion as "ultimate concern" that need not inhere in the transcendent or spiritual realm.

45. See Roger Williams, *The Bloudy Tenet of Persecution, for Cause of Conscience*, 1644, in *On Religious Liberty: Selections from the Words of Roger Williams*, ed. James Calvin Davis (Cambridge, MA: Harvard University Press, 2008); John Henry Newman, "Letter to the Duke of Norfolk," 1874, in *Newman Reader*: https://www.newmanreader.org/works/anglicans/volume2/gladstone/index.html; and James Madison, "Memorial and Remonstrance Against Religious Assessments," 1785, https://founders.archives.gov/documents/Madison/01-08-02-0163.

46. Rajdeep Singh Jolly, interview with author by former leader within the Sikh Coalition, Washington, DC, conducted in 2009.

47. For the importance of the right of exit, see Albert O. Hirschman, *Exit, Voice and Loyalty: Responses to Decline in Firms, Organizations, and States* (Cambridge, MA: Harvard University Press, 1970).

48. The Pew Research Center reported that 79 countries and territories out of the 198 studied in 2019 (or 40 percent) had laws against blasphemy, while another 11 percent (22 countries) had laws against apostasy: See Virginia Villa, "Four-in-ten countries and territories worldwide had blasphemy laws in 2019," Pew Research Center, January 25, 2022, https://www.pewresearch.org/short-reads/2022/01/25/four-in-ten-countries-and-territories-worldwide-had-blasphemy-laws-in-2019-2/. On anti-conversion laws, the United States Commission on International Religious Freedom (USCIRF) reported that 46 countries have at least one anti-conversion law in force. See "USCIRF Releases Report on National Level Anti-Conversion Laws around the World," November 28, 2023, https://www.uscirf.gov/news-room/releases-statements/uscirf-releases-report-national-level-anti-conversion-laws-around#:~:text=In%20total%2C%2046%20countries%20have,anti%2Dconversion%20law%20in%20force.

49. Glenn W. LaFantasie, ed., "From a Letter to Major John Wilson and Governor Thomas Prence," *The Correspondence of Roger Williams*, Volume 2: 1654-1682 (Providence, RI: Brown University Press, 1988): 617-18.

50. Lihui Zhang, "Are International Human Rights Organizations Effective in Protecting Religious Freedom?" *Religions* 12, no. 7, 2021, 479. https://www.mdpi.com/2077-1444/12/7/479.

51. *Freedom of Religious Institutions in Society*, eds. Timothy S. Shah and Nathan Berkeley, special issue of *Religions* (Basel, Switzerland: MDPI 2022): https://www.mdpi.com/journal/religions/special_issues/free_reli.

52. Adam Smith, "Of the Expense of the Institutions for the Instruction of People of All Ages," *The Wealth of Nations*, 1776, Book 5, Chapter 1, Part 3, Article 3. https://press-pubs.uchicago.edu/founders/documents/amendI_religions31.html.

53. In July of 2025 the Internal Revenue Service in the Trump administration declared that churches *can* endorse candidates, which is a clear violation of the 1954 statute prohibiting churches and other nonprofit agencies from engaging in partisan political campaigning. While it is not clear how the courts will deal with this discrepancy, as of this writing, American public opinion strongly opposes churches endorsing candidates. See "Most Americans Oppose Churches Endorsing Political Candidates," PRRI, July 8, 2025, https://prri.org/spotlight/most-americans-oppose-churches-endorsing-political-candidates/.

54. After the collapse of communism, the new Czech Republic initially allowed official recognition for any church that could gather 300 signatories on a petition claiming allegiance to a recognizable faith. Catholic leaders lobbied to have this threshold raised to 0.1 percent of the population, a seemingly small percentage until one realizes that for a church to qualify for tax-exempt status and various property permissions, it would need to have over 10,000 members,

effectively eliminating access to public accommodations to nearly every upstart denomination. See Anthony Gill, *Rending unto Caesar: The Catholic Church and the State in Latin America* (Chicago: University of Chicago Press, 1998): 14.

55. Mariz Tadros documents how authorities in Egypt make it arduous for Coptic Christian communities to get a permit to repair a church. Mariz Tadros, "Copts of Egypt: Defiance, Compliance, and Continuity," in *Christianity and Freedom, Volume 2: Contemporary Perspectives*, eds. Allen D. Hertzke and Timothy Samuel Shah (New York: Cambridge University Press, 2016).

56. See Thomas F. Farr, *World of Faith and Freedom: Why International Religious Liberty is Vital to American National Security* (New York: Oxford University Press, 2008); Barbara Ann Rieffer-Flanagan, *Promoting Religious Freedom in an Age of Intolerance* (Cheltenham, UK: Edard Elgar, 2022); and a special journal issue: "Strategies of Advocacy for International Religious Freedom," Allen D. Hertzke, Guest Editor, *The Review of Faith & International Affairs,* Vol. 10, No. 3 (Fall 2012).

57. H. Knox Thames, *Ending Persecution: Charting the Path to Global Religious Freedom* (Notre Dame, IN: University of Notre Dame Press, 2024).

58. These include the United States Commission on International Religious Freedom (USCIRF), https://www.uscirf.gov/; the Religious Freedom Institute, https://religiousfreedominstitute.org/; and the International Institute for Religious Freedom, https://iirf.global/. USCIRF acts as a watchdog on policies of the U.S. State Department and presidential administrations, often prodding them to take more assertive measures to address religious persecution around the world. Its 2025 report contains detailed policy recommendations for how the U.S. government and other entities can better promote international religious freedom, https://www.uscirf.gov/sites/default/files/2025-03/2025%20USCIRF%20Annual%20Report.pdf.

59. A more formal way to capture the centrality of religious freedom to human personhood and experience is to say that it is central to *human ontology*.

60. Roger Finke, "Origins and Consequences of Religious Freedoms: A Global Overview," *Sociology of Religion* 43, no. 3 (2013): 297.

61. The biography of Brian Grim, along with a link to his CV, is provided by the Religious Freedom and Business Foundation: https://religiousfreedomandbusiness.org/brian-j-grim.

62. Roger Finke developed the Association of Religion Data Archives at Penn State University, a huge repository of quantitative data on religion. For examples of his systematic use of religious data, see: Roger Finke and Rodney Stark, *The Churching of America, 1776-2005: Winners and Losers in Our Religious Economy* (New Brunswick, NJ: Rutgers University Press, 2005); and Amy Adamczyk, John Wybraniec, and Roger Finke, "Religious Regulation and the Courts: Documenting the Effects of Smith and RFRA," *Journal of Church and State* 46 (2004).

63. Pew Research Center, "Government Restrictions Stayed at Peak Levels Globally in 2022."

64. "Double-blind" means coders work independently and cannot see each other's answers, thus ensuring high inter-coder reliability. In the few cases where discrepancies emerge, research leaders then meet with the coders to discuss and iron out.

65. Pew Research Center, "Government Restrictions Stayed at Peak Levels Globally in 2022," December 18, 2024: https://www.pewresearch.org/religion/2024/12/18/restrictions-on-religion-2022-methodology/. This document provides a lucid and detailed elaboration of the methodology Pew employs to develop its indexes of Government Restrictions on Religion Index (GRI) and Social Hostilities Index (SHI). The GRI is derived from twenty indicators of how national and local governments restrict religion, while the SHI includes thirteen ways that private individuals and social groups infringe on religious beliefs and practices. The GRI includes questions on government support for some religions not provided to others. Each indicator includes a question or questions that coders answer, with each question coded as a 0.0 or 1.0. In cases where the indicator involves different dimensions or degrees of severity, answers to questions are recorded in fractions, such as one-half, one-third, or one-fifth of a point each. All scores are summed and adjusted into a 0–10 index.

66. Pew Research Center, "Government Restrictions on Religion Stayed at Peak Levels Globally in 2022," https://www.pewresearch.org/religion/2024/12/18/restrictions-on-religion-2022-methodology/. Numerous statistical tests are employed to validate the reliability of the Pew indexes. Because the Pew Center replicates the methodology in each successive report, scholars can track changes over time and across countries, regions, and religions.

67. Brian J. Grim, "Economic Growth."

68. Pew Research Center, see Appendix to coding instrument for "Government Restrictions on Religion Stayed at Peak Levels Globally in 2022," https://www.pewresearch.org/wp-content/uploads/sites/20/2024/12/PR_2024.12.18_restrictions-on-religion-2022_appendix-d.pdf.

69. I was at the Pew Research Center when the staff debated what to do about the highly repressive North Korea regime. While I thought they should include it in the category of very high government restrictions, the decision to omit it (with an asterisk noting its repressive character) reflected an impressive adherence to employing only comparable metrics in their coding.

70. Grim and Finke, *The Price of Freedom Denied.*

71. "Religion and State (RAS) Project."

72. The following, by Jonathan Fox, are the successive books that analyze RAS data: Jonathan Fox, *A World Survey of Religion and the State* (New York, NY:

Cambridge University Press, 2008); *Political Secularism, Religion, and the State: A Time Series Analysis of Worldwide Data* (New York: Cambridge University Press, 2015); *The Unfree Exercise of Religion: A World Survey of Religious Discrimination Against Religious Minorities* (New York: Cambridge University Press, 2016); *Thou Shalt Have No Other Gods Before Me: Why Governments Discriminate Against Religious Minorities* (New York: Cambridge University Press, 2020); and Matthias Basedau, Jonathan Fox, and Ariel Zellman, *Religious Minorities at Risk* (New York: Oxford University Press, 2023).

73. The RAS project provides detailed summaries of the numerous indicators coded for different waves of the major categories, and scholars can download data sets for free at https://ras.thearda.com/ras-downloads.

74. The Association of Religion Data Archives (ARDA) serves as a repository of the RAS data sets, including a detailed summary of the methodology employed by Fox's team to derive scales from 0–3 for 175 nations for each of the major categories: State Funding of Religion, Societal Discrimination of Minority Religions, State Regulation of Majority or All Religions, and State Discrimination of Minority Religions: https://www.thearda.com/ARDA/pdf/RASIndexes.pdf. ARDA also maintains a system on its website that enables a quick view of the summary scores for each of the four RAS indexes for each country, along with other dimensions, such as constitutional provisions, provided by other research centers. See https://www.thearda.com/world-religion/national-profiles.

75. The world is a vast laboratory, as a growing number of independent organizations and academic institutes catalogue and measure a wide variety of variables. For over 50 years, Freedom House has produced a Freedom Score that tracks trends on two dimensions, political rights and civil liberties, each of which is measured on a 50-point scale to produce a composite measure of freedom on a 100-point scale (https://freedomhouse.org/report/freedom-world). The libertarian Cato Institute produces its own 10-point Freedom Index based on a combination of personal freedom and economic freedom (https://www.cato.org/human-freedom-index/2024). For measures of the level and varieties of democracy, see the V-Dem Institute, University of Gothenburg, Gothenburg, Sweden (https://www.v-dem.net/). A cooperative institute, V-Dem, enlists several thousand scholars from around the world and measures over 600 different attributes of democracy for 202 countries (https://www.v-dem.net/). The Center for Systematic Peace produces a 21-point scale of "Polity" scores that annually measure the spectrum of national governments from complete autocracies to anocracies, mixing autocratic and democratic features, to fully consolidated democracies (https://www.systemicpeace.org/polityproject.html). ARDA sponsors the Religious Characteristics of States Project, which includes national religious demographics (https://

www.thearda.com/data-archive?fid=RCSDEM2), and measures of government-level of favoritism toward, or disfavor against, religious denominations (https://www.thearda.com/data-archive?fid=GRPCOMP). The National Consortium for the Study of Terrorism and Responses to Terrorism, hosted by the University of Maryland, produces the Global Terrorism Database, which includes systematic data on national and transnational terrorist incidents (https://www.start.umd.edu/data-tools/GTD). The International Institute for Religious Freedom maintains a Violent Incidents Database that records and counts such incidents each year (https://iirf.global/vid/). Since 2006, the World Economic Forum has produced an annual gender parity index across four dimensions—economic participation, educational attainment, health and survival, and political empowerment—for all countries in the world (https://www.weforum.org/publications/global-gender-gap-report-2024/). The Heritage Foundation produces an annual Index of Economic Freedom on a hundred-point scale for countries in the world (https://www.heritage.org/index/). The Fund for Peace sponsors the Fragile States Index, which ranks nations from most fragile to least fragile based on 12 indicators. In 2024, it ranged from Somalia to Norway (https://fragilestatesindex.org/). Transparency International produces an annual Corruption Perceptions Index for nations on a scale of 0–100, based on diverse sources that show the perceptions of business persons and country experts on the levels of corruption (https://www.transparency.org/en/cpi/2024). The World Bank produces the premier multidimensional index of development and progress of nations, based on numerous indicators of poverty and inequality, health, literacy, environmental quality, and economic development (https://datatopics.worldbank.org/world-development-indicators/). Diverse national economic measures, of course, are readily available through the World Bank (https://datatopics.worldbank.org/world-development-indicators/themes/economy.html#:~:text=Economic%20indicators%20include%20measures%20of,and%20the%20balance%20of%20payments). On global and national religious demographic patterns and changes, see the World Religion Database, sponsored by the Institute on Culture, Religion, and World Affairs at Boston University (https://www.worldreligiondatabase.org/); and the Pew-Templeton Global Religious Futures Project (https://www.pewresearch.org/religion/2022/12/21/key-findings-from-the-global-religious-futures-project/). These wide-ranging indexes and measures enable scholars to perform rigorous statistical tests on the role of religious freedom by different dimensions, to control for diverse variables, and to explore alternative explanations—all hallmarks of good science.

76. Mauro Gatti, Pasquale Annicchino, Judd Birdsall, Valeria Fabretti, and Marco Ventura, "Quantifying Persecution: Developing an International Law-based Measurement of Freedom of Religion or Belief," *The Review of Faith &*

International Affairs 17, no. 2 (May 2019): https://doi.org/10.1080/15570274.2019.1608648.

77. This clearinghouse, the Religious Freedom Data Spectrum, is produced through a partnership between the International Institute for Religious Freedom and 21 Wilberforce, a religious advocacy organization. See https://iirf.global/global-religious-freedom-data-spectrum/.

78. On the importance of replication in the social sciences, see Gary King, "Replication, Replication," *PS: Political Science and Politics* 28 (1995): 444–52, https://tinyurl.com/mvc5kg5.

79. Jo Howard and Mariz Tadros, editors, *Using Participatory Methods to Explore Freedom of Religion and Belief* (Bristol, UK: Bristol University Press, July 27, 2023): https://doi.org/10.51952/9781529229295. This book contains chapters by scholars and practitioners that illuminate the benefits and insights of using participatory methods. Chapter 2, "Participatory Methods and the Freedom of Religion and Belief," by Rebecca Shah and Timothy Shah, provides a vivid depiction of how visual techniques enabled groups of Dalit men and women in India to tell their stories of navigating the COVID-19 pandemic and lockdowns.

80. Judd Birdsall and Lori Beaman, "Faith in Numbers: Can We Trust Quantitative Data on Religious Affiliation and Religious Freedom?" *The Review of Faith & International Affairs* 18, no. 3 (2020): 60–68, was originally released as a report from the Transatlantic Policy Network on Religion and Diplomacy and commissioned by the Cambridge Institute of Religion & International Studies (Cambridge, UK). Birdsall and Beaman provide some useful caveats about how Pew measures religious restrictions, and they end by making the case for the indispensability of narrative accounts. As an ethnographic scholar myself, I can hardly disagree. Indeed, my nearly three-decade immersion in the milieu of international networks of religious freedom advocacy and scholarship has enabled and deeply informed this book.

81. Thomas S. Kuhn, *The Structure of Scientific Revolutions* (Chicago: University of Chicago Press, 1962). As a historian of science, Kuhn famously contended that scientific revolutions take place through shifts in the paradigms under which research takes place. A new paradigm, he argues, is not merely a better theory but instead reflects an entirely new way of seeing the world. What strikes me about global research on religious freedom is how much it conforms to Kuhn's idea. The paradoxical findings of this research, when theoretically explained, often reflect a paradigm shift: a new way of seeing the world. Indeed, as Kuhn suggests, we cannot see the world the same way after that paradigm shift. That has certainly been the case for me in the process of researching and writing this book.

Chapter Two

1. Brian Grim, "Globally, Restrictions on Religion Reach 14-Year High," Religious Freedom and Business Foundation, March 21, 2024: https://religiousfreedomandbusiness.org/2/post/2024/03/globally-restrictions-on-religion-reach-14-year-high.html.

2. Brian Grim, "Religious Freedom: Good for What Ails Us?" *The Review of Faith & International Affairs* 6, no. 2 (2008): 3–7.

3. Grim, "Religious Freedom: Good for What Ails Us?" In this article, Grim develops his causal theory, backed by statistical analysis, for why religious freedom in society produces these beneficial outcomes.

4. Anthony Gill, *The Political Origins of Religious Liberty* (New York: Cambridge University Press, 2008): 86–89.

5. Gill, *The Political Origins of Religious Liberty*, 62.

6. "Mary Dyer," *Encyclopedia Britannica,* May 28, 2023, https://www.britannica.com/biography/Mary-Barrett-Dyer.

7. Kevin Seamus Hasson, *The Right to be Wrong* (San Francisco: Encounter Books, 2005), chapter 7.

8. William Penn, *The Great Case of Liberty of Conscience,* 1670, University of Michigan Library Digital Collections, Early English Books Online, https://quod.lib.umich.edu/e/eebo/A54146.0001.001?rgn=main;view=fulltext.

9. The role of religious revivals and competition in paving the way for the American Revolution is recounted in Sidney Ahlstrom, *A Religious History of the American People,* 2nd ed. (New Haven: Yale University Press, 2004), and Allen Hertzke, *Echoes of Discontent: Jesse Jackson, Pat Robertson, and the Resurgence of Populism* (Washington DC, CQ Press, 1993), chapter 2. The full John Adams quote is: "The Revolution was effected before the War commenced. The Revolution was in the minds and hearts of the people; a change in their religious sentiments of their duties and obligations. . . . This radical change in the principles, opinions, sentiments, and affections of the people, was the real American Revolution." From a letter from John Adams to N. Niles, February 13, 1818: "Teaching American History," http://teachingamericanhistory.org/library/document/john-adams-to-h-niles/

10. Gill, *The Political Origins of Religious Liberty*, 75; Carl H. Esbeck and Jonathan J. Den Hartog, eds., *Disestablishment and Religious Dissent: Church-State Relations in the New American States, 1776–1833* (Columbia: MO: University of Missouri Press, 2019).

11. Tocqueville, Alexis de. 1835. *Democracy in America*, vol. 1, translated by Harvey Mansfield (New York: University of Chicago Press, 2000).

12. John Owen, *Confronting Political Islam: Six Lessons from the West's Past.* (Princeton: Princeton University Press, 2014), chapter 3.

13. Mark Lilla, *The Stillborn God: Religion, Politics, and the Modern West* (New York: Knopf, 2007).

14. John Smyth, "Propositions and Conclusions Concerning True Christian Religion, Containing a Confession of Faith of Certain English People, Living at Amsterdam" (1612), in *Baptist Confessions of Faith,* 2nd ed., eds. William L. Lumpkin and Bill J. Leonard (Valley Forge: Judson Press, 2011).

15. Roger Williams, *The Bloudy Tenet of Persecution, for Cause of Conscience* (1644), in *On Religious Liberty: Selections from the Words of Roger Williams,* ed. James Calvin Davis (Cambridge, MA: Harvard University Press, 2008).

16. Edward J. Eberle, "Roger Williams's Gift: Religious Freedom in America." *Roger Williams University Law Review* 4, no. 2, Article 3 (1999).

17. Penn, *The Great Case of Liberty of Conscience.*

18. John Locke, *A Letter Concerning Toleration.* Trans. William Popple, 1689: (www.constitution.org/jl/tolerati.htm#01).

19. Brian Grim and Roger Finke, *The Price of Freedom Denied: Religious Persecution and Conflict in the Twenty-First Century* (New York: Cambridge University Press, 2011).

20. James Madison, "Memorial and Remonstrance Against Religious Assessments" (1785), https://founders.archives.gov/documents/Madison/01-08-02-0163.

21. Leonard Levy, "Virginia Declaration of Rights and Constitution of 1776" (June 12 and 29, 1776). *Encyclopedia of the American Constitution, 6,* 2799–2800 (2000), https://constitution.org/2-Authors/bcp/virg_dor.htm.

22. Madison, "Memorial and Remonstrance."

23. Robert D. Putnam, *Bowling Alone: The Collapse and Revival of American Community* (New York: Simon & Schuster, 2000).

24. Abdolkarim Soroush, *Reason, Freedom, and Democracy in Islam* (New York: Oxford University Press, 2000).

25. Abdolkarim Soroush, *Reason, Freedom, and Democracy,* Ch. 9.

26. Abdolkarim Soroush, "Religious Tyranny is Crumbling: Rejoice!" Open Letter to Mr. Khamenei, September 13, 2009, https://drsoroush.com/en/religious-tyranny-is-crumbling-rejoice/; "You Have Turned Iran into a Grim Land," Open letter to Mr. Seyyed Ali Khamenei, leader of the Islamic Republic of Iran, December 22, 2011, https://drsoroush.com/en/you-have-turned-iran-into-a-grim-land/.

27. Yana Gorokhovskaia and Cathryn Grothe, *Freedom in the World 2025: The Uphill Battle to Safeguard Rights.* (Washington, DC: Freedom House, February 2025): https://freedomhouse.org/sites/default/files/2025-03/FITW_World

2025digitalN.pdf. As reported here, political rights and civil liberties worldwide declined for the nineteenth consecutive year.

28. Jonathan Fox, *The Unfree Exercise of Religion: A World Survey of Discrimination Against Religious Minorities* (New York: Cambridge University Press, 2016).

29. Nilay Saiya, "The Rise of Theocratic Democracy," *Journal of Democracy* 24, no. 4 (October 2023): 66–79.

30. Brian Grim, "Restrictions on Religion in the World: Measures and Implications," in *The Future of Religious Freedom: Global Challenges,* ed. Allen D. Hertzke (New York: Oxford University Press, 2013), 102; Karrie Koesel, *Religion and Authoritarianism: Cooperation, Conflict, and the Consequences* (Cambridge: Cambridge University Press, 2014); Ani Sarkissian, *The Varieties of Religious Repression: Why Governments Restrict Religion* (New York: Oxford University Press, 2015).

31. Anthony Gill, "Religious Liberty and Economic Development: Exploring the Causal Connections," *The Review of Faith and International Affairs* 11, no. 4 (2013): 5–23.

32. Alfred Stepan, "Religion, Democracy, and the 'Twin Tolerations,'" *Journal of Democracy* 11, no. 4 (October 2000): 37–57: https://doi.org/10.1353/jod.2000.0088.

33. Stepan, "Twin Tolerations."

34. Elliot Abrams, "In Russia, 'Liquidating' Churches," *The Washington Post,* November 14, 2000, https://www.uscirf.gov/news-room/op-eds/russia-liquidating-churches-washington-post.

35. Daniel Philpott, "Explaining the Political Ambivalence of Religion," *American Political Science Review* 101, no. 3 (2007): 505–25.

36. Daniel Philpott, "The Catholic Wave," *Journal of Democracy* 15, no. 2 (2004): 32–46.

37. Allen Hertzke, "The Catholic Church and Catholicism in Global Politics," in *Routledge Handbook of Religion and Politics,* 2nd ed., ed. Jeffrey Haynes (Abingdon, UK: Routledge, 2016), and "Roman Catholicism and the Faith-Based Movement for Global Human Rights," *The Review of Faith & International Affairs* 3, no. 3 (2005): 19–24.

38. Anthony Gill, *Rending unto Caesar: The Catholic Church and the State in Latin America* (Chicago: University of Chicago Press, 1998).

39. Philpott, "The Catholic Wave."

40. Samuel P. Huntington, *The Third Wave: Democratization in the Late Twentieth Century* (Norman: University of Oklahoma Press, 1991).

41. Monica Duffy Toft, Daniel Philpott, and Timothy Shah, *God's Century: Resurgent Religion and Global Politics* (New York: W.W. Norton, 2011), chapter 4.

42. As summarized by Brian Grim, "Religious Freedom was more than 2 times higher in countries where Catholics are the majority population." The Weekly Number Blog, 2015, http://theweeklynumber.com/weekly-number-blog/category/government%20restrictions.

43. Robert Woodberry, "The Missionary Roots of Liberal Democracy," *American Political Science Review* 106, no. 2 (2012): 244–74.

44. Grim and Finke, *The Price of Freedom Denied,* chapter 6.

45. Mustafa Akyol, *Islam Without Extremes: A Muslim Case for Liberty* (New York: W.W. Norton, 2011); Abdullah Saeed, *Islam and Belief: At Home with Religious Freedom* (Palo Alto: Zephyr Institute, 2014); Abdolkarim Soroush, *Reason, Freedom, and Democracy in Islam* (New York: Oxford University Press, 2000); Abdullahi Ahmed An-Na'im, *Islam and the Secular State* (Cambridge, MA: Harvard University Press, 2008); Recep Senturk, "Human Rights in Islamic Jurisprudence: Why Should All Human Beings Be Inviolable," in *The Future of Religious Freedom: Global Challenges*, ed. Allen D. Hertzke (New York: Oxford University Press, 2013), 290–311; Asma Afsaruddin, "Making the Case for Religious Freedom Within the Islamic Tradition," *The Review of Faith & International Affairs* 6, no. 2 (June 1, 2008): 57–60.

46. These include the following: "There is no compulsion in religion" (Surah 2 verse 256); a reference to the sanctity of all worship sites (Surah 22 verse 40), and God-ordained religious pluralism so that people "vie one with another in virtue" (Surah 5 verse 48). *My Mercy Encompasses All: The Koran's Teachings on Compassion, Peace & Love,* Gathered & Introduced by Reza Shah-Kazemi (Emeryville, CA: Shoemaker & Hoard, 2007).

47. Daniel Philpott, *Religious Freedom in Islam: The Fate of a Universal Right in the Muslim World Today* (New York: Oxford University Press, 2019); Mustafa Akyol, *Islam Without Extremes.*

48. Philpott, *Religious Freedom in Islam,* chapter 2. Religiously free states make up 23 percent of all Muslim majority countries, 50.

49. Alfred Stepan and Graeme B. Robertson, "An 'Arab' More than 'Muslim' Electoral Gap," *Journal of Democracy* 14, no. 3 (July 2003): 30–44; https://doi.org/10.1353/jod.2003.0064.

50. Stepan and Robertson, "An 'Arab' More than 'Muslim' Electoral Gap"; Kuru, *Islam, Authoritarianism, and Underdevelopment,* 53. Kuru updated Stepan and Robertson a decade later, finding fewer overachievers overall but still finding that non-Arab states generally eschew government enforcement of Islamic law.

51. Robet W. Hefner, *Civil Islam: Muslims and Democratization in Indonesia* (Princeton, NJ: Princeton University Press, 2000).

52. Krithika Varagur, "How Saudi Arabia's Religious Project Transformed Indonesia," *The Guardian*, April 16, 2020: https://www.theguardian.com/news/2020/apr/16/how-saudi-arabia-religious-project-transformed-indonesia-islamaragur. Nahdlatul Ulama: https://www.nu.or.id/.

53. Philpott, *Religious Freedom in Islam*, "Chapter 3: Secular Repressive States in the Muslim World."

54. Pew Research Center, "Government Restrictions on Religion Stayed at Peak Levels Globally in 2022," December 8, 2024, https://www.pewresearch.org/religion/2024/12/18/government-restrictions-on-religion-stayed-at-peak-levels-globally-in-2022/.

55. Timur Kuran, *Freedoms Delayed: Political Legacies of Islamic Law in the Middle East* (New York: Cambridge University Press, 2023), chapter 1.

56. Kuran, *Freedoms Delayed*. This project serves as the companion of Kuran's previous work, *The Long Divergence: How Islamic Law Held Back the Middle East* (Princeton: Princeton University Press, 2010), which documented how the social mechanisms of Islamic law retarded economic development.

57. Kuran. *Freedoms Delayed*, chapters 2–4.

58. Kuran, *Freedoms Delayed*, chapters 4–5.

59. Paul Marshall and Nina Shea, *Silenced: How Apostasy and Blasphemy Codes are Choking Freedom Worldwide* (New York: Oxford University Press, 2011).

60. Kuran, *Freedoms Delayed*, preface, chapter 1, and chapter 9.

61. Ani Sarkissian, "Religious Regulation and the Muslim Democracy Gap," *Politics and Religion* 5, no. 3 (2012): 501–27, https://doi.org/10.1017/S1755048312000284. The quote is from the Abstract on page 501.

62. Sarkissian, "Religious Regulation and the Muslim Democracy Gap."

63. John Owen, *Confronting Political Islam: Six Lessons from the West's Past* (Princeton: Princeton University Press, 2014).

64. Nina Shea, *In the Lion's Den: A Shocking Account of Persecution and Martyrdom of Christians Today and How We Should Respond* (Nashville: B&H Publishing Group, 1997).

65. Toft, Philpott, and Shah, *God's Century: Resurgent Religion and Global Politics*, chapter 4.

66. Karrie J. Koesel and Ani Sarkissian, "Religion and the Authoritarian Toolkit: Are Carrots Substitutes for Sticks?" *Democratization* (May 18, 2025): 1–24, https://doi.org/10.1080/13510347.2025.2489024.

67. From the beginning of Russia's invasion of Ukraine, the leading Orthodox leaders blessed the war and parroted Putin's rationale. This even led to the declaration by the Church that the invasion was a "holy war." Brian Mefford,

"Russian Orthodox Church Declares 'Holy War' Against Ukraine and West," *Atlantic Council*, April 9, 2024, https://www.atlanticcouncil.org/blogs/ukrainealert/russian-orthodox-church-declares-holy-war-against-ukraine-and-west/.

68. Karrie Koesel, *Religion and Authoritarianism: Cooperation, Conflict, and the Consequences* (Cambridge: Cambridge University Press, 2014).

69. Karrie Koesel, "The Political Economy of Religious Revival," *Politics and Religion* 8, no. 2 (2015): 211–35.

70. Koesel, *Religion and Authoritarianism.*

71. Ani Sarkissian, *The Varieties of Religious Repression: Why Governments Restrict Religion* (New York: Oxford University Press, 2015), 185.

72. The most recent report by Freedom House categorizes Turkey as "Not Free" because of the regime's move toward autocratic control. See https://freedomhouse.org/country/turkey/freedom-world/2025.

73. Sarkissian, *The Varieties of Religious Repression,* 191.

74. Religion and State Project, Round 2 dataset, https://www.thearda.com/data-archive?fid=RAS2012.

75. Ani Sarkissian, "Sacred or Strategic? State Regulation of Religion Across Religious and Secular Regimes," Presented at the Annual Meeting of the American Political Science Association, San Francisco, CA, September 3–6, 2015, unpublished paper. Sarkissian is a professor of political science at Michigan State University.

76. Karrie J. Koesel and Ani Sarkissian, "Religion and the Authoritarian Toolkit."

77. Koesel and Sarkissian use data from the third round of the Religion and State (RAS) Project, which distinguishes different co-optive and repressive strategies toward religion, https://ras.thearda.com/.

78. Koesel and Sarkissian, "Religion and the Authoritarian Toolkit."

79. Koesel and Sarkissian, "Religion and the Authoritarian Toolkit."

80. Koesel and Sarkissian, "Religion and the Authoritarian Toolkit."

81. Gorokhovskaia and Grothe, *Freedom in the World 2025.*

82. Nilay Saiya, "The Rise of Theocratic Democracy," *Journal of Democracy* 34, no. 4 (October 2023): 66–79, https://doi.org/10.1353/jod.2023.a907688. The quote is on page 67.

83. Ani Sarkissian, "Religious Reestablishment in Post-Communist Polities," *Journal of Church and State* 51, no. 3 (Summer 2009): 472-501, https://www.jstor.org/stable/23921633.

84. Nilay Saiya, "The Rise of Theocratic Democracy." Saiya terms the movement "theocratic democracy" because it involves using democratic means to achieve illiberal ends, but ultimately results in the *erosion* of democracy. To avoid

confusion in my narrative, I omit the term and instead emphasize religious privilege and democratic backsliding.

85. Saiya, "Theocratic Democracy," 71.

86. Saiya, "Theocratic Democracy," 74.

Chapter Three

1. Rhys Isaac, "Religion and Authority: Problems of the Anglican Establishment in Virginia in the Era of the Great Awakening and the Parsons' Cause," *The William and Mary Quarterly* 30, no. 1 (January 1973): 3–36.

2. Brian J. Grim and Roger Finke, *The Price of Freedom Denied: Religious Persecution and Conflict in the Twenty-First Century* (Cambridge: Cambridge University Press, 2011).

3. The most common measure of economic growth is by Gross Domestic Product (GDP), which is the measure used in the graph produced by Brian Grim.

4. Anthony Gill, "Religious Liberty and Economic Development: Exploring the Casual Connections," *The Review of Faith & International Affairs* 2, no. 4 (Winter 2013); Anthony Gill and John Owen IV, "Religious Liberty and Economic Prosperity: Four Lessons from the Past," *Cato Journal* 37, no. 1 (2017): 115–34; Anthony Gill and Timothy Shah, "Religious Freedom, Democratization, and Economic Development: A Survey of the Causal Pathways Linking Religious Freedom to Economic Freedom and Prosperity and Political Freedom and Democracy," Annual Meeting of the Association for the Study of Religion, Economics, and Culture (ASREC), Washington, DC, April 13, 2013, https://www.asrec.org/wp-content/uploads/2015/10/Gill-Shah-Religious-freedom-democratization-and-economic-development.pdf.

5. Brian J. Grim and Melissa E. Grim, "The Socio-Economic Contribution of Religion to American Society: An Empirical Analysis," *Interdisciplinary Journal of Research on Religion* 12, Article 3 (2016).

6. Gill, "Religious Liberty and Economic Development," and Gill and Shah, "Religious Freedom, Democratization, and Economic Development."

7. Robert Woodberry, "The Missionary Roots of Liberal Democracy," *American Political Science Review* 106, no. 2 (2012): 244–74.

8. Gill, "Religious Liberty and Economic Development."

9. Gill, "Religious Liberty and Economic Development."

10. Anthony Gill and John Owen IV, "Religious Liberty and Economic Prosperity: Four Lessons from the Past."

11. Adam Smith, *The Wealth of Nations,* originally published in 1776, republished in 1976 by The Liberty Fund, Volume 1, Book 5, 793.

12. Voltaire, *Letters on the English,* "Letter 6. On the Presbyterians," originally published in 1733 and republished in 2011 by Dover Publishing, http://public-library.uk/ebooks/58/98.pdf.

13. Rhys Isaac, "Religion and Authority: Problems of the Anglican Establishment in Virginia in the Era of the Great Awakening and the Parsons' Cause," *The William and Mary Quarterly* 30, no. 1 (1973): 27. In the seventeenth century, the common language for greater religious freedom was religious toleration. See John Locke, *A Letter Concerning Toleration*, published in 1689, www.constitution.org/jl/tolerati.htm#01.

14. Anthony Gill, *The Political Origins of Religious Liberty* (Cambridge: Cambridge University Press, 2007).

15. Gill and Owen IV, "Religious Liberty and Economic Prosperity," 119.

16. Peter Berger and Anton Zijderveld, *In Praise of Doubt: How to Have Convictions Without Becoming a Fanatic* (New York: HarperOne, 2009).

17. Gill and Owen IV, "Religious Liberty and Economic Prosperity," 123.

18. Gill and Owen IV, "Religious Liberty and Economic Prosperity."

19. Warren C. Scoville, "The Huguenots and the Diffusion of Technology II," *Journal of Political Economy* 60, no. 5 (October 1952): 392–411.

20. Gill, *The Political Origins*, 78.

21. Gill and Owen IV, "Religious Liberty and Economic Prosperity."

22. Warren C. Scoville, "The Huguenots and the Diffusion of Technology I," *Journal of Political Economy* 60, no. 4 (August 1952): 294–311; and "The Huguenots and the Diffusion of Technology II," *Journal of Political Economy* 60, no. 5 (October 1952): 392–411.

23. Scoville, "The Huguenots I," and "The Huguenots II," 398.

24. Scoville, "The Huguenots I."

25. Gill and Owen IV, "Religious Liberty and Economic Prosperity," 127.

26. Gill and Owen IV, "Religious Liberty and Economic Prosperity," 130.

27. Religious Freedom and Business Foundation, "Pew Research Work on Global Restrictions to Continue," *Monthly Archives*, January 31, 2014, https://religiousfreedomandbusiness.org/2/post/2014/01.

28. United Nations, "Academic Impact: Sustainability," 2025, https://www.un.org/en/academic-impact/sustainability.

29. Brian J. Grim, "Seven Ways Religious Freedom Contributes to Sustainable Development," in *Religious Freedom and Sustainable Development*, on-line series, August 10, 2015, http://religiousfreedomandbusiness.org/2/post/2015/08/seven-ways-religious-freedom-contributes-to-sustainable-development.html; Religious Freedom & Business Foundation, "Socioeconomic Impact of Religious

Freedom," 2025, https://religiousfreedomandbusiness.org/socioeconomic-impact-of-religious-freedom.

30. Brian Grim, G. Clark, and R. E. Snyder, "Is Religious Freedom Good for Business? A Conceptual and Empirical Analysis," *Interdisciplinary Journal of Research on Religion* 4 (2014): 1–19.

31. Jerome Hergueux, "How Does Religion Bias the Allocation of Foreign Direct Investment?," *International Economics* 128 (4), 2012: 53–76; Ilan Alon, Shaomin Li, and Jun Wu, "An Institutional Perspective on Religious Freedom and Economic Growth," *Politics and Religion* 10 (2017): 689–716.

32. Alon, Li, and Wu, "An Institutional Perspective on Religious Freedom and Economic Growth," 707.

33. Mack Ott, "Religious Freedom and Economic Progress: A Philosophical and Empirical Exploration, *Journal of Private Enterprise* 20, no. 2 (Spring 2005): 68–96.

34. Religious Freedom and Business Foundation, "Socioeconomic Impact."

35. Brian Grim, "Losing DEI May Cost More Than You Think," *Patheos*, March 31, 2025, https://www.patheos.com/blogs/coalitionforfaithandmedia/2025/03/losing-dei-may-cost-more-than-you-think-including-faith/. Grim showed that President Trump's sweeping elimination of federal DEI programs in his second administration also eliminated religious liberty efforts of a State Department Christian employee group (created by Secretary of State Mike Pompeo in the first Trump administration) to promote "faith-and-belief friendly workplace policies" in China.

36. Ilan Alon and G. Chase, "Religious Freedom and Economic Prosperity," *Cato Journal* 2 (2005): 399–406.

37. Ilan Alon and John Spitzer, "Does Religious Freedom Affect Country Risk Assessment?" *Journal of International and Area Studies* 10, no. 2 (2003): 51–62.

38. Allen Hertzke, *Freeing God's Children: The Unlikely Alliance for Global Human Rights* (Lanham, MD: Rowman & Littlefield, 2004), chapter 7.

39. Allen Hertzke, "Genocide Fueled by Oil," *Weekly Standard* (July 22, 2002): 27–29.

40. Nina Shea, "Religious Freedom in American Foreign Policy," in *Religious Freedom in the World: A Global Report on Freedom and Persecution*, ed. Paul Marshall (Nashville: Tennessee: Broadman & Holman Publishers, 2000): 1–8.

41. Sudan Peace Act, Public Law 107-245, October 21, 2002.

42. Alon, Li, and Wu, "An Institutional Perspective on Religious Freedom and Economic Growth," 2017.

43. Alon, Li, and Wu, "An Institutional Perspective on Religious Freedom and Economic Growth."

44. Timur Kuran, *Freedoms Delayed: Political Legacies of Islamic Law in the Middle East* (Cambridge: Cambridge University Press, 2023); *The Long Divergence: How Islamic Law Held Back the Middle East* (Princeton: Princeton University Press, 2011); *Islam and Mammon: The Economic Predicaments of Islamism* (Princeton, NJ: Princeton University Press, 2004); Ahmet T. Kuru, *Islam, Authoritarianism, and Underdevelopment: A Global and Historical Comparison* (Cambridge: Cambridge University Press, 2019).

45. Kuru, in *Islam, Authoritarianism, and Underdevelopment* especially develops this relationship.

46. Kuru, *Islam*, 3.

47. Kuru, *Islam*, 227.

48. Kuru documents that, from the 8th through the mid-11th century, over 70 percent of "Islamic scholars or families worked in commerce or industry." See Kuru, *Islam*, 3.

49. Kuru, *Islam*, 227.

50. Kuru, *Islam*, 69

51. Kuru, *Islam*, chapter 4.

52. Kuru, *Islam*, 90.

53. Kuru, *Islam*, 69.

54. Kuru, *Islam*, 93–117.

55. Kuru, *Islam*, 227.

56. The sad spectacle of Russian Orthodox leaders blessing Putin's brutal invasion of Ukraine illustrates what co-opted religion looks like.

57. Nilay Saiya, "The Rise of Theocratic Democracy," *Journal of Democracy* 34, no. 4 (October 2023): 66–79.

58. Kuru, *Islam*, 111.

59. Paul Marshall and Nina Shea, *Silenced: How Apostasy and Blasphemy Codes Are Choking Freedom Worldwide* (New York: Oxford University Press, 2011).

60. Kuru, *Islam*, 101–117.

61. Kuru, *Islam*, 162.

62. Kuru, *Islam*, 234.

63. Kuru, *Islam*, 235.

64. Timur Kuran, *Islam and Mammon;* Timur Kuran, *The Long Divergence;* and Timur Kuran, *Freedoms Delayed.*

65. Timur Kuran, *Freedoms Delayed*, 6.

66. Kuran, *Freedoms Delayed*, chapter 7.

67. Kuran, *Freedoms Delayed*, 117.

68. Kuran, *Freedoms Delayed*, 124.

69. Kuran, *Freedoms Delayed*, 125.

70. Kuran, *Freedoms Delayed,* 126.

71. Kuran, *Freedoms Delayed,* 17 and 126.

72. Kuran, *Freedoms Delayed,* Part 3, especially 124–25.

73. Kuran, *Freedoms Delayed,* 17.

74. Kuran, *Freedoms Delayed,* Ch. 4–6. These chapters probe in detail the historical roots and long shadow of Waqfs in stunting civil society.

75. Kuran, *Freedoms Delayed,* Ch. 3–4.

76. Timur Kuran and Jared Rubin, "The Financial Power of the Powerless: Socio-Economic Status and Interest Rates under Partial Rule of Law." *The Economic Journal* (London) 128, no. 609 (2018): 758–96, https://doi-org.ezproxy.lib.ou.edu/10.1111/ecoj.12389.

77. Timur Kuran and Jared Rubin, "The Financial Power of the Powerless."

78. Marshall and Shea, *Silenced.*

79. Brian J. Grim and Melissa E. Grim, "The Socio-Economic Contribution of Religion to American Society: An Empirical Analysis," *Interdisciplinary Journal of Research on Religion* 12, Article 3 (2016).

80. Grim and Grim, "Socio-economic Contribution of Religion to American Society."

81. Grim and Grim, "Socio-economic Contribution of Religion to American Society."

82. *The Review of Faith & International Affairs* published back-to-back special issues with multiple articles on the religious provision of health care and education in Sub-Saharan Africa. See Jill Oliver and Quentin Wodon, "Faith-Inspired Health Care in Sub-Saharan Africa: An Introduction to the Spring 2014 Issue," *The Review of Faith & International Affairs* 12, no. 1 (Spring 2014); Quentin Wodon, "Faith-Inspired Schools in Sub-Saharan Africa: An Introduction to the Summer 2014 Issue," *The Review of Faith & International Affairs* 12, no. 2 (Summer 2014). On the role of religious communities in reconciliation, see Richard Burgess and Danny McCain, "Christianity and the Challenge of Religious Violence in Northern Nigeria," in Allen D. Hertzke and Timothy Samuel Shah, eds., *Christianity and Freedom Volume 2: Contemporary Perspectives* (New York: Cambridge University Press, 2016).

83. Ram Cnaan, Stephanie C. Boodie, Charlene C. McGrew, and Jennifer J. Kang, *The Other Philadelphia Story: How Local Congregations Support Quality of Life in Urban America* (Philadelphia: University of Pennsylvania Press, 2006; Ram Cnaan, Thome Forrest, Joseph Carlsmith, and Kelsey Karsh, "If You Don't Count It, It doesn't Count: A Pilot Study of Valuing Urban Congregations," *Journal of Management, Spirituality and Religion* 10 (2013): 3–36; and Ram Cnaan, Robert J. Wineburg and Stephanie Boodie, *Newer Deal: Social Work and Religion in Partnership* (New York: Columbia University Press, 1999).

84. Tyler J. VanderWeele, "Chapter 4: Spiritual Well-Being and Human Flourishing," in Adam Cohen, ed., *Religion and Human Flourishing* (Waco, TX: Baylor University Press, 2020), 58–59.

85. *The Global Flourishing Study: What Contributes to a Life Well-Lived?* Sponsored by Gallup, Baylor University's Institute for Studies of Religion, Harvard University's Human Flourishing Program, and Center for Open Science, 2025, https://globalflourishingstudy.com/wp-content/uploads/2025/04/GFS_Report-1.pdf.

86. Putnam, *Bowling Alone: The Collapse and Revival of Community in America* (New York: Simon and Schuster, 2001).

87. Adam Cohen, "Chapter 7: Religions Help Us Trust One Another," in *Religion and Human Flourishing.*

88. Byron Johnson, Sung Joon Jang, David B. Larson, and Spencer De Li, "Does Adolescent Religious Commitment Matter? A Reexamination of the Effects of Religiosity on Delinquency," *Journal of Research in Crime and Delinquency* 38, no. 1 (2001): 22–44; Byron Johnson, *More God, Less Crime: Why Religion Matters and How It Could Matter More* (Conshohocken, PA: Templeton Press, 2011).

89. Byron Johnson is the leading authority on religion and crime prevention, rehabilitation, and the transformation of prison environments. See Byron Johnson, "How Religion Contributes to the Common Good, Positive Criminology, and Justice Reform," *Religions* 12, no. 6 (2021): 402; Byron Johnson, "Chapter 10: Offender-Led Religious Movements," in *Religion and Human Flourishing*; Grant Duwe and Byron Johnson, "Estimating the Benefits of a Faith-Based Correctional Program," *International Journal of Criminology and Sociology* 2 (2013): 227–39.

90. Jeff Levin, "Religion and Mental Health: Theory and Research," *International Journal of Applied Psychoanalytic Studies* 7, Issue 2 (2010): 102–15.

91. Harold Koenig, Dana King, and Verna B. Carson, *Handbook of Religion and Health* (Oxford: Oxford University Press, 2012).

92. Tyler J. VanderWeele, "Association Between Religious Service Attendance and Lower Suicide Rates Among US Women," *JAMA Psychiatry* 8 (2016): 845–51.

93. Rodney Stark, *America's Blessings: How Religion Benefits Everyone, Including Atheists* (Conshohocken, PA: Templeton Foundation Press, 2012).

94. Gill and Shah, "Religious Freedom, Democratization, and Economic Development," 22.

95. The first "World Happiness Report" survey was launched in 2012 under the direction of Columbia University's Earth Institute with contributions from the world's leading happiness researchers. Subsequent World Happiness Reports were produced through a partnership of Gallup, the University of Oxford Wellbeing Research Center, and the UN Sustainable Development Solutions Network, under the direction of the Editorial Board of the World Happiness Report, https://world

happiness.report/ed/2023/. See John F. Helliwell, Richard Layard, Jeffrey D. Sachs, Jan-Emmanuel De Neve, Lara B. Aknin, and Shun Wang, eds. *World Happiness Report 2023*, 11th ed. (Sustainable Development Solutions Network, 2023).

96. Gill and Shah, "Religious Freedom, Democratization, and Economic Development," 23.

97. Christos Andreas Makridis, "Human Flourishing and Religious Liberty: Evidence from 150 Countries," *PLOS ONE* 15, no. 10 (October 1, 2020).

98. Martha C. Nussbaum, *Creating Capabilities*. (Cambridge: Harvard University Press, 2011).

99. The John Templeton Foundation funded a conference held in 2018 at Harvard University to bring together scholars who explored the broad questions of religion's relationship to human flourishing. The product of that conference was an edited volume (see Cohen, *Religion and Human Flourishing*), which helped launch the five-year Global Flourishing Study, co-directed by Tyler VanderWeele and Byron Johnson, funded by Templeton and others, and sponsored by Gallup, Baylor University's Institute for Studies of Religion, Harvard University's Human Flourishing Project, and the Center for Open Science. See *The Global Flourishing Study: What Contributes to a Life Well-Lived?* (2025), 4–6.

100. *The Global Flourishing Study*, 21. The exceptions to the positive link between religious service attendance and flourishing include religiously-repressive China, Nigeria, which is afflicted by violent religious strife, and Egypt, where the state privileges Sunni Islam.

101. See Philip S. Gorski and Samuel L. Perry, *The Flag and the Cross: White Christian Nationalism and the Threat to Democracy* (New York: Oxford University Press, 2022).

102. Nilay Saiya, *The Global Politics of Jesus: A Christian Case for Church-State Separation* (New York: Oxford University Press, 2022).

103. Nilay Saiya, *God's Warriors: Religious Violence and the Global Crisis of Secularism* (New York: Oxford University Press, 2005).

104. Stella Yifan Xie and Jason Douglas, "China's Fading Recovery Reveals Deeper Economic Struggles," *The Wall Street Journal*, May 30, 2023, https://www.wsj.com/world/chinas-fading-recovery-reveals-deeper-economic-struggles-31f4097b.

105. Brian Grim, "The Modern Chinese Secret to Sustainable Economic Growth: Religious Freedom and Diversity," *The Review of Faith & International Affairs* 13, no. 2 (Summer 2015): 13–24.

106. Grim, "The Modern Chinese Secret."

107. Grim, "The Modern Chinese Secret."

108. Helen Davidson, "China in Darkest Period for Human Rights Since Tiananmen, says Human Rights Group," *The Guardian* (January 13, 2021), https://

www.theguardian.com/world/2021/jan/13/china-in-darkest-period-for-human-rights-since-tiananmen-says-rights-group.

109. Lingling Wei, "Xi Jinping Chokes Off Crucial Engine of China's Economy," *The Wall Street Journal*, July 13, 2023, https://www.wsj.com/world/xi-china-economy-capital-investment-3439d31a.

110. Fenggang Yang, "The Growth and Dynamism of Chinese Christianity," in *Christianity and Freedom: Contemporary Perspectives*, eds. Allen D. Hertzke and Timothy Samuel Shah (Cambridge: Cambridge University Press, 2016). Fenggang Yang, Director of the Center on Religion and the Global East at Purdue University, is the leading authority on religion in China. While the religious crackdown by the Xi regime may be slowing the growth rates of Christianity in China that Yang documented in 2016, he expects to see compounding growth into the future (personal conversation with the author, July 28, 2023).

111. Fenggang Yang, "The Growth and Dynamism of Chinese Christianity."

112. Nanlai Cao, "Boss Christians: The Business of Religion in the 'Wenzhou Model' of Christian Revival," *The China Journal*, no. 59 (January 2008): 63–87.

113. Joy K. C. Tong and Fenggang Yang, "Trust at Work: A Study on Faith and Trust of Protestant Entrepreneurs in China," *MDPI Religions* 7, no. 12 (2016); and Xiangping Li and Fenggang Yang, "Protestant Ethics and the Construction of Social Trust: Christian Enterprises in Contemporary China," In *From the Armchair to the Field: Selected Articles of the Beijing Summit on Chinese Spirituality and Society* 2, eds. Shining Gao and Fenggang Yang (Beijing: China Social Sciences Press, 2010): 287–302.

114. Qunyong Wang and Xinyu Lin, "Does Religious Beliefs Affect Economic Growth? Evidence From Provincial-Level Data in China," *China Economic Review*, 31 (2014): 277–87. The quote is from the abstract on page 277.

115. Qunyong Wang and Xinyu Lin, "Does Religious Beliefs Affect Economic Growth?," 284.

116. Qunyong Wang and Xinyu Lin, "Does Religious Beliefs Affect Economic Growth?"

117. See Grim, "The Modern Chinese Secret" and Brian Grim and Liu Peng, "The Achilles Heel of China's Rise: Belief," Beijing: Pu Shi Institute for Social Sciences, July 25, 2012, https://www.asianews.it/news-en/The-Achilles%27-Heel-of-China%27s-Rise:-Belief--25379.html.

118. According to Pew, China's Government Restriction Index (GRI) went from 7.8 to 9.1 on a 10-point scale between 2007 to 2022, the highest GRI in the world. Pew Research Center, "Government Restrictions on Religion Stayed at Peak Levels Globally in 2022," Appendix C, December 18, 2024: https://

www.pewresearch.org/wp-content/uploads/sites/20/2024/12/PR_2024.12.18_restrictions-on-religion-2022_appendix-c.pdf.

119. Alexandra Stevenson and Zixu Wang, "China's Population Falls, Heralding a Demographic Crisis," *The New York Times* (January 16, 2023), https://www.nytimes.com/2023/01/16/business/china-birth-rate.html.

120. Pew Research Center, "The Future of World Religions: Population Growth Projections: 2010–2050" (April 2 2015), http://www.pewforum.org/2015/04/02/religious-projections-2010-2050/.

121. Yang, "The Growth and Dynamism of Chinese Christianity."

Chapter Four

1. Robert D. Putnam, *Bowling Alone: The Collapse and Revival of Community in America* (New York: Simon & Schuster, 2001).

2. *The Hidden Form of Capital: Spiritual Influences in Societal Progress*, ed. Peter L. Berger and Gordon Redding (London: Anthem Press, 2010).

3. Timothy Samuel Shah, *Religious Freedom: Why Now?* (Princeton: The Witherspoon Institute, Inc., 2012).

4. The first Global Restrictions report by the Pew Research Center, issued in December of 2009 but covering the year 2007, found that 70 percent of the world's population lived in countries with high or very high restrictions on religion. Pew Research Center, "Global Restrictions on Religion," Pew Forum on Religion and Public Life, December 17, 2009, http://www.pewforum.org/2009/12/17/global-restrictions-on-religion/. A decade later, that figure rose to 85 percent, according to an analysis of the Pew report for 2017 by Brian Grim, "Economic Growth Slowed by Decline in Religious Freedom," Religious Freedom and Business Foundation, 2019, https://religiousfreedomandbusiness.org/economic-growth-slowed-by-decline-in-religious-freedom. Pew Research Center, "A Closer Look at How Religious Restrictions Have Risen Around the World," July 15, 2019, https://www.pewresearch.org/wp-content/uploads/sites/20/2019/07/Restrictions_X_WEB_7-15_FULL-VERSION-1.pdf. Note: Pew reports have a two-year lag time between the year covered and the publishing year.

5. Jonathan Fox, *The Unfree Exercise of Religion: A World Survey of Discrimination Against Religious Minorities* (New York: Cambridge University Press, 2016), and *Political Secularism, Religion, and the State* (New York: Cambridge University Press, 2015).

6. Brian J. Grim, "Seven Ways Religious Freedom Contributes to Sustainable Development," in *Religious Freedom and Sustainable Development*, online

series, August 10, 2015, http://religiousfreedomandbusiness.org/2/post/2015/08/seven-ways-religious-freedom-contributes-to-sustainable-development.html, accessed April 24, 2017.

7. Robert Woodberry, "The Missionary Roots of Liberal Democracy," *American Political Science Review* 106, no. 2 (2012): 244–74.

8. Brian J. Grim and Roger Finke, *The Price of Freedom Denied: Religious Persecution and Conflict in the Twenty-First Century* (New York: Cambridge University Press, 2010).

9. Brian Grim and Jo-Ann Lyon, "Religion Holds Women Back: Or Does It?" World Economic Forum, November 17, 2015, https://www.weforum.org/agenda/2015/11/religion-holds-women-back-or-does-it. Grim and Lyon compare the Gender Inequality Index in the UN Human Development Reports and find a strong correlation between gender inequality and countries with high restrictions on religion.

10. Grim and Lyon, "Religion Holds Women Back," 4

11. Grim and Lyon, "Religion Holds Women Back."

12. Nicholas Kristof and Sheryl WuDunn, *Half the Sky: Turning Oppression into Opportunity for Women Worldwide* (New York: Vintage, 2010).

13. Rebecca Samuel Shah and Timothy Samuel Shah, "Chapter 10: Religious Freedom Among the Marginalized in Bangalore, India," in *Christianity in India: Conversion, Community Development, and Religious Freedom*, Rebecca Samuel Shah and Joel Carpenter, eds. (Minneapolis: Fortress Press, 2018).

14. Brian Grim and Roger Finke, *The Price of Freedom Denied.*

15. Amartya Sen, *Development as Freedom* (New York: Knopf, 1999). Rebecca Shah expands on his and other research by developing the idea of spiritual capital. See Rebecca S. Shah, "Religion and Economic Empowerment Among the Enterprising Poor," *The Review of Faith & International Affairs* 11 (Winter 2013).

16. See Sabina Alkire, *Valuing Freedoms* (Oxford: Oxford University Press, 2005); Deepa Narayan, *Voices of the Poor: Can Anyone Hear Us* (Oxford: Oxford University Press, 2000); Rebecca and Timothy Shah, "Spiritual Capital and Economic Enterprise," Oxford Centre for Religion & Public Life, June 26, 2007, http://www.ocrpl.org/2007/spiritual-capital-and-economic-entrerprise/; Rebecca S. Shah and Robert Woodberry, "Religion and Economic Empowerment: A Growing but Still Tentative Relationship," a literature review working paper, August 2015; Rebecca Shah, "Christianity Among the Marginalized: Empowering Poor Women in India," in *Christianity and Freedom Volume II: Contemporary Perspectives*, Allen D. Hertzke and Timothy Samuel Shah, eds. (New York: Cambridge University Press, 2016).

17. Rebecca Shah, "Religion and Economic Empowerment Among the Enterprising Poor," *Review of Faith & International Affairs* 11, no. 4 (December 2013): 41–45, https://doi-org.ezproxy.lib.ou.edu/10.1080/15570274.2013.857121. See also Rebecca and Timothy Shah, "Spiritual Capital and Economic Enterprise," Oxford Centre for Religion & Public Life, June 26, 2007, http://www.ocrpl.org/2007/spiritual-capital-and-economic-entrerprise/.

18. Shah, "Religion and Economic Empowerment."

19. Shah, "Religion and Economic Empowerment," 41–42.

20. "India: Official Dalit Population Exceeds 200 Million," International Dalit Solidarity Network, May 29, 2013, http://idsn.org/india-official-dalit-population-exceeds-200-million/.

21. Shah, "Christianity Among the Marginalized: Empowering Poor Women in India."

22. Bruce Wydick, Robert Dowd, and Travis J. Lybbert, "Hope and Human Dignity: Exploring Religious Belief, Hope, and Transition out of Poverty in Oaxaca, Mexico," in *The Practice of Human Development and Dignity*, eds. Paolo G. Carozza and Clemens Sedmak (Notre Dame, IN: University of Notre Dame Press, 2020): 139–62.

23. Rebecca Shah and her colleagues conducted waves of surveys (totaling over 7,600) among the poor in India and Sri Lanka from 2016 until 2019, along with case studies of thirty Dalit women entrepreneurs, for the Religion and Economic Empowerment Project (REEP), funded by the Templeton Religion Trust. For initial findings of this project, see Rebecca Supriya Shah and Timothy Samuel Shah, "Chapter 4—The Other Invisible Hand: How Freedom of Religion and Belief Fosters Pro-Social and Pro-Development Outcomes for the Poor," in *What About Us? Global Perspectives on Redressing Religious Inequalities*, Mariz Tadros, editor (Sussex: UK: Institute of Development Studies, University of Sussex, 2022).

24. Shah and Shah, "The Other Invisible Hand," 96.

25. Shah and Shah, "The Other Invisible Hand," 107.

26. Shah and Shah, "The Other Invisible Hand," 96.

27. Rebecca Shah and Timothy Shah, "Participatory Methods and the Freedom of Religion and Belief," in *Using Participatory Methods to Explore Freedom of Religion and Belief: Whose Reality Counts?*, eds. Jo Howard and Mariz Tadros (Bristol, UK: Bristol University Press, 2023), 51.

28. I elaborate on the "paradox of privilege" in chapters 5 and 6.

29. Shah and Shah, "The Other Invisible Hand," 90

30. Shah and Shah, "The Other Invisible Hand," 91.

31. Elizabeth E. Brusco, *The Reformation of Machismo: Evangelical Conversion and Gender in Colombia* (Austin: University of Texas Press, 1995).

32. Roger Finke and Rodney Stark, *The Churching of America, 1776-2005: Winners and Losers in Our Religious Economy* (New Brunswick: Rutgers University Press, 2005).

33. Anthony Gill, *Rending unto Caesar: The Catholic Church and the State in Latin America* (Chicago: University of Chicago Press, 1998).

34. Daniel Philpott, "The Catholic Wave," *Journal of Democracy* 15, no. 2 (April 2004).

35. Robert Woodberry, "The Missionary Roots of Liberal Democracy."

36. Guillermo Trejo, *Popular Movements in Autocracies: Religion, Repression, and Indigenous Collective Action in Mexico* (New York: Cambridge University Press, 2012).

37. Trejo, *Popular Movements*, xv.

38. The Mexican Indigenous Insurgency Database (MII) contains information on over 3,500 acts of rural indigenous protest, along with thousands of legal claims and government actions between 1970 and 2000. See Trejo, *Popular Movements*, page 21.

39. Trejo, *Popular Movements*, 7.

40. To scientific purists, the controlled experiment is the surest means of testing theories and showing causation. For obvious reasons, it is difficult, if not impossible, to conduct experiments in the social and political world. However, sometimes scholars identify conditions in the real world that constitute a kind of "natural experiment," as we saw in chapter 2 on the Catholic wave of democratization after the Church's doctrinal embrace of religious freedom at Vatican II.

41. Trejo also noted that this move was based on a Vatican practice of transferring bishops for practical considerations, not ideology; thus, it contributed to the natural experiment. Trejo, *Popular Movements*, 22.

42. Trejo, *Popular Movements*, 22.

43. Trejo, *Popular Movements*, 7.

44. Trejo, *Popular Movements*, 85–86.

45. Trejo, *Popular Movements*, 36.

46. Trejo, *Popular Movements*, 19.

47. Trejo, *Popular Movements*, 229.

48. Christopher W. Hale, *Divined Intervention: Religious Institutions and Collective Action* (Ann Arbor: University of Michigan Press, 2020).

49. Mariz Tadros is Professor of Politics and Development and Director of the Coalition for Religious Equality and Inclusive Development, Institute for Development Studies, University of Sussex, United Kingdom.

50. At a Zoom presentation to the Orthodox Christian Studies Center of Fordham University, July 23, 2020, Tadros provided a vivid account of her

background as a Coptic Orthodox Christian in Egypt, and how unexpected immersion in a local Coptic church launched her quest to address inequality: https://www.youtube.com/watch?v=crgcdRZ1d6Y.

51. A good example of this approach is her book chapter, "Copts of Egypt: Defiance, Compliance, and Continuity," in *Christianity and Freedom, Volume 2: Contemporary Perspectives*, eds. Allen D. Hertzke and Timothy Samuel Shah. See also her Fordham University presentation: https://www.youtube.com/watch?v=crgcdRZ1d6Y.

52. Guided by a religiously diverse steering committee, CREID was cofounded in 2018 and is currently directed by Mariz Tadros, Institute of Development Studies Research Fellow at the University of Sussex, who specializes in the politics and human development in the Middle East. See https://creid.ac/.

53. *What About Us? Global Perspectives on Redressing Religious Inequalities.*

54. Asif Aqeel and Mary Gill, "International Assistance and Impoverished Religious Minorities in Pakistan," in *What About Us?*, chapter 8.

55. Moses Muhumuza, Tom Vanwing, and Mark Kaahwa, "The Integration of Traditional Religious Beliefs in the Conservation of the Rwenzori Mountains National Park, Uganda: Processes and Lessons Learned," in *What About Us?*, chapter 7.

56. Rifqah Tifloen and Matome Jacky Makgoba, "Sustainable Faith and Livelihoods: Promoting Freedom of Religion and Belief in Development," in *What About Us?*, chapter 6.

57. Miram Feldmann Kaye, "Intercultural Training, Interfaith Dialogue, and Religious Literacy: Minority Groups in the Israeli Health-Care System," in *What About Us?*, chapter 2.

58. Jo Howard, "Understanding Intersecting Vulnerabilities Experienced by Religious Minorities Living in Poverty in the Shadows of Covid-19," April 30, 2021, Coalition for Religious Equality and Inclusive Development, https://en.unesco.org/inclusivepolicylab/system/files/teams/discussion/comments/2021/11/CRIED_Intersections_Series_Religious_Inequalities_and_Covid-19.pdf. CRIED enlisted teams of local researchers and investigators in different sites in Nigeria and India, to conduct qualitative and participatory methods that included semi-structured interviews, visual methods in which participants traced their lives before, during, and after the peak of the pandemic, and group-based discussions.

59. Rebecca Supriya Shah and Timothy Samuel Shah, "The Other Invisible Hand."

60. Philip Mader, "'We Put God and Drums in the Front': Spirituality as Strategy in Adivasi Self-Empowerment Movement," in *What About Us?*, chapter 5. Scheduled Tribes, the official designation of the Adivasi peoples, comprise 8.6 percent of the Indian population, or 104 million people. They suffer even worse health

outcomes than Dalits, or untouchables, which make up another 8 percent of the Indian population, an indication of why uplift for this huge population would represent such a large global impact.

61. Howard and Tadros, eds., *Using Participatory Methods to Explore Freedom of Religion and Belief: Whose Reality Counts?*

62. Brian Grim, "Religious Freedom and LGBT Rights: Do They Have Common Ground," Religious Freedom and Business Foundation, 2020, https://religiousfreedomandbusiness.org/wp-content/uploads/2020/11/COMMON-GROUND-LGBT-Rights-and-Religious-Freedom.pdf.

63. Virginia Villa, "Religiously Unaffiliated People Face Harassment in a Growing Number of Countries," Pew Research Center, August 12, 2019.

64. The great champion of religious freedom, Roger Williams, defended both unbelief and religious beliefs he found repugnant because he believed that conscience is from God and thus no political authority has the right to violate that sacred haven. A person can be persuaded to embrace sacred truths but cannot be forced by the state to do so. See *Bloody Tenet of Persecution for the Cause of Conscience*, first published in 1644, in *On Religious Liberty: Selections from the Words of Roger Williams*, ed. James Calvin Davis. (Cambridge, MA: Harvard University Press, 2008).

65. Article 18, International Covenant on Civil and Political Rights, 1976; UN Declaration of Human Rights, 1948.

66. Grim, "Religious Freedom and LGBT Rights," 2020.

67. Leaders of the Religious Freedom Institute charged that the Equality Act before Congress goes beyond protecting LGBT persons from discrimination and instead is aimed at forcing religious institutions with traditional beliefs on marriage and sexuality out of public life. See Thomas Farr, "The Equality Act Will Harm Religious Freedom," https://www.realclearreligion.org/articles/2019/05/16/the_equality_act_will_hurt_religious_freedom_110219.html; David Trimble and Nathaniel Hurd, "Why Does the Infrastructure Bill Include Sexual Orientation and Gender Identity Language," Religious Freedom Institute Blog, August 6, 2021, https://www.religiousfreedominstitute.org/blog/why-does-the-infrastructure-bill-include-sexual-orientation-and-gender-identity-language.

68. Grim, "Religious Freedom and LGBT Rights."

69. Grim, "Religious Freedom and LGBT Rights."

70. Gary A. Haugen and Victor Boutros, *The Locust Effect: Why the End of Poverty Required the End of Violence* (New York: Oxford University Press, 2014), x.

71. Haugen, *The Locust Effect*, xii.

72. Paul Marshall and Nina Shea, *Silenced: How Apostasy and Blasphemy Codes Are Choking Freedom Worldwide* (New York: Oxford University Press, 2011).

73. This insight was pointed out to me by Shino Yokotsuka, a graduate student at the University of Delaware, who is exploring the value of religious freedom to the inclusion of outsiders to Japanese culture.

74. Pew Research Center, "Government Restrictions on Religion Stayed at Peak Levels Globally in 2022," Pew Research Center, December 18, 2024, https://www.pewresearch.org/wp-content/uploads/sites/20/2024/12/PR_2024.12.18_restrictions-on-religion-2022_report.pdf.

75. Stephen V. Monsma, "Faith-Based NGOs and the Government Embrace," in *The Influence of Faith: Religious Groups and U.S. Foreign Policy,* ed. Elliott Abrams (Lanham, MD: Rowman and Littlefield, 2001).

76. Andrew S. Natsios, "Faith-Based NGOs and U.S. Foreign Policy," in *The Influence of Faith: Religious Groups and U.S. Foreign Policy*, ed. Elliot Abrams (Lanham, MD: Rowman & Littlefield, 2001).

77. Allen Hertzke, "Globalization of Advocacy," in *The Politics and Practices of Religious Diversity*, ed. Andrew Dawson (New York: Routledge, 2016).

78. Rabbi David Saperstein, "Event transcript: Lobbying for the Faithful," Pew Research Center, November 21, 2011, https://www.pewresearch.org/religion/2011/11/21/lobbying-for-the-faithful-event-transcript/.

79. Hertzke, "Globalization of Advocacy."

80. Scott Baldauf and Jina Moore, "Bush Sees Results of His AIDS Plan in Africa," *The Christian Science Monitor*, February 20, 2008.

81. "The United States President's Emergency Plan for AIDS Relief," United States Department of State, https://www.state.gov/pepfar/.

82. This is the figure given by the 2014 State Department's Trafficking in Persons report. See http://www.state.gov/j/tip/rls/tiprpt/2014/index.htm. Kevin Bales estimates 27 million persons in conditions of slavery. Kevin Bales, *Disposable People: New Slavery in the Global Economy* (Berkeley: University of California Press, 2000).

83. Allen Hertzke, *Freeing God's Children: The Unlikely Alliance for Global Human Rights (*Lanham, MD: Rowman & Littlefield, 2006), chapter 8.

84. Quentin Hardy, "Hitting Slavery Where It Hurts," *Forbes* 172, no. 14 (2004): 76.

85. As Haugen writes, the "good news" about injustice is that God is against it, which mandates that believers must fight against it as well. See Gary Haugen, *The Good News About Injustice* (Downers Grove, IL: InterVarsity Press, 1999).

86. See Talith Kum's website, www.talithakum.info, for its mission statement and additional information.

87. U.S. Embassy to the Holy See Conference on Building Bridges of Freedom, May 18, 2011, http://vatican.usembassy.gov/news-events/launch-talitha-kums-countering-trafficking-in-persons.html.

88. Hertzke, *Freeing God's Children*, chapter 8. For text of the act and subsequent reauthorizations, see the State Department office website, http://www.state.gov/j/tip/laws/.

89. Allen Hertzke, *Freeing God's Children.*

Chapter Five

1. Monica Duffy Toft, "Religion, Terrorism, and Violence," in *Rethinking Religion and World Affairs,* eds. Timothy Samuel Shah, Alfred Stepan, and Monica Duffy Toft (New York: Oxford University Press, 2012); Nilay Saiya, *Weapon of Peace: How Religious Liberty Combats Terrorism* (Cambridge: Cambridge University Press, 2018).

2. Monica Duffy Toft, Daniel Philpott, and Timothy Samuel Shah, *God's Century: Resurgent Religion and Global Politics* (New York: W.W. Norton, 2011).

3. Toft, Philpott, and Shah, *God's Century*, 153.

4. Saiya, *Weapon of Peace*, 1.

5. Saiya, *Weapon of Peace*, 14–19.

6. Saiya, *Weapon of Peace,* 5.

7. Toft, Philpott, and Shah, *God's Century,* chapter 4.

8. W. Cole Durham Jr. and Elizabeth A. Clark, "The Place of Religious Freedom in the Structure of Peacebuilding," in *The Oxford Handbook of Religion, Conflict, and Peacebuilding,* eds. Atalia Omer, R. Scot Appleby, and David Little (New York: Oxford University Press, 2015), 298.

9. This argument about modernization and plurality is made by Peter Berger. He made the specific quip in a presentation at a conference in Istanbul on global religious freedom, which I organized for the John Templeton Foundation, April 2009. See Peter Berger, *The Many Altars of Modernity: Toward a Paradigm for Religion in a Pluralist Age* (Boston and Berlin: Walter de Gruyter, 2014).

10. These examples are provided by Brian Grim and Roger Finke, *The Price of Freedom Denied: Religious Persecution and Conflict in the Twenty-First Century* (Cambridge: Cambridge University Press), chapter 1.

11. For a summary of foundational thinkers, see Allen Hertzke, "Introduction: A Madisonian Framework for Applying Constitutional Principles on Religion," *Religious Freedom in America: Constitutional Roots and Contemporary Challenges*, ed. Allen D. Hertzke (Norman: University of Oklahoma Press, 2015).

12. Pew Research Center, "Government Restrictions on Religion Stayed at Peak Levels Globally in 2022, December 18, 2024, https://www.pewresearch.org/wp-content/uploads/sites/20/2024/12/PR_2024.12.18_restrictions-on-religion-2022_report.pdf.

13. Brian Grim and Roger Finke, *Price of Freedom Denied: Religious Persecution and Conflict in the Twenty-First Century* (New York: Cambridge University Press, 2011), 70–74.

14. Between 900 thousand and 1.8 million Uyghurs were held in these camps at the end of 2019. United States Commission for International Religious Freedom, "USCIRF Warns that Forced Sterilization of Uyghur Muslims is Evidence of Genocide," 2020, https://www.uscirf.gov/news-room/press-releases-statements/uscirf-warns-forced-sterilization-uyghur-muslims-evidence.

15. "USCIRF Warns that Forced Sterilization of Uyghur Muslims Is Evidence of Genocide," United States Commission on International Religious Freedom, June 30, 2020, Washington, DC, https://www.uscirf.gov/release-statements/uscirf-warns-forced-sterilization-uyghur-muslims-evidence-genocide; Lindsay Maizland, "China's Repression of Uyghurs in Xinjiang," Council on Foreign Relations, September 22, 2022, https://www.cfr.org/backgrounder/china-xinjiang-uyghurs-muslims-repression-genocide-human-rights.

16. Daniel Philpott, "Why Religious Freedom is a Human Right," *The American Journal of Jurisprudence* 68, no. 3 (December 2023), 5.

17. Pew Research Center, "Government Restrictions on Religion Stayed at Peak Levels Globally in 2002." In "Appendix C," China's score on Pew's 10-point scale was 9.1, the highest in the world. China's only competitor as the most repressive government is North Korea, but because the "Hermit Kingdom" is such a closed system, comparable data by which to code its restrictions is unavailable; as a result, the Pew Research Center omits it from its scoring.

18. Jonathan Fox, *A World Survey of Religion and the State* (New York: Cambridge University Press, 2008); and Jonathan Fox, *Thou Shalt Have No Other Gods Before Me: Why Governments Discriminate Against Religious Minorities* (Cambridge: Cambridge University Press, 2020). For access to the Religion and State (RAS) data sets, see https://ras.thearda.com/ras-downloads/.

19. "Myanmar Rohingya: What You Need to Know about the Crisis," BBC, January 23, 2020, https://www.bbc.com/news/world-asia-41566561.

20. Toft, Philpott, and Shah, *God's Century*, 80–82.

21. Grim and Finke, *Price of Freedom Denied*, provide the statistical model of this "religious violence cycle," presented in the "Appendix," 217.

22. Pew Research Center, "Government Restrictions on Religion Stayed at Peak Levels Globally in 2022." While social hostilities were not quite at peak levels, this report showed that social hostilities increased substantially from the baseline period of 2007–2008.

23. Pew's global reports measure two distinct types of restrictions on religion: government restrictions and social hostilities.

24. Because of their ancient gnostic faith, Yazidis were considered devil worshipers by the Sunni militants of the Islamic State. When ISIS overran the Sinjar province of northern Iraq, it unleashed a genocidal campaign of mass executions, forced conversions, and sexual violence against Yazidis. The terror and ethnic cleansing resulted in the displacement of some 400,000 Yazidis, which sparked international outrage and Western military strikes and rescue efforts. See "USCIRF Solemnly Commemorates the Tenth Anniversary of ISIS Genocide Against Iraqi and Syrian Religious Minorities," United States Commission on International Religious Freedom, Washington, DC, August 2, 2024, https://www.uscirf.gov/news-room/releases-statements/uscirf-solemnly-commemorates-tenth-anniversary-isiss-genocide-against.

25. Matthew Barber, "They That Remain: Syrian and Iraqi Christian Communities amid the Syria Conflict and the Rise of the Islamic State," in *Christianity and Freedom Volume II: Contemporary Perspectives*, eds. Allen D. Hertzke and Timothy Samuel Shah (New York: Cambridge University Press, 2016).

26. Grim and Finke, *Price of Freedom Denied.*

27. Grim and Finke, *Price of Freedom Denied,* 70–79.

28. In the Appendix of *The Price of Freedom Denied*, Grim and Finke employ structural equation modeling to show statistically how the religious violence cycle works.

29. Toft, Philpott, and Shah, *God's Century,* 49.

30. Toft, Philpott, and Shah, *God's Century,* chapter 5.

31. Thomas F. Farr, *World of Faith and Freedom: Why International Religious Liberty is Vital to American National Security* (New York: Oxford University Press, 2008).

32. William Inboden, "Religious Freedom and National Security," *Policy Review* 175 (October and November 2012): 57.

33. Inboden, "Religious Freedom and National Security," 56.

34. Inboden, "Religious Freedom and National Security," 57.

35. William Inboden, "Jihadist Ideology, Religious Intolerance, and the Anathema of Democracy," presented at Religious Freedom Project Symposium, Georgetown University, November 15, 2016, unpublished paper cited with permission of author.

36. John Owen, *The Clash of Ideas in World Politics: Transnational Networks, States and Regime Change, 1510–2010* (Princeton, NJ: Princeton University Press, 2010).

37. Owen, *The Clash of Ideas in World Politics.*

38. Farr, *World of Faith and Freedom.* A different problem manifested itself during the Trump administration. On the one hand, Secretary of State Mike

Pompeo and Ambassador for International Religious Freedom Sam Brownback elevated religious freedom in a variety of initiatives and helped craft the Trump administration's Executive Order on Advancing International Religious Freedom. On the other hand, Trump himself undermined these initiatives by appeasing autocrats who repress religious freedom, most egregiously when he apparently gave a nod of approval to the Chinese regime's massive repression of its Uyghur Muslim population and, later, seemed to take the side of Vladimir Putin in his military aggression against Ukraine. See John Bolton, *The Room Where it Happened: A White House Memoir* (New York: Simon and Schuster, 2020).

39. To measure religious terrorist attacks, Saiya codes data from the Global Terrorism Database (GTD), hosted by the National Consortium for the Study of Terrorism and Responses to Terrorism, and the RAND Database of Worldwide Terrorist Incidents. To assess the impact of religious civil wars, he codes data from the Religious Civil Wars database compiled by Monica Duffy Toft. For measures of religious restrictions, he uses three sources: International Religious Freedom Data compiled by Brian Grim and Roger Finke, the Pew Research Center's Global Restrictions on Religion reports, and data from the Religion and State (RAS) Project run by Jonathan Fox at Bar Ilan University. To demonstrate the wider impact of religious freedom, and to control for variables that might reduce religious violence, he incorporates measures of democracy and civil liberties from the Polity database, along with measures of wealth, population, and geographic area. "Appendix," Saiya, *Weapon of Peace.*

40. Saiya, *Weapon of Peace*, 192.

41. Nilay Saiya and Anthony Scime, "Explaining Religious Terrorism: A Data-Mined Analysis," *Conflict Management and Peace Science* 32, no. 5 (2014): 487–512.

42. Countries with low government restrictions suffered less than one terrorist attack per year (.30); those with moderate restrictions, 5.37 attacks per year; and those in the high category, 7.35 attacks annually, or nearly 25 times as many attacks as countries with low restrictions. See Saiya, *Weapon of Peace*, 44.

43. Saiya, *Weapon of Peace*, 52.

44. Saiya, *Weapon of Peace*, 52. For earlier research findings, see Nilay Saiya, "Religion, State, and Terrorism: A Global Analysis," *Terrorism and Political Violence* 31, no. 2 (2016), 204–23; Nilay Saiya, "The Religious Freedom Peace." *The International Journal of Human Rights* 19, no. 3 (2015): 369–82; and Saiya and Scime, "Explaining Religious Terrorism."

45. Figure 5.3 in this chapter is an earlier version of the one Saiya included in *Weapon of Peace,* 53. In the book, Saiya expands the recording period from 1991 to 2013 and increases country years to over 3,500. But the pattern is exactly the same as figure 5.3.

46. There is a robust debate about how, or whether, the social sciences can yield the experimental findings of natural science. But with the growing volume and quality of global data over time, and with creative methods, scholars like Saiya can reveal and analyze patterns of the "natural experiment" of changing government policies and regimes. Saiya enhances his "natural experiment" by lagging (by one year) his measure of terrorist attacks to ensure he captures the direction of causality. Saiya, *Weapon of Peace.*

47. Saiya, *Weapon of Peace,* 34.

48. Prime Minister Indira Gandhi was assassinated by two of her own Sikh guards in 1984. See Saiya, *Weapon of Peace,* 37.

49. Allen Hertzke, "State Failure and International Response: The Lessons of South Sudan," in *Nation, State, Nation-State,* Vittorio Hosle, Marcelo Sanchez, and Stefano Zamagni, eds. (Vatican City: Pontifical Academy of Social Sciences, 2020), 183–213.

50. Saiya, Weapon of Peace, 38–39.

51. Dalits and other lower caste Indians, not surprisingly, have converted from Hinduism to Buddhism, Islam, or Christianity. Hindu nationalists see these conversions as a transitive act, as something done to the former Hindus, or an assault on the Hindu heritage of India, rather than a voluntary and reasonable decision on the part of people. See Rebecca S. Shah, "Christianity Among the Marginalized: Empowering Poor Women in India," in *Christianity and Freedom Volume II: Contemporary Perspectives,* eds. Allen Hertzke and Timothy Shah.

52. Sara Singha, "The Challenge and Leaven of Christianity in Pakistan," and Richard Burgess and Danny McCain, "Christianity and the Challenge of Religious Violence in Nigeria," both in *Christianity and Freedom Volume II.* See also Open Doors, "Situation of Religious Freedom for Christians: Nigeria," *World Watch List 2025.*

53. Robert A. Dowd, "Religious Diversity and Religious Tolerance: Lessons from Nigeria," *Journal of Conflict Resolution* 60, no. 4 (2014): 617–44.

54. Saiya, *Weapon of Peace,* 48.

55. Saiya, *Weapon of Peace,* 48. It should be noted that transnational support for co-religionists is not restricted to backing violent rebellions. Many persecuted religious groups, from Iranian Baha'is to Iraqi Yazidis and Chinese Christians and Uyghurs, mobilize co-religionists to bring peaceful economic and diplomatic international pressure on persecuting regimes. See Allen Hertzke, *Freeing God's Children: The Unlikely Alliance for Global Human Rights* (Lanham, MD: Rowman & Littlefield, 2004).

56. The former Soviet republics of Tajikistan, Turkmenistan, Kazakhstan, Kyrgyzstan, Uzbekistan, and Azerbaijan are often ruled by former Communist

officials who employ ruthless means of repressing independent Muslim practice. While they co-opt Islamic symbols for legitimacy, their regimes are more accurately described as secular authoritarian. Saiya, *Weapon of Peace,* 49.

57. Saiya, *Weapon of Peace,* 49.

58. Grim and Finke, *Price of Freedom Denied,* 177-78. The one exception is Nigeria, where Muslims hold a slight majority over the Christian population, and where Muslim majority states have enacted strict Sharia.

59. Saiya, *Weapon of Peace,* 47–53. Grim and Finke, *Price of Freedom Denied,* provide documentation of this wide variability of religious regulation in Muslim-majority countries, especially the dramatic difference between the Middle East and North Africa region (MENA) and sub-Saharan Africa. Daniel Philpott provides the most systematic examination of the sources of support for religious freedom in Islam and the variable patterns of practices in different Islamic societies in *Religious Freedom in Islam: The Fate of a Universal Human Right in the Muslim World Today* (New York: Oxford University Press, 2019).

60. Saiya, *Weapon of Peace,* 51.

61. Thomas F. Farr, *World of Faith and Freedom: Why International Religious Liberty Is Vital to American National Security* (New York: Oxford University Press, 2008).

62. See a detailed account of this conflict in Hertzke, *Freeing God's Children,* chapter 7.

63. The late Macram Max Gassis was bishop of the sprawling Catholic diocese of El Obeid in the Nuba Mountains of Sudan, a center of African population besieged by the Islamist regime of Sudan. He was in Washington, DC, to testify before the U.S. Commission of International Religious Freedom on February 8 and spoke to Christian and advocacy groups as well. For an account of the human rights campaign for the African Sudanese people, see Hertzke, *Freeing God's Children,* chapter 7.

64. *The Baha'i Question: Cultural Cleansing in Iran,*" Baha'i International Community, September 2008, https://www.bic.org/sites/default/files/pdf/TheBahaiQuestion.pdf.

65. *The Baha'i Question.* The account of the ten teachers executed is on pages 46–47 of the report.

66. Valerie M. Hudson and Kaylee B. Hodgson, "Sex and Terror: Is the Subordination of Women Associated with the Use of Terror?," *Terrorism and Political Violence* 34, no.3 (2022): 605–32; Nilay Saiya, Tasneem Zaihra, and Joshua Fidler, "Testing the Hillary Doctrine: Women's Rights and Anti-American Terrorism," *Political Research Quarterly* 70, no. 2 (June 2017): 421–32; Kyle Kattelman and Courtney Burns, "Unpacking the Concepts: Examining the Link Between Women's Status and Terrorism," *Journal of Peace Research* 60, no. 5 (2023): 792–806; Cameron Harris

and Daniel James Milton, "Is Standing for Women a Stand Against Terrorism? Exploring the Connection Between Women's Rights and Terrorism," *Journal of Human Rights* 15, no. 1 (2015): 60–78; Daniel Meierrieks and Laura Renner, "Islamist Terrorism and the Status of Women," *European Journal of Political Economy* 78C, Article 102364 (June 2023), https://www.sciencedirect.com/journal/european-journal-of-political-economy/vol/78/suppl/C.

67. Hillary Clinton, *Hard Choices* (New York: Simon & Schuster, 2014), 562. Her speeches articulating the Hillary Doctrine are summarized by Saiya, Zaihra, and Fidler, "Testing the Hillary Doctrine," 421.

68. Saiya, Zaihra, and Fidler, "Testing the Hillary Doctrine," 428.

69. Harris and Milton, "Is Standing for Women a Stand Against Terrorism?," and Hudson and Hodgson, "Sex and Terror."

70. Hudson and Hodgson, "Sex and Terror," 611.

71. Harris and Milton, "Is Standing for Women a Stand Against Terrorism?," 64, 73.

72. Saiya, Zaihra, and Fidler, "Testing the Hillary Doctrine," 425.

73. Hudson and Hodgson, "Sex and Terror," 611.

74. Meierrieks and Renner, "Islamist Terrorism and the Status of Women," Introduction.

75. Kettleman and Burns, "Unpacking the Concepts: Examining the Link Between Women's Status and Terrorism."

76. Ozgur Özdamar and Yasemin Akbaba, "Religious Discrimination and International Crises: International Effects of Domestic Inequality," *Foreign Policy Analysis* 10, no. 4 (2014): 413–30.

77. Mary Caprioli and Peter Trumbore, "Ethnic Discrimination and Interstate Violence: Testing the International Impact of Domestic Behavior," *Journal of Peace Research* 40, no. 1 (2003): 5–23.

78. Nilay Saiya, "The Religious Freedom Peace."

79. William Inboden, "Religious Freedom and National Security," *Policy Review*, no. 175 (October/November 2012).

80. Saiya initially capitalized on new data from the RAS Round Three Data Set (2023), produced by Jonathan Fox and his team. But to cover more years, Saiya discovered that embedded in Pew's annual reports on government restrictions were eight components of majority privilege that enabled him to construct a new "Religious Privilege" measure. See Nilay Saiya, *God's Warriors: Religious Violence and the Global Crisis of Secularism* (New York: Oxford University Press, 2025), 229.

81. Nilay Saiya, *God's Warriors*, 22.

82. Saiya first coined the term in *The Global Politics of Jesus: A Christian Case for Church-State Separation* (New York: Oxford University Press, 2022), chapter 7. He then elaborated and developed it in *God's Warriors.*

83. Nilay Saiya, *God's Warriors.*

84. In the natural sciences and physics, we see how new data and better measurements lead to refinements of existing theories or the development of new theories. This is exactly what happened in scholarship on religious repression and violence. Existing theories suggested that religious violence stemmed primarily from aggrieved minorities. New measurement enabled Saiya to challenge that view and replace it with a better theoretical explanation, the paradox of privilege.

85. Saiya's statistical operationalization is the following: The dependent variable (DV), the thing to be explained, is the number of attacks by majority actors on minority communities for 157 countries between 2008 and 2018. The independent variable (IV), the thing that explains, is the "Religious Privilege" measure Saiya developed from Pew's annual government restriction index (GRI) components. An alternative dependent variable that Saiya also tested is the number of victims of attacks by majority actors. Analyses found that both dependent variables were strongly associated with the degree of religious privilege. "Appendix," *God's Warriors.*

86. Saiya, *God's Warriors,* 230.

87. Saiya, *God's Warriors,* back cover.

88. Saiya, *God's Warriors,* 58.

89. Nilay Saiya and Stuti Manchanda, "Monks Behaving Badly: Explaining Buddhist Violence in Asia," *International Security* 49, no. 4 (Spring 2025): 119–59.

90. Saiya and Manchanda, "Monks Behaving Badly."

91. Saiya, *God's Warriors,* chapter 1.

92. Saiya, *Weapon of Peace,* 55–56.

93. Saiya, *Weapon of Peace.* 57–58.

94. Grim and Finke, *Price of Freedom Denied*

95. Saiya, *Weapon of Peace,* 58.

96. Toft, Philpott, and Shah, *God's Century,* chapter 7.

97. Douglas Johnston and Cynthia Sampson, eds. *Religion, the Missing Dimension of Statecraft* (New York: Oxford University Press, 1995).

98. Toft, Philpott, and Shah, *God's Century,* chapter 7; Daniel Philpott, ed., *The Politics of Past Evil: Religion, Reconciliation, and the Dilemmas of Transitional Justice* (Notre Dame, IN: University of Notre Dame Press, 2006).

99. Daniel Philpott, *Just and Unjust Peace: An Ethic of Political Reconciliation* (New York: Oxford University Press, 2012).

100. Saiya, "The Religious Freedom Peace," reinforced by Saiya, *Weapon of Peace*, and Saiya, *God's Warriors*.

Chapter Six

1. An excellent example concerns the pivotal role of the Catholic Church in propelling the last wave of global democracy, as discussed in Chapter 2. As powerful and singular as the transformation of the church's teaching on religious freedom was, the Catholic wave of democratization was aided by key political actors, such as President Ronald Reagan, who teamed up with Pope John Paul II to undermine the Communist Warsaw Pact. See Paul Kengor, *A Pope and a President: John Paul II, Ronald Reagan, and the Extraordinary Untold Story of the 20th Century* (Wilmington, DE: ISI Books, 2017).

2. The civil war that erupted in South Sudan in 2013 arose from long-standing tribal conflicts; religious clashes had little to do with it. See Allen Hertzke, "State Failure and International Response: The Lessons of South Sudan," in *Nation, State, Nation-State*, Vittorio Hosle, Marcelo Sanchez Sorondo, and Stefano Zamagni, eds. (Vatican City: Pontifical Academy of Social Sciences, 2020), 183–213, https://www.pass.va/content/dam/casinapioiv/pass/pdf-volumi/acta/acta22pass.pdf.

3. Thomas S. Kuhn, *The Structure of Scientific Revolutions* (Chicago: University of Chicago Press, 1962). Kuhn contended that great advances in knowledge happen when a new and better paradigm alters the very way scientists see the world. My use of paradigm here also applies to how political leaders and religious authorities see the world.

4. Daniel Philpott, "Has the Study of Global Religion Found Religion," *Annual Review of Political Science* 12 (2009): 183–202. The quote is on page 185.

5. Abdullahi Ahmed An-Naim, *Islam and the Secular State* (Cambridge, MA: Harvard University Press, 2008); Jacques Berlinerblau, *How to Be Secular: A Call to Arms for Religious Freedom* (New York: Mariner Books, 2013). An-Naim argues that Muslims need a secular state while Berlinerblau calls for a reclaiming of the American tradition of secularism that protects freedom from and for all religions.

6. The late Pope Benedict used these exact terms in contrasting the United States and Europe. See Mary Ann Glendon, *In the Courts of Three Popes: An American Lawyer and Diplomat in the Last Absolute Monarchy of the West* (New York: Image, 2024), 110. Elizabeth Shakman Hurd, similarly, contrasts the ideal of laicism versus the more accommodating Judeo-Christian form of secularism, but she also argues that shifting understandings of secularism are heavily contingent on time and context. Elizabeth Shakman Hurd, "The Politics of Secularism," in

Rethinking Religion and World Affairs, eds. Timothy Samuel Shah, Alfred Stepan, and Monica Duffy Toft (New York: Oxford University Press, 2012).

7. Ahmet T. Kuru, *Secularism and State Policies Toward Religion: The United States, France, and Turkey* (New York: Cambridge University Press, 2009). At the time this book was published, Ahmet Kuru depicted both France and Turkey as examples of "aggressive secularism," but Turkey has moved away from that tradition through the policies of long-time President Recep Erdoğan.

8. Jonathan Fox, *Political Secularism, Religion, and the State: A Time Series Analysis of Worldwide Data* (New York: Cambridge University Press, 2015); Jonathan Fox, *Thou Shalt Have No Other Gods Before Me: Why Governments Discriminate Against Religious Minorities* (Cambridge: Cambridge University Press, 2020). In the latter, Fox documents how aggressive secularism often falls more heavily on religious minorities.

9. Nilay Saiya, *God's Warriors: Religious Violence and the Global Crisis of Secularism* (New York: Oxford University Press, 2025). In defining "political secularism," Saiya argues that to be truly secular, states must be independent of religious dogma but also of anti-religious dogma.

10. Allen D. Hertzke, "Introduction," *Religious Freedom in America: Constitutional Roots and Contemporary Standards*, ed. Allen D. Hertzke (Norman: University of Oklahoma Press, 2015). In this introduction, I provide a litany of contemporary examples of government agencies interpreting mandates in ways that trump legitimate religious free exercise claims.

11. The term "benevolent neutrality" was coined by Chief Justice Warren Berger in *Walz v. Tax Commission of the City of New York*, 397 U.S. 664 (1970). As the principle has evolved, it combines neutrality among different religions with generous accommodation of religious practice. See *Toward Benevolent Neutrality: Church, State, and the Supreme Court*, edited by Robert T. Miller and Ronald B. Flowers (Waco, TX: Baylor University Press Imprint, 2020). In the "Introduction" to *Religious Freedom in America*, I write that to preserve "religious freedom in full," something akin to the American Supreme Court's "compelling interest test" best shields the rights of religious minorities and faith institutions from government encroachments, especially in an age of powerful administrative bureaucracies. This most exacting standard is employed by the Court to etch the limits of government actions that burden a fundamental right. When government actions impose a substantial burden on religious free exercise, even from a law of general applicability, the state must show that it used "the least restrictive means of achieving a compelling state interest." If not, religious claimants gain reasonable "accommodations." Statistical analyses show that when this standard is applied by the courts, religious

litigants win far more often, but that governments still prevail when they show that accommodating the religious claimant would undermine a compelling governmental interest. See Amy Adamczyk, John Wybraniec, and Roger Finke, "Religious Regulation and the Courts: Documenting the Effects of Smith and RFRA," *Journal of Church and State* 46 (2004); and Robert Martin and Roger Finke, "Defining and Redefining Religious Freedom: A Quantitative Assessment of Free Exercise Cases in the U.S. State Courts, 1981–2011," Chapter 4 in *Religious Freedom in America*, ed. Hertzke. Similarly, international law expert Cole Durham finds that an accommodationist posture is the sweet spot for maximum protection of religious freedom. See W. Cole Durham Jr., "Perspectives on Religious Liberty: A Comparative Framework," in *Religious Human Rights in Global Perspective: Legal Perspectives*, eds. Johan D. van der Vyver and John Witte Jr. (The Hague, Netherlands: Martin Nihoff Publishers, 1996). Sometimes the accommodation of conscience rights can even extend to beliefs that are not strictly religious, such as a philosophical opposition to all wars, which the U.S. government and the courts recognize for conscientious objector status to military conscription.

12. On *benevolentia*, see Pope Francis, *Fratelli Tutti: On Fraternity and Social Friendship*, Encyclical Letter, Vatican Publication House, Vatican City (October 3, 2020), paragraph 112, https://www.vatican.va/content/francesco/en/encyclicals/documents/papa-francesco_20201003_enciclica-fratelli-tutti.html.

13. In the United States, this sense of lost position in society is captured by the idea that traditional Christians have entered a "negative world" of prevailing hostility toward their beliefs within elite sectors of society, such as higher education, law, public policy, and entertainment. See Aaron M. Renn, *Life in the Negative World: Confronting Challenges in an Anti-Christian Culture* (Grand Rapids, MI: Zondervan, 2024).

14. Saiya, *God's Warriors*; Jonathan Fox, *Thou Shalt Have No Other Gods Before Me*, and Matthias Basedau, Jonathan Fox, and Ariel Zellman, *Religious Minorities at Risk* (New York: Oxford University Press, 2023).

15. Nilay Saiya first used the term "paradox of privilege" in an exploration of the ways in which state privileges for Christianity tend to pervert the faith, violate the teachings of Jesus, and paradoxically produce violence in the name of the Prince of Peace. See Nilay Saiya, *The Global Politics of Jesus: A Christian Case for Church-State Separation* (New York: Oxford University Press, 2022).

16. In *God's Warriors*, Saiya shows that, whether from Muslim, Buddhist, Christian, Hindu, or Jewish sources, most religious violence stems from dominant and privileged religious majorities, not persecuted minorities.

17. Nilay Saiya and Stuti Manchanda, "Monks Behaving Badly: Explaining Buddhist Violence in Asia," *International Security* 49, no. 4 (Winter 2024–2025).

18. Jonathan Fox, *Thou Shalt Have No Other Gods Before Me*; and Jonathan Fox, *The Unfree Exercise of Religion: A World Survey of Discrimination Against Religious Minorities* (New York: Cambridge University Press, 2016).

19. Samuel P. Huntington, *The Third Wave: Democratization in the Late Twentieth Century* (Norman: University of Oklahoma Press, 1991); Daniel Philpott, "Christianity and Democracy: The Catholic Wave," *Journal of Democracy* 15, no. 2 (April 2004). Considerable historical scholarship also suggests that when the Catholic Church was deeply embedded with the state, it was similarly corruptible and less likely to fulfill its Christian mission. See *Christianity and Freedom: Historical Perspectives*, eds. Timothy Samuel Shah and Allen D. Hertzke (New York: Cambridge University Press, 2016).

20. Jonathan Fox and Jori Breslawski, "State Support for Religion and Government Legitimacy in Christian-Majority Countries," *The American Political Science Review* 117, no. 4 (November 2023): 1395–1409: DOI:10.1017/S00030554 22001320.

21. This literature is nicely summarized by Nilay Saiya and Stuti Manchanda, "Paradoxes of Pluralism, Privilege, and Persecution: Explaining Christian Growth and Decline Worldwide," *Sociology of Religion: A Quarterly Review* 83, no. 1 (2022), 60–78.

22. A large survey of Iranians found a striking decline in allegiance to Shia Islam (less than a third of the respondents in 2020) compared to an increase in the number who report their religion as "none," "atheist," or "agnostic" (nearly 37%). See Ammar Maleki and Pooyan Tamimi Arab, "Iranians' Attitudes Toward Religion: A 2020 Survey Report," GAMAAN: The Group for Analyzing and Measuring Attitudes in Iran, August 2020, https://gamaan.org/wp-content/uploads/2020/09/GAMAAN-Iran-Religion-Survey-2020-English.pdf.

23. Nilay Saiya, *The Global Politics of Jesus*; Saiya and Manchanda, "Paradoxes of Pluralism, Privilege, and Persecution."

24. Saiya brings a unique perspective to his argument. As he discussed in the Introduction of *The Global Politics of Jesus*, he was raised by Indian immigrant parents who worshiped in evangelical Christian churches in central Pennsylvania, a religious culture he describes as akin to "Alabama." He then moved as a professor to Singapore and discovered a similar Christian culture that sees certain nations as divinely chosen, thus justifying state support for the faith. With his unique blend of theological depth, methodological sophistication, and profound theoretical insights, Nilay Saiya is one of the most important global Christian voices in a generation.

25. Great figures of the past, like John Locke and Roger Williams, made this very argument, as noted in Chapter 1.

26. Gregory A. Boyd, *The Myth of a Christian Nation: How the Quest for Political Power Is Destroying the Church* (Grand Rapids, MI: Zondervan, 2007), 94–95. I credit Nilay Saiya for finding this illustrative citation.

27. Saiya, *Global Politics of Jesus*, 229–34.

28. Saiya and Manchanda, "Paradoxes of Pluralism, Privilege, and Persecution."

29. Sociologist Peter Berger attributed the secularization of European societies to widespread state sponsorship, including tax support, which conforms to the patterns that Saiya finds. See Gregor Thuswaldner, "A Conversation with Peter L. Berger: 'How My Views Have Changed,'" *The Cresset* 77, no. 3 (Lent 2014): 16–20. The link between state support and religious decline is the theme of the market school of religious sociology, which analogizes religious monopolies or oligopolies to economic ones that become lax with state subsidies, versus the vibrance of institutions under competition. See Roger Finke and Rodney Stark, *The Churching of America, 1776–2005: Winners and Losers in Our Religious Economy* (New Brunswick, NJ: Rutgers University Press, 2005).

30. Saiya and Manchanda, "Paradoxes of Pluralism, Privilege, and Persecution."

31. To develop measures of privilege for Catholic majority nations, Nilay Saiya created his own five-point scale using Pew's GRI.Q20 indicator, which contained five items of government privileges. See Pew Research Center, Appendix D: "Summary of Results for its December 2022 Religious Restrictions report," https://www.pewresearch.org/wp-content/uploads/sites/20/2024/12/PR_2024.12.18_restrictions-on-religion-2022_appendix-d.pdf. Saiya found that Catholic majority nations where privilege was highest (a 4 or 5 on his scale) saw the Catholic share of the population fall by an average of 2 percent from 2010 to 2020, while those where the privilege is lowest (1 or 2) saw the Catholic share of the population grow by around 1 percent, as measured by Pew's global demographic figures. As Saiya conveyed to me, this gap is quite remarkable given that levels of privilege for Catholic majority countries are relatively low to begin with and that the figures account for other explanations of growth or decline. Personal email from Nilay Saiya, Associate Professor of Public Policy & Global Affairs, Nanyang Technological University, February 18, 2024.

32. David E. Campbell, Geoffrey C. Layman, and John C. Green, *Secular Surge: A New Faultline in American Politics* (New York: Cambridge University Press, 2020); David E. Campbell, "The Perils of Politicized Religion," *Daedalus* 149, no. 3 (Summer, 2020), 87–104. This latter essay provides the remarkable—and to Campbell, troubling—findings that Trump appears to be leading his Christian supporters to abandon their own religious principles about moral behavior.

33. In his first administration, U.S. President Trump appointed three justices who provided the crucial votes to overturn *Roe v. Wade*, and in his second administration pardoned pro-life activists who had been jailed for blocking access to abortion clinics. During Trump's presidencies, Catholic leaders also welcomed relief from what they saw as aggressively secular or culturally progressive policies of the Obama and Biden administrations, which to them undermined conscience rights and the autonomy of their institutions.

34. Catholic social teaching exhibits a long tradition of concern for refugees and exiles, most recently by Pope Francis in his vigorous critique of nativism and call to treat migrating persons with dignity. See Pope Francis, *Fratelli Tutti: On Fraternity and Social Friendship*. On the responses of the new pontiff to religious nationalism and nativism, see Leon Krauze, "An Immigrant Pope Meets the Nativist Movement," *Washington Pos*t, May 21, 2025; Julian Coman, "MAGA Catholics are on a Collision Course with Leo XIV," *The Guardian*, May 21, 2025.

35. The head of the Heritage Foundation that produced the Project 2025 plan for the Trump administration is Kevin Roberts, an Opus Dei-associated Catholic who seeks to deploy the institutions of state power to realize his vision of Catholic integration with the nation. Similarly, Leonard Leo, formerly of the Federalist Society and who vetted justices for President Trump, now controls a billion-dollar dark money fund to advance his project of "weaponizing" the conservative movement; Trump strategist Steve Bannon, a right-wing Catholic, proudly calls himself a "Christian Nationalist;" and Vice-President J. D. Vance, a visible Catholic convert, has embraced the MAGA movement's nativism, even when it runs contrary to Catholic social teaching. See Rachel Leingang and Stephanie Kirchgaessner, "Kevin Roberts, Architect of Project 2025, Has Close Ties to Radical Group Opus Dei," *The Guardian*, July 26, 2024, https://www.theguardian.com/us-news/article/2024/jul/26/kevin-roberts-project-2025-opus-dei; Hans Nichols, "Scoop: Activist Leonard Leo Pushes to 'Weaponize' Conservatives," *Axios*, September 12, 2024, https://www.axios.com/2024/09/12/leonard-leo-conservative-groups-funding; Shirin Ali, "Well, This Letter from a Conservative Kingmaker is Downright Chilling!" *Slate*, September 13, 2024, https://slate.com/news-and-politics/2024/09/leonard-leo-letter-85-fund-network-conservative-agenda-weaponize.html; Ruth Braunstein, "Catholic Christian Nationalism is Having a Moment, *Religion News Service*, July 23, 2024, https://religionnews.com/2024/07/23/jd-vance-catholic-christian-nationalism-is-having-a-moment/; Jack Jenkins, "5 Facts About JD Vance, Catholic Convert and Trump's VP Pick," *Religion News Service,* July 24, 2024, https://www.americamagazine.org/politics-society/2024/07/16/five-faith-facts-jd-vance-trump-vp-248368; Gareth Gore,

Opus: The Cult of Dark Money, Human Trafficking, and Right-Wing Conspiracy Inside the Catholic Church (New York: Simon & Schuster, 2024), especially Chapters 13 and 14.

36. In a test case of whether a fully tax-funded Catholic charter school was constitutional, a deadlocked Supreme Court (with justices voting 4-4 and Amy Coney Barrett recusing) left standing an Oklahoma Supreme Court ruling that such a school violated the Oklahoma and federal constitutions (*St. Isidore of Seville Catholic Virtual School, Petitioner v. Gentner Drummond, Attorney General of Oklahoma, ex rel. Oklahoma,* Docketed October 9, 2024). This leaves open the possibility that a future court will find in favor of tax-funded Catholic charter schools.

37. Nilay Saiya, "The Rise of Theocratic Democracy, *Journal of Democracy* 34, no. 4 (October 2023), 66–79; Nilay Saiya, "Christian Nationalism's Threat to Global Democracy," *The Review of Faith & International Affairs* 22, no. 1 (2024), https://www-tandfonline-com.ezproxy.lib.ou.edu/doi/full/10.1080/15570274.2023.2204679. Nilay Saiya's current research project is an exploration of the different forms of Christian nationalism and its threat to democracy. I served as an evaluator of his proposed research project as a Yang Visiting Scholar at Harvard Divinity School (2024–2025 academic year).

38. Kenneth L. Woodward, "How I Became a 'Christian Nationalist,'" *Washington Post,* May 16, 2023.

39. Andrew L. Whitehead and Samuel L. Perry, *Taking America Back for God: Christian Nationalism in the United States* (New York: Oxford University Press, 2020); Allyson Shortle, Eric L. McDaniel, and Irfan Nooruddin, *The Everyday Crusade: Christian Nationalism in American Politics* (New York: Cambridge University Press, 2022); Philip S. Gorski and Samuel L. Perry, *The Flag and the Cross: White Christian Nationalism and the Threat to American Democracy* (New York: Oxford University Press, 2022); Matthew D. Taylor, *The Violent Take It by Force: The Christian Movement That Is Threatening Our Democracy* (Minneapolis: Broadleaf Books, 2024); Nilay Saiya, "The Rise of Theocratic Democracy."

40. For the autocratic tendencies of the New Apostolic Reformation Movement, the cutting edge of Christian Nationalism in the MAGA movement of Donald Trump, see Matthew D. Taylor, *The Violent Take It by Force;* and Stephanie McCrummen, "The Army of God Comes Out of the Shadows," *The Atlantic,* February 2025, https://www.theatlantic.com/magazine/archive/2025/02/new-apostolic-reformation-christian-movement-trump/681092/. A key aim of the movement is to take dominion of the "Seven Mountains" of society: family, religion, education, media, arts and entertainment, business, and government. Its leaders see President Trump providing unique access to the power they need to realize this vision. Keen observers document how MAGA influencers and politicians

increasingly criticize the central Christian norm of "empathy" (or compassion) because it undercuts tough measures necessary to crush the "woke" state or expel refugees. See Cathy Young, "The Bizarre Right-Wing War on Empathy?," *The Bulwark*, April 21, 2025, https://www.thebulwark.com/p/bizarre-right-wing-war-empathy-misogynistic-abrego-garcia-suicidal-civilizational-musk-barrett-gad-saad. On the prominence of Christian nationalists and Christian symbols on January 6, 2021, see Nilay Saiya, "The Rise of Theocratic Democracy," 71. The cruelty of the Trump immigration crackdown was exemplified by the swift "abduction" and deportation, without any due process, of Kilmar Abrego Garcia, a father of three living in Maryland legally, to a notorious prison in El Salvador, and then the refusal to bring him back after admitting his deportation was in error. The Court of Appeals declared that this was a "shocking" violation of the "foundation of our constitutional order." United States Court of Appeals for the Fourth Circuit, *Kilmar Armando Abrego Garcia v. Kristi Noem et al.*, No. 25-1404 (8:25-cv-00951-PX), April 17, 2025, https://www.ca4.uscourts.gov/docs/pdfs/251404order.pdf?sfvrsn=b404b209_2. Cruelty continued with sweeps by masked ICE agents, often of legal residents, and detentions to other states, makeshift camps, or foreign countries, which appeared designed to terrorize immigrant communities.

41. Allen Hertzke, "The Constitutional Roots of American Global Leadership on Religious Freedom," *Starting Points Journal,* March 5, 2019, https://startingpointsjournal.com/constitutional-roots-american-global-leadership-religious-freedom/.

42. The International Religious Freedom Act (IRFA) of 1998 established the infrastructure for America's contemporary global leadership on religious freedom. For a listing and discussion of the eighteen nations that have also developed their own initiatives, see Jeremy P. Barker, Andrew Bennett, and Thomas Farr, *Surveying the Landscape of International Religious Freedom Policy*, Religious Freedom Institute, Washington, DC, 2019, https://religiousfreedominstitute.org/surveying-the-landscape-irf-policy/.

43. The early Trump administration cut programs vital to American soft power: Voice of America, the U.S. Agency for International Development (USAID), including the President's Emergency Plan for AIDS Relief, PEPFAR. While some of these programs may be revived in some form, as of this writing, serious damage has been done both to these initiatives and to the nation's reputation. In addition, Trump deemphasized human rights in foreign policy, excused Putin, cut support for Ukraine, curried favor with the autocratic Gulf states, and bullied international friends and allies, including our closest neighbor, Canada, with tariffs and heated rhetoric, undermining the great legacy of goodwill built up for decades. A good summary of the autocratic moves of the administration comes

from a survey of 500 U.S. political scientists. See Frank Langfitt, "Hundreds of Scholars Say U.S is Swiftly Heading Toward Authoritarianism," National Public Radio, April 25, 2025, https://www.npr.org/2025/04/22/nx-s1-5340753/trump-democracy-authoritarianism-competive-survey-political-scientist.

44. *Christianity and Freedom, Volume I: Historical Perspectives,* ed. Timothy Samuel Shah and Allen D. Hertzke (New York: Cambridge University Press, 2016); *Christianity and Freedom, Volume II: Contemporary Perspectives,* ed. Allen D. Hertzke and Timothy Samuel Shah (New York: Cambridge University Press, 2016).

45. Saiya, *The Global Politics of Jesus*, Chapter 5; Monica Duffy Toft, Daniel Philpott, and Timothy Shah. *God's Century: Resurgent Religion and Global Politics* (New York: W.W. Norton, 2011), Chapter 7.

46. Peter Berger, *The Many Altars of Modernity: Toward a Paradigm for Religion in a Pluralist Age* (Berlin: De Gruyter, 2014).

47. Daniel Philpott, "Explaining the Political Ambivalence of Religion," *American Political Science Review* 101, no. 3 (August 2007): 505–25; DOI, https://doi.org/10.1017/S0003055407070372.

48. Political patronage likely held a similarly corrupt influence in the past. Certainly, that was the case with Catholic Popes sanctioning brutal imperialism in the New World by Spain and Portugal. But in a less globalized and less pluralistic world, societies could theoretically benefit from what was termed in Russia the "symphony" between church and state.

49. In the United States and elsewhere, we see the language of religious freedom sometimes employed by Christian nationalists to gain government privileges for Christian communities in different states or nationally. See Whitehead and Perry, *Taking America Back for God*; and Gorski and Perry, *The Flag and the Cross.* Sometimes efforts are overtly partisan; sometimes well-meaning. Yet seeking state favor is always perilous, as we have learned.

50. Mariz Tadros, "Conclusion," in *What About Us? Global Perspectives on Redressing Religious Inequalities*, ed. Mariz Tadros (Sussex, United Kingdom: Institute of Development Studies, 2022).

51. Rebecca Supriya Shah and Timothy Samuel Shah, "The Other Invisible Hand: How Freedom of Religion and Belief Fosters Pro-Social and Pro-Development Outcomes for the Poor," in *What About Us?*, Chapter 4.

52. Winnifred Fallers Sullivan, Elizabeth Shakman Hurd, Saba Mahmood, and Peter G. Danchin, eds., *The Politics of Religious Freedom* (Chicago: University of Chicago Press, 2015).

53. Elizabeth Shakman Hurd, "The Politics of International Religious Freedom," in *Routledge Handbook of Religion and Politics*, 3rd ed., ed. Jeffrey Haynes (Abingdon, UK: Routledge, 2023), 145.

54. Katherine Marshall, "Towards Enriching Understandings and Assessments of Freedom of Religion or Belief: Politics, Debates, Methodologies and Practices," CREID Working Paper 6, Coalition for Religious Equality and Inclusive Development (Brighten, UK: Institute of Development Studies, 202), 30. Quote provided by Tadros, *What About Us?*, 325.

55. I am not referring here to the long and tragic history of government actions against tribal peoples and lands, even though they illustrate the problem, but to more recent examples. In the Supreme Court case, *Lyng v. Northwest Indian Cemetery Protective Association*, the Court majority, while conceding that allowing the government to build a road through sacred forests would irreparably damage or destroy a California tribe's spiritual practice, nonetheless found for the government. *Lyng v. Northwest Indian Cemetery Protective Association,* No. 86-1013, 1988, 485 U.S. 439. Thankfully, public reaction against the *Lyng* decision led Congress to designate the forest as a national recreation area to prevent the road from being built (Smith River National Recreation Area Act of 1990, Pub L. No. 101–612, 104 Stat. 3209) (1990).

56. The site is central to the multiday coming of age ceremony for young women, as summarized by Justice Gorsuch's dissenting opinion in *Apache Stronghold v. United States,* Petition for a Writ of Certiorari, No. 24-292, May 27, 2025.

57. The petition for a Writ of Cert was denied in *Apache Stronghold v. United States,* Justice Gorsuch dissenting. The Becket Fund, a religious freedom legal advocacy organization, which joined in the appellate process, provides an excellent summary of the issue: https://www.becketlaw.org/case/apache-stronghold-v-united-states/?section=caseDetail.

58. See Sullivan, Hurd, Mahmood, and Danchin, eds., *Politics of Religious Freedom*; Winnifred Fallers Sullivan, *The Impossibility of Religious Freedom* (Princeton, NJ: Princeton University Press, 2005); Elizabeth Shakman Hurd, *Beyond Religious Freedom: The New Global Politics of Religion* (Princeton, NJ: Princeton University Press, 2015); and Saba Mahmood, *Religious Difference in a Secular Age: A Minority Report* (Princeton, NJ: Princeton University Press, 2015). For a systematic critique of this scholarship skeptical of religious freedom, see Daniel Philpott and Timothy Samuel Shah, "In Defense of Religious Freedom: New Critics of a Beleaguered Human Right," *Journal of Law and Religion* 31, no. 3 (2016), 380–95.

59. As Philpott and Shah observe, the collective literature against the "religious freedom industry" draws heavily on deconstructionist, post-modern hermeneutics, with Michel Foucault making obligatory appearances. Philpott and Shah, "In Defense of Religious Freedom."

60. Philpott and Shah, "In Defense of Religious Freedom," 383.

61. Philpott and Shah, "In Defense of Religious Freedom," 391–92, document the variety of ancient declarations of the normative ideal of religious liberty. The modern promotion of religious freedom, moreover, was launched by the *Universal Declaration of Human Rights*, which was drafted by an international body of commissioners not exclusively from the West. See Mary Ann Glendon, *A World Made New: Eleanor Roosevelt and the Universal Declaration of Human Rights* (New York: Random House, 2001).

62. Philpott and Shah, "In Defense of Religious Freedom," 388.

63. Elizabeth Shakman Hurd, "The International Politics of Religious Freedom," *India International Centre Quarterly* 40, no. 3/4 (Winter 2013–Spring 2014): 225–37: https://www.jstor.org/stable/24394399.

64. Philpott and Shah, "In Defense of Religious Freedom," 394.

65. For a good summary of these clashes in the United States, see Stephanie Slade, "The Fight for Religious Liberty is Never Going to End: We'd Better Get Used to It," *America Magazine*, February 15, 2017, https://www.americamagazine.org/politics-society/2017/02/15/fight-religious-liberty-never-going-end-wed-better-get-used-it.

66. Christian Munthe, "Conscience Refusal in Healthcare: The Swedish Solution," *Journal of Medical Ethics* 43, no. 4 (April 2017): 257–59, https://doi.org/10.1136/medethics-2016-103752.

67. *Little Sisters of the Poor v. Pennsylvania*, No. 19–431 (2020). See also Allen D. Hertzke, "A Meditation on Hanukkah and Religious Freedom," RFI blog, July 5, 2016, https://religiousfreedominstitute.org/2016-7-5-a-meditation-on-hanukkah-and-religious-freedom/.

68. See *Burwell v. Hobby Lobby Stores, Inc.*, 573 U.S. 682 (2014).

69. In Finland, a member of parliament, Päivi Räsänen, was charged with hate speech for tweeting Bible passages on homosexuality and marriage. After a five-year process, she won acquittal at trial, but the state appealed to the Supreme Court in 2024, in a move that gained international attention for its threat to free speech. Sean Nelson and Paul Teller, "The Bible is Yet Again on Trial in Finland," *National Review*, May 24, 2024, https://www.nationalreview.com/2024/05/the-bible-is-yet-again-on-trial-in-finland/.

70. See Allen Hertzke, "Introduction," *Religious Freedom in America.*

71. Becket, the nation's leading religious legal advocacy organization, has taken on such cases. See https://www.becketlaw.org/case/our-lady-of-guadalupe-school/.

72. The journal, *MDPI* produced a special issue on institutional religious freedom, which reinforces the centrality of protecting religious institutions, https://www.mdpi.com/journal/religions/special_issues/free_reli.

73. The Religious Freedom Institute and others have provided congressional testimony and sent letters to Congress, charging that the law would dramatically undermine the autonomy of religious institutions and their contributions to civil society, particularly since it would overturn conscience right protections in prior congressional legislation, the Religious Freedom Restoration Act. See the Religious Freedom Institute blog on Sexual Orientation and Gender Identity Policy: https://religiousfreedominstitute.org/category/topic-guides/sexual-orientation-and-gender-identity-policy/.

74. Emily Bazelon, "In Defense of Religious Freedom," *Slate,* March 14, 2014, https://slate.com/news-and-politics/2014/03/religious-liberty-the-owners-of-hobby-lobby-have-it-wrong-but-religious-rights-are-worth-defending.html.

75. See Becket, the leading legal advocacy organization for religious liberty for all, https://www.becketlaw.org/. A 2024 example involves a lawsuit filed by Becket for Catholic Charities of Superior, Michigan, which was deemed not a part of the religious mission of the Catholic Church and thus prevented from leaving the state's unemployment program for the Wisconsin Catholic Church's better option. See https://www.becketlaw.org/media/catholic-charities-asks-supreme-court-to-protect-its-right-to-serve-the-needy/. Another vivid example involved the District of Columbia's historical preservation agency, which denied the Christian Science Church the right to tear down an ugly and costly concrete church structure, because the preservationists deemed it an excellent example of "brutalist architecture." After years of costly litigation, Becket and the Church finally prevailed. See https://www.becketlaw.org/case/third-church-christ-scientist-v-district-columbia/.

76. One possible exception is Uganda, which, under conservative religious influences, passed draconian laws against homosexual behavior. But since Uganda's record on religious freedom is marked by privilege for established Christian communities, it would be inaccurate to describe it as religiously free.

77. Stuart Adams, Brady Brammer, Michael Petersen, Chris Wilson, Todd Weiler, and Robin Fretwell Wilson, "Opinion: Fairness for All—The Utah Compromise in Laws Across the Decade," *Deseret News*, March 11, 2025, https://www.deseret.com/opinion/2025/03/11/utah-compromise-anniversary-fairness-for-all-religion-lgbt/; *Religious Freedom, LGBT Rights, and the Prospects for Common Ground*, ed. William N. Eskridge and Robin Fretwell Wilson (New York: Cambridge University Press, 2018).

78. Kelsey Dallas, "Five Years Ago, Utah Passed Landmark Legislation on LGBTQ and Religious Rights. Why Didn't Other States Follow Its Lead?" *Deseret News*, March 11, 2020, https://www.deseret.com/indepth/2020/3/11/21163307/utah-lgbtq-rights-religious-freedom-lgbt-fairness-for-all-mormon-equality-act

-congress/. This is an excellent summary of the vision and actors behind the Utah Compromise.

79. Alliance for Lasting Liberty, https://fairnessforall.org/ and https://fairnessforall.org/about-the-alliance/.

80. For a nuanced critique of "fairness for all" compromises, see Ryan Anderson, "How to Think About Sexual Orientation and Gender Identity (SOGI) Policies and Religious Freedom," *The Heritage Foundation*, February 13, 2017, https://www.heritage.org/sites/default/files/2017-03/BG3194.pdf. A Yale conference on the debate featured figures such as Robert George, who remains skeptical that any conscience clause in SOGI legislation will effectively protect religious liberty. See Kelsey Dallas, "Religious Freedom Advocates Are Divided over How to Address LGBT Rights," CRUX, January 16, 2017, https://cruxnow.com/rns/2017/01/religious-freedom-advocates-divided-address-lgbt-rights.

81. Alliance for Lasting Liberty, https://fairnessforall.org/ and https://fairnessforall.org/about-the-alliance/.

82. See Shirley Hoogstra and Robin Fretwell Wilson, "Fairness as a Path Toward LGBTQ Rights and Religious Liberty," in *The Routledge Handbook of Religious Literacy, Pluralism, and Global Engagement*, eds. Chris Seiple and Dennis R. Hoover (New York: Routledge, 2022). Professor Wilson has been intensively engaged in efforts to replicate the Utah Compromise.

83 A number of these figures, including Brian Grim, are featured in *The Routledge Handbook of Religious Literacy, Pluralism, and Global Engagement.*

84. Chris Seiple, "The Call of Covenantal Pluralism: Defeating Religious Nationalism with Faithful Patriotism," *Foreign Policy Research Institute*, October 13, 2018, https://www.fpri.org/article/2018/11/the-call-of-covenantal-pluralism-defeating-religious-nationalism-with-faithful-patriotism/. The mission statement of the Institute for Global Engagement is as follows: "Promote societal flourishing in nations by equipping citizens to engage, respect, and protect one another regardless of faith or none." See https://globalengage.org/.

85. W. Christopher Stewart, Chris Seiple, and Dennis R. Hoover, "Toward a Global Covenant of Peaceable Neighborhood: Introducing the Philosophy of Covenantal Pluralism," *The Review of Faith & International Affairs* (RFIA) 18, no. 4 (Winter 2020).

86. Seiple is the principal advisor, and Hoover is the research advisor for the Covenantal Pluralism Initiative, Templeton Religion Trust. See https://templetonreligiontrust.org/areas-of-focus/covenantal-pluralism/#:~:text=Covenantal%20pluralism%20calls%20people%2C%20not,relationships%2C%20collaboration%2C%20and%20understanding.

87. Chris Seiple, "The Call of Covenantal Pluralism."

88. Stewart, Seiple, and Hoover, "Toward a Global Covenant of Peaceable Neighborhood," 9.

89. Templeton Religion Trust, Covenantal Pluralism, https://templeton religiontrust.org/areas-of-focus/covenantal-pluralism/.

90. Jonathan Sacks, *The Dignity of Difference: How to Avoid the Clash of Civilizations* (London: Continuum, 2003), https://rabbisacks.org/.

91. Mary Ann Glendon, *A World Made New*.

92. Nilay Saiya, in the "Conclusion" of *God's Warriors*, develops Covenantal Pluralism as the antidote to weaponized religion.

93. Stewart, Seiple, and Hoover, "Toward a Global Covenant."

94. *The Routledge Handbook of Religious Literacy, Pluralism, and Global Engagement.*

95. Betsy Hammond, "Governor Signs Repeal on Teachers' Religious Dress; Ban Will Lift in July 2011," *The Oregonian/OregonLive*, April 1, 2010, https://www .oregonlive.com/education/2010/04/governor_signs_repeal_on_teach.html.

96. I attended the Seventh Day Adventist banquet in Washington, DC, at which religious liberty awards for 2010 were presented.

97. Interfaith America, https://www.interfaithamerica.org/. The quote is from the video presentation on the organization's front page of its website. For his story and vision, see Eboo Patel, *Acts of Faith: The Story of an American Muslim, the Struggle for the Soul of a Generation* (Boston: Beacon Press, 2010).

98. Nahdlatul Ulama (NU), led by Sheikh Yahya Choil Staquf, with 50 million members and 14,000 Madrasahs, is the world's largest Muslim organization. Based in Indonesia, it established the Center for Shared Civilizational Values, "to preserve and strengthen a rules-based international order founded upon universal ethics and humanitarian values," https://civilizationalvalues.org/.

99. Nahdlatul Ulama issued its "Civilizational Strategy" on January 29, 2024, https://civilizationalvalues.org/media/political-communiques/2024/2024_01_29 _Nahdlatul-Ulama's-Civilizational-Strategy/2024_01_29_Nahdlatul-Ulama's -Civilizational-Strategy.pdf. Robert W. Hefner, professor of anthropology and international relations at Boston University and a leading authority on Islam in Indonesia, provided his endorsement and analysis of this initiative. See https:// civilizationalvalues.org/media/2024/Moral-leadership-at-a-critical-juncture _Professor-Robert-W-Hefner.pdf.

100. Institute for Global Engagement, focus on Uzbekistan, https://global engage.org/programs/uzbekistan/.

101. Allen D. Hertzke, *Freeing God's Children: The Unlikely Alliance for Global Human Rights* (Lanham, MD: Rowman & Littlefield, 2004).

102. Edward Pentin, "Interreligious Leaders to Sign Historic Declaration Against Human Trafficking," *National Catholic Register*, December 2, 2014, https://

www.ncregister.com/blog/interreligious-leaders-to-sign-historic-joint-declaration-against-human-trafficking.

103. "A Joint Message for the Protection," signed by Pope Francis, Ecumenical Patriarch Bartholomew, and Archbishop of Canterbury Justin, September 1, 2021, https://www.vatican.va/content/francesco/en/messages/pont-messages/2021/documents/20210901-messaggio-protezionedelcreato.htm.

104. Paul Woodruff, *Reverence: Renewing a Forgotten Virtue* (New York: Oxford University Press, 2001).

105. *My Mercy Encompasses All: The Koran's Teachings on Compassion, Peace & Love*, Gathered & Introduced by Reza Shah-Kazemi (Emeryville, CA: Shoemaker & Hoard, 2007).

106. Knox Thames, *Ending Persecution: Charting the Path to Global Religious Freedom* (Notre Dame, IN: University of Notre Dame Press, 2024). A veteran of decades of advocacy for global religious freedom, inside and outside government, Knox Thames brings this wealth of experience to show how diverse stakeholders can move toward that noble end.

BIBLIOGRAPHY

Abrams, Elliot. "In Russia, 'Liquidating' Churches." *The Washington Post*, November 14, 2000. https://www.uscirf.gov/news-room/op-eds/russia-liquidating-churches-washington-post.

Adamczyk, Amy, John Wybraniec, and Roger Finke. "Religious Regulation and the Courts: Documenting the Effects of *Smith* and RFRA." *Journal of Church and State* 46, no. 2 (Spring 2004): 237–62.

Adams, Stuart, Brady Brammer, Michael Petersen, Chris Wilson, Todd Weiler, and Robin Fretwell Wilson. "Opinion: Fairness for All—The Utah Compromise in Laws Across the Decade." *Deseret News*, March 11, 2025. https://www.deseret.com/opinion/2025/03/11/utah-compromise-anniversary-fairness-for-all-religion-lgbt/.

Ahlstrom, Sydney. *A Religious History of the American People*, 2nd ed. New Haven: Yale University Press, 2004.

Akyol, Mustafa. *Islam Without Extremes: A Muslim Case for Religious Liberty.* New York: W. W. Norton, 2011.

Ali, Shirin. "Well, This Letter from a Conservative Kingmaker is Downright Chilling!" *Slate*, September 13, 2024. https://slate.com/news-and-politics/2024/09/leonard-leo-letter-85-fund-network-conservative-agenda-weaponize.html.

Alkire, Sabina. *Valuing Freedoms.* Oxford: Oxford University Press, 2005.

Alon, Ilan, and John Spitzer. "Does Religious Freedom Affect Country Risk Assessment?" *Journal of International and Area Studies* 10, no. 2 (2003): 51–62.

Alon, Ilan, Shaomin Li, and Jun Wu. "An Institutional Perspective on Religious Freedom and Economic Growth." *Politics and Religion* 10, no. 3 (2017): 689–716.

Alon, Ilan, and Gregory Chase. "Religious Freedom and Economic Prosperity." *Cato Journal* 25, no. 2 (Spring/Summer 2005): 399–406.

An-Naim, Abdullahi Ahmed. *Islam and the Secular State: Negotiating the Future of Shari'a.* Cambridge, MA: Harvard University Press, 2008.

Anderson, Ryan. "How to Think About Sexual Orientation and Gender Identity (SOGI) Policies and Religious Freedom." The Heritage Foundation, February 13, 2017. https://www.heritage.org/sites/default/files/2017-03/BG3194.pdf.

Aqeel, Asif, and Mary Gill. "International Assistance and Impoverished Religious Minorities in Pakistan." In *What About Us? Global Perspectives on Redressing Religious Inequalities*. Edited by Mariz Tadros, 221–49. Brighton, UK: University of Sussex Institute of Development Studies, 2022.

The Baha'i Question: Cultural Cleansing in Iran. Baha'i International Community, September 2008. https://www.bic.org/sites/default/files/pdf/TheBahaiQuestion.pdf.

Baldauf, Scott, and Jina Moore. "Bush Sees Results of His AIDS Plan in Africa." *The Christian Science Monitor*, February 20, 2008. https://www.csmonitor.com/World/Africa/2008/0220/p07s07-woaf.html.

Bales, Kevin. *Disposable People: New Slavery in the Global Economy*. Berkeley: University of California Press, 2000.

Barber, Matthew. "They That Remain: Syrian and Iraqi Christian Communities amid the Syrian Conflict and the Rise of the Islamic State." In *Christianity and Freedom, Volume II: Contemporary Perspectives.* Edited by Allen D. Hertzke and Timothy Samuel Shah. New York: Cambridge University Press, 2016.

Barker, Jeremy P., Andrew Bennett, and Thomas Farr, *Surveying the Landscape of International Religious Freedom Policy*. Religious Freedom Institute, Washington, DC, 2019. https://religiousfreedominstitute.org/surveying-the-landscape-irf-policy/,

Basedau, Matthias, Jonathan Fox, and Ariel Zellman. *Religious Minorities at Risk*. New York: Oxford University Press, 2023.

Bazelon, Emily. "In Defense of Religious Freedom." *Slate*, March 14, 2014. https://slate.com/news-and-politics/2014/03/religious-liberty-the-owners-of-hobby-lobby-have-it-wrong-but-religious-rights-are-worth-defending.html.

BBC. "Myanmar Rohingya: What You Need to Know about the Crisis." British Broadcasting Corporation, January 23, 2020. https://www.bbc.com/news/world-asia-41566561.

Berger, Peter. "Epistemological Modesty: An Interview with Peter Berger." *The Christian Century* 114 (October 29, 1997): 972–75, 978.

Berger, Peter. *The Many Altars of Modernity: Toward a Paradigm for Religion in a Pluralist Age.* Boston and Berlin: Walter de Gruyter, 2014.

Berger, Peter, and Anton Zijderveld. *In Praise of Doubt: How to Have Convictions Without Becoming a Fanatic.* New York: HarperOne, 2009.

Berger, Peter, and Gordon Redding, eds. *The Hidden Form of Capital: Spiritual Influences in Societal Progress*. Anthem Press, 2010.

Berlinerblau, Jacques. *How to Be Secular: A Call to Arms for Religious Freedom*. New York: Mariner Books, 2013.

Birdsall, Judd, and Lori Beaman. "Faith in Numbers: Can We Trust Quantitative Data on Religious Affiliation and Religious Freedom?" *The Review of Faith & International Affairs* 18, no. 3 (2020): 60–68.

Bolton, John. *The Room Where It Happened: A White House Memoir*. New York: Simon and Schuster, 2020.

Boyd, Gregory A. *The Myth of a Christian Nation: How the Quest for Political Power Is Destroying the Church*. Grand Rapids: Zondervan, 2007.

Braunstein, Ruth. "Catholic Christian Nationalism Is Having a Moment." *Religion News Service*, July 23, 2024. https://religionnews.com/2024/07/23/jd-vance-catholic-christian-nationalism-is-having-a-moment/.

Brusco, Elizabeth E. *The Reformation of Machismo: Evangelical Conversion and Gender in Colombia*. Austin: University of Texas Press, 1995.

Bunn-Livingstone, Sandra L. "A Historical Analysis: International Religious Freedom 1998–2008." Paper presented at the Pew Charitable Trusts Conference, April 30–May 2, 2008.

Burgess, Richard, and Danny McCain, "Christianity and the Challenge of Religious Violence in Nigeria." In *Christianity and Freedom Volume II: Contemporary Perspectives*. Edited by Allen Hertzke and Timothy Samuel Shah. New York: Cambridge University Press, 2016.

Campbell, David E. "The Perils of Politicized Religion." *Daedalus* 149, no. 3 (Summer 2020): 87–104.

Campbell, David E., Geoffrey C. Layman, and John C. Green. *Secular Surge: A New Faultline in American Politics*. New York: Cambridge University Press, 2020.

Cao, Nanlai. "Boss Christians: The Business of Religion in the 'Wenzhou Model' of Christian Revival." *The China Journal* 59 (January 2008): 63–87.

Caprioli, Mary, and Peter Trumbore. "Ethnic Discrimination and Interstate Violence: Testing the International Impact of Domestic Behavior." *Journal of Peace Research* 40, no.1 (2003): 5–23.

Casanova, Jose. *Public Religions in the Modern World*. Chicago: University of Chicago Press, 2011.

Cnaan, Ram, Robert J. Wineburg, and Stephanie Boddie. *Newer Deal: Social Work and Religion in Partnership*. New York: Columbia University Press, 1999.

Cnaan, Ram, Thome Forrest, Joseph Carlsmith, and Kelsey Karsh. "If You Don't Count It, It Doesn't Count: A Pilot Study of Valuing Urban Congregations." *Journal of Management, Spirituality and Religion* 10 (2013): 3-36.

Cnaan, Ram, Stephanie C. Boodie, Charlene C. McGrew, and Jennifer J. Kang. *The Other Philadelphia Story: How Local Congregations Support Quality of Life in Urban America.* Philadelphia: University of Pennsylvania Press, 2006.

Cohen, Adam B., ed. *Religion & Human Flourishing.* Waco, TX: Baylor University Press, 2020.

Cohen, Adam, "Chapter 7: Religions Help Us Trust One Another." In *Religion and Human Flourishing.*

Dallas, Kelsey. "Five Years Ago, Utah Passed Landmark Legislation on LGBTQ and Religious Rights. Why Didn't Other States Follow Its Lead?" *Deseret News,* March 11, 2020. https://www.deseret.com/indepth/2020/3/11/21163307/utah-lgbtq-rights-religious-freedom-lgbt-fairness-for-all-mormon-equality-act-congress/.

Dallas, Kelsey. "Religious Freedom Advocates are Divided over How to Address LGBT Rights." *CRUX,* January 16, 2017. https://cruxnow.com/rns/2017/01/religious-freedom-advocates-divided-address-lgbt-rights.

Davidson, Helen. "China in Darkest Period for Human Rights Since Tiananmen, Says Human Rights Group." *The Guardian,* January 13, 2021. https://www.theguardian.com/world/2021/jan/13/china-in-darkest-period-for-human-rights-since-tiananmen-says-rights-group.

Dowd, Robert A. "Religious Diversity and Religious Tolerance: Lessons from Nigeria." *Journal of Conflict Resolution* 60, no. 4 (2014): 617–44.

Durham Jr., W. Cole. "Perspectives on Religious Liberty: A Comparative Framework." In *Religious Human Rights in Global Perspective: Legal Perspectives.* Edited by Johan D. van der Vyver and John Witte Jr. The Hague, Netherlands: Martin Nihoff Publishers, 1996.

Durham Jr., W. Cole, and Elizabeth A. Clark. "The Place of Religious Freedom in the Structure of Peacebuilding." In *The Oxford Handbook of Religion, Conflict, and Peacebuilding.* Edited by Atalia Omer, R. Scot Appleby, and David Little. New York: Oxford University Press, 2015.

Dreher, Rod. *The Benedict Option: A Strategy for Christians in a Post-Christian Nation.* New York: Sentinel, 2017.

Duwe, Grant, and Byron Johnson. "Estimating the Benefits of a Faith-Based Correctional Program." *International Journal of Criminology and Sociology* 2 (2013): 227–39.

Eberle, Edward J. "Roger Williams's Gift: Religious Freedom in America." *Roger Williams University Law Review* 4, no. 2 (1999): Article 3.

Esbeck, Carl H., and Jonathan J. Den Hartog, eds. *Disestablishment and Religious Dissent: Church-State Relations in the New American States, 1776–1833.* Columbia: University of Missouri Press, 2019.

Eskridge. William N., and Robin Fretwell Wilson, eds. *Religious Freedom, LGBT Rights, and the Prospects for Common Ground.* New York: Cambridge University Press, 2018.

Farr, Thomas. "The Equality Act Will Harm Religious Freedom." *Real Clear Religion,* March 16, 2016. https://www.realclearreligion.org/articles/2019/05/16/the_equality_act_will_hurt_religious_freedom_110219.html.

Farr, Thomas. *World of Faith and Freedom: Why International Religious Liberty Is Vital to American National Security.* New York: Oxford University Press, 2008.

Finke, Roger. "Origins and Consequences of Religious Freedoms: A Global Overview." *Sociology of Religion* 43, no. 3 (2013): 297.

Finke, Roger, and Rodney Stark. *The Churching of America, 1776–2005: Winners and Losers in Our Religious Economy.* New Brunswick: Rutgers University Press, 2005.

Fox, Jonathan. *Political Secularism, Religion, and the State: A Time Series Analysis of Worldwide Data.* New York: Cambridge University Press, 2015.

Fox, Jonathan. *Thou Shalt Have No Other Gods Before Me: Why Governments Discriminate Against Religious Minorities.* Cambridge: Cambridge University Press, 2020.

Fox, Jonathan. *The Unfree Exercise of Religion: A World Survey of Discrimination Against Religious Minorities.* New York: Cambridge University Press, 2016.

Fox, Jonathan. *A World Survey of Religion and the State.* New York: Cambridge University Press, 2008.

Fox, Jonathan, and Jori Breslawski. "State Support for Religion and Government Legitimacy in Christian-Majority Countries." *The American Political Science Review* 117, no. 4 (November 2023): 1395-1409. DOI:10.1017/S0003055422001320.

Froese, Paul. *The Plot to Kill God: Findings from the Soviet Experiment in Secularization.* Berkeley: University of California Press, 2008.

Gill, Anthony. *The Political Origins of Religious Liberty.* New York: Cambridge University Press, 2008.

Gill, Anthony. "Religious Liberty and Economic Development: Exploring the Causal Connections." *The Review of Faith and International Affairs* 1, no. 4 (2013): 5–23.

Gill, Anthony. *Rending unto Caesar: The Catholic Church and the State in Latin America.* Chicago: University of Chicago Press, 1998.

Gill, Anthony, and Timothy Shah. "Religious Freedom, Democratization, and Economic Development: A Survey of the Causal Pathways Linking Religious Freedom to Economic Freedom and Prosperity and Political Freedom and Democracy." Annual Meeting of the Association for the Study of Religion, Economics, and Culture (ASREC), Washington, DC, April 13, 2013. https://www.asrec

.org/wp-content/uploads/2015/10/Gill-Shah-Religious-freedom-democratization-and-economic-development.pdf.

Gill, Anthony, and John Owen IV. "Religious Liberty and Economic Prosperity: Four Lessons from the Past." *Cato Journal* 37, no. 1 (2017): 115–34.

Glendon, Mary Ann. *A World Made New: Eleanor Roosevelt and the Universal Declaration of Human Rights.* New York: Random House, 2002.

Glendon, Mary Ann. *In the Courts of Three Popes: An American Lawyer and Diplomat in the Last Absolute Monarchy of the West.* New York: Image, 2024.

"Global Flourishing Study: Highlights from the Inaugural Wave of Data Collection." Sponsored by Gallup, Baylor University Institute for Studies of Religion, Harvard University Human Flourishing Program, and Center for Open Science, 2025. https://globalflourishingstudy.com/wp-content/uploads/2025/04/GFS_Report-1.pdf.

Gore, Gareth. *Opus: The Cult of Dark Money, Human Trafficking, and Right-Wing Conspiracy Inside the Catholic Church.* New York: Simon & Schuster, 2024.

Gorokhovskaia, Yana, and Cathryn Grothe. *Freedom in the World 2025: The Uphill Battle to Safeguard Rights.* Washington, DC: Freedom House. February 2025. https://freedomhouse.org/sites/default/files/2025-03/FITW_World2025digitalN.pdf.

Gorski, Philip S., and Samuel L. Perry. *The Flag and the Cross: White Christian Nationalism and the Threat to Democracy.* New York: Oxford University Press, 2022.

Grim, Brian. "Economic Growth Slowed by Decline in Religious Freedom." *Religious Freedom and Business Foundation,* 2019. https://religiousfreedomandbusiness.org/economic-growth-slowed-by-decline-in-religious-freedom#:~:text=RFBF's%20analysis%20of%20Pew's%20study,7.7%20billion%20%E2%80%94%20live%20today%20in.

Grim, Brian. "Globally, Restrictions on Religion Reached 14-Year High." Religious Freedom and Business Foundation, March 21, 2024. https://religiousfreedomandbusiness.org/2/post/2024/03/globally-restrictions-on-religion-reach-14-year-high.html.

Grim, Brian. "The Modern Chinese Secret to Sustainable Economic Growth: Religious Freedom and Diversity." *The Review of Faith & International Affairs* 13, no. 2 (Summer 2015): 13–24.

Grim, Brian. "Religious Freedom and LBGT Rights: Do They Have Common Ground?" *Religious Freedom and Business Foundation,* 2020. https://religiousfreedomandbusiness.org/religious-freedom-and-lgbt-rights.

Grim, Brian. "Religious Freedom: Good for What Ails Us?" *The Review of Faith & International Affairs* 6, no. 2 (2008): 3–7.

Grim, Brian. "Religious Freedom Was More Than 2 Times Higher in Countries Where Catholics Are the Majority Population." *The Weekly Number Blog,* 2015. http://theweeklynumber.com/weekly-number-blog/category/government%20restrictions.

Grim, Brian. "Restrictions on Religion in the World: Measures and Implications." In *The Future of Religious Freedom: Global Challenges.* Edited by Allen D. Hertzke. New York: Oxford University Press, 2013.

Grim, Brian. "Seven Ways Religious Freedom Contributes to Sustainable Development." *Religious Freedom & Sustainable Development,* August 10, 2015. http://religiousfreedomandbusiness.org/2/post/2015/08/seven-ways-religious-freedom-contributes-to-sustainable-development.html.

Grim, Brian. "The Social and Economic Impact of Religious Intolerance." Religious Freedom and Business Foundation, March 15, 2014. https://religiousfreedomandbusiness.org/2/post/2014/03/the-social-and-economic-impact-of-religious-intolerance.html.

Grim, Brian J., Greg Clark, and Robert Edward Snyder. "Is Religious Freedom Good for Business? A Conceptual and Empirical Analysis." *Interdisciplinary Journal of Research on Religion* 4 (2014): 1–19.

Grim, Brian J., and Philip Connor. "Changing Religion, Changing Economies: Future Global Religious and Economic Growth." *Religious Freedom & Business Foundation,* October 21, 2015. https://religiousfreedomandbusiness.org/wp-content/uploads/2015/10/Changing-religion-Changing-economies-Religious-Freedom-Business-Foundation-October-21-2015.pdf.

Grim, Brian J., and Roger Finke. *The Price of Freedom Denied: Religious Persecution and Conflict in the Twenty-First Century.* Cambridge: Cambridge University Press, 2011.

Grim, Brian J., and Roger Finke. "Religious Persecution in Cross-National Context: Clashing Civilizations or Regulated Religious Economies?" *American Sociological Review* 72, no. 4 (Aug. 2007): 633–58.

Grim, Brian J., and Melissa E. Grim. "The Socio-Economic Contribution of Religion to American Society: An Empirical Analysis," *Interdisciplinary Journal of Research on Religion* 12, Article 3 (2016). https://religiousfreedomandbusiness.org/wp-content/uploads/2020/04/1.2-trillion-US-Religious-Economy-2-page-summary.pdf.

Grim, Brian J., and JoAnn Lyon. "Religion Holds Women Back: Or Does It?" *World Economic Forum,* November 17, 2015. https://www.weforum.org/agenda/2015/11/religion-holds-women-back-or-does-it.

Grim, Brian, and Liu Peng. "The Achilles Heel of China's Rise: Faith." Beijing: Pu Shi Institute for Social Sciences, 2011. https://www.asianews.it/news-en/The-Achilles%27-Heel-of-China%27s-Rise:-Belief--25379.html.

Grim, Brian, and Lingling Wei. "Xi Jinping Chokes Off Crucial Engine of China's Economy." *The Wall Street Journal*, July 13, 2023. https://www.wsj.com/world/xi-china-economy-capital-investment-3439d31a.

Hale, Christopher W. *Divined Intervention: Religious Institutions and Collective Action*. Ann Arbor: University of Michigan Press, 2020.

Hammond, Betsy. "Governor Signs Repeal on Teachers' Religious Dress; Ban Will Lift in July 2011." *The Oregonian/OregonLive*, April 1, 2010. https://www.oregonlive.com/education/2010/04/governor_signs_repeal_on_teach.html.

Hardy, Quentin. "Hitting Slavery Where It Hurts (Gary Haugen of International Justice Mission)." *Forbes* 172, no.14 (2014): 76.

Harris, Cameron, and Daniel James Milton. "Is Standing for Women a Stand Against Terrorism? Exploring the Connection Between Women's Rights and Terrorism." *Journal of Human Rights* 15, no. 1 (2016): 60–78.

Harris, Elise. "Anti-Human Trafficking Effort Launched Ahead of World Cup." *Catholic News Agency*, 2014. http://www.catholicnewsagency.com/news/anti-human-trafficking-effort-launched-ahead-of-world-cup/.

Hasson, Kevin Seamus. *The Right to Be Wrong: Ending the Culture War over Religion in America*. San Francisco: Encounter Books, 2005.

Haugen, Gary. *The Good News About Injustice*. Downers Grove, IL: InterVarsity Press, 2014.

Haugen, Gary A., and Victor Boutros. *The Locust Effect: Why the End of Poverty Required the End of Violence*. New York: Oxford University Press, 2014.

Hefner, Robert W. *Civil Islam: Muslims and Democratization in Indonesia*. Princeton, NJ: Princeton University Press, 2000.

Helliwell, John F., Richard Layard, Jeffrey D. Sachs, Jan-Emmanuel De Neve, Lara B. Aknin, and Shun Wang, eds. *World Happiness Report 2023*, 11th ed. The University of Oxford's Wellbeing Research Centre, in partnership with Gallup, the UN Sustainable Partnership Solutions Network, and the World Happiness Report's Editorial Board, 2023.

Hergueux, Jerome. "How Does Religion Bias the Allocation of Foreign Direct Investment?" *International Economics* 128, no. 4 (2012): 53–76.

Hertzke, Allen D. "The Catholic Church and Catholicism in Global Politics." *Routledge Handbook of Religion and Politics,* 2nd ed., edited by Jeffrey Haynes. Abingdon: Routledge, 2016.

Hertzke, Allen D. "The Constitutional Roots of American Global Leadership on Religious Freedom." *Starting Points Journal*, March 5, 2019. https://startingpointsjournal.com/constitutional-roots-american-global-leadership-religious-freedom/.

Hertzke, Allen D. *Echoes of Discontent: Jesse Jackson, Pat Robertson, and the Resurgence of Populism.* Washington, DC: CQ Press, 1993.

Hertzke, Allen D. *Freeing God's Children: The Unlikely Alliance for Global Human Rights.* Lanham, MD: Rowman & Littlefield, 2004.

Hertzke, Allen D, ed. *The Future of Religious Freedom: Global Challenges.* New York: Oxford University Press, 2013.

Hertzke, Allen D. "Genocide Fueled by Oil." *Weekly Standard,* July 22, 2002.

Hertzke, Allen D. "Globalization of Advocacy." In *The Politics and Practices of Religious Diversity.* Edited by Andrew Dawson. Abingdon: Routledge, 2016.

Hertzke, Allen D. "A Meditation on Hanukkah and Religious Freedom." Blog. Religious Freedom Institute, July 5, 2016. https://religiousfreedominstitute.org/2016-7-5-a-meditation-on-hanukkah-and-religious-freedom/.

Hertzke, Allen D, ed. *Religious Freedom in America: Constitutional Roots and Contemporary Challenges.* Norman: University of Oklahoma Press, 2015.

Hertzke, Allen D. "Roman Catholicism and the Faith-Based Movement for Global Human Rights." *The Review of Faith & International Affairs* 3, no. 3 (2005): 19–24.

Hertzke, Allen D. "State Failure and International Response: The Lessons of South Sudan." In *Nation, State, Nation-State,* edited by Vittorio Hosle. Vatican City: Pontifical Academy of Social Sciences, 2020. https://www.pass.va/content/dam/casinapioiv/pass/pdf-volumi/acta/acta22pass.pdf.

Hertzke, Allen D, guest ed. "Strategies of Advocacy for International Religious Freedom." *The Review of Faith & International Affairs* 10, no. 3 (Fall 2012).

Hertzke, Allen, and Timothy Samuel Shah, eds. *Christianity and Freedom, Volume II: Contemporary Perspectives.* New York: Cambridge University Press, 2016.

Hirschman, Albert O. *Exit, Voice, and Loyalty: Responses to Decline in Firms, Organizations, and States.* Cambridge, MA: Harvard University Press, 1970.

Hoogstra, Shirley, and Robin Fretwell Wilson. "Fairness as a Path Toward LGBTQ Rights and Religious Liberty." In *The Routledge Handbook of Religious Literacy, Pluralism, and Global Engagement,* edited by Chris Seiple and Dennis R. Hoover. New York: Routledge, 2022.

Howard, Jo, and Mariz Tadros, eds. *Using Participatory Methods to Explore Freedom of Religion and Belief.* Bristol, UK: Bristol University Press, July 27, 2023. https://doi.org/10.51952/9781529229295.

Hudson, Valerie M., and Kaylee B. Hodgson. "Sex and Terror: Is the Subordination of Women Associated with the Use of Terror?" *Terrorism and Political Violence* 34, no. 3 (2022): 605–32.

Huntington, Samuel P. *The Clash of Civilizations and the Remaking of World Order.* New York: Touchstone, 1996.

Huntington, Samuel P. *The Third Wave: Democratization in the Late Twentieth Century*. Norman: University of Oklahoma Press, 1991.

Hurd, Elizabeth Shakman. "The International Politics of Religious Freedom." *India International Centre Quarterly* 40, no. 3/4 (Winter 2013–Spring 2014): 225–37. https://www.jstor.org/stable/24394399.

Hurd, Elizabeth Shakman. *Beyond Religious Freedom: The New Global Politics of Religion*. Princeton, NJ: Princeton University Press, 2015.

Hurd, Elizabeth Shakman. "The Politics of International Religious Freedom." In *Routledge Handbook of Religion and Politics*, 3rd ed., edited by Jeffrey Haynes (Abingdon, UK: Routledge, 2023).

Hurd, Elizabeth Shakman. "The Politics of Secularism." In *Rethinking Religion and World Affairs*, edited by Timothy Samuel Shah, Alfred Stepan, and Monica Duffy Toft. New York: Oxford University Press, 2012.

Inboden, William. "Jihadist Ideology, Religious Intolerance, and the Anathema of Democracy." Presented at Religious Freedom Project Symposium, Georgetown University, November 15, 2016. Unpublished paper cited with permission of author.

Inboden, William. "Religious Freedom and National Security: Why the U.S. Should Make the Connection." *Policy Review* 175 (October 2012): 55–68.

"India: Official Dalit Population Exceeds 200 million." International Dalit Solidarity Network, May 29, 2013. http://idsn.org/india-official-dalit-population-exceeds-200-million/.

Inglehart, Ronald F. *Religion's Sudden Decline: What's Causing It, and What Comes Next?* Oxford: Oxford University Press, 2021.

Isaac, Rhys. "Religion and Authority: Problems of the Anglican Establishment in Virginia in the Era of the Great Awakening and the Parsons' Cause." *The William and Mary Quarterly* 30, no. 1 (1973): 4–36.

Jenkins, Jack. "5 Facts About JD Vance, Catholic Convert and Trump's VP Pick." *Religion News Service,* July 24, 2024. https://www.americamagazine.org/politics-society/2024/07/16/five-faith-facts-jd-vance-trump-vp-248368.

Jenkins, Philip. *The Next Christendom: The Coming of Global Christianity*, 2nd ed. New York: Oxford University Press, 2007.

Johnson, Byron R. *More God, Less Crime: Why Religion Matters and How It Could Matter More.* Conshohocken, PA: Templeton Press. 2011.

Johnson, Bryon R. "Chapter 10: Offender-Led Religious Movements." In *Religion & Human Flourishing*. Waco, TX: Baylor University Press, 2020.

Johnson, Byron R. "How Religion Contributes to the Common Good, Positive Criminology, and Justice Reform." *Religions* 12: 402 (2021): 213–23. https://doi.org/10.3390/rel12060402.

Johnson, Byron, Sung Joon Jang, David B. Larson, and Spencer De Li. "Does Adolescent Religious Commitment Matter? A Reexamination of the Effects of Religiosity on Delinquency." *Journal of Research in Crime and Delinquency* 38, no. 1 (2001): 22–44.

Johnston, Douglas, and Cynthia Sampson. *Religion, the Missing Dimension of Statecraft.* New York: Oxford University Press, 1994.

Kattelman, Kyle, and Courtney Burns. "Unpacking the Concepts: Examining the Link Between Women's Status and Terrorism." *Journal of Peace Research* 60, no. 5 (2023): 792–806.

Kengor, Paul. *A Pope and a President: John Paul II, Ronald Reagan, and the Extraordinary Untold Story of the 20th Century.* Wilmington, DE: ISI Books, 2017.

Kepel, Gilles. *The Revenge of God: The Resurgence of Islam, Christianity, and Judaism in the Modern World.* University Park: The Pennsylvania State University Press, 1994.

King, Gary. "Replication, Replication." *PS: Political Science and Politics* 28 (1995): 444–52. https://tinyurl.com/mvc5kg5.

Koenig, Harold G., Dana E. King, and Verna B. Carson. *Handbook of Religion and Health*, 2nd ed. Oxford: Oxford University Press, 2012.

Koesel, Karrie. *Religion and Authoritarianism: Cooperation, Conflict, and the Consequences.* Cambridge: Cambridge University Press, 2014.

Koesel, Karrie. "The Political Economy of Religious Revival." *Politics and Religion* 8, no. 2 (2015): 211–35.

Koesel, Karrie J., and Ani Sarkissian. "Religion and the Authoritarian Toolkit: Are Carrots Substitutes for Sticks?" *Democratization*, May 18, 2025: 1–24. https://doi.org/10.1080/13510347.2025.2489024.

Kristof, Nicholas, and Sheryl WuDunn. *Half the Sky: Turning Oppression into Opportunity for Women Worldwide.* New York: Vintage, 2010.

Kuhn, Thomas S. *The Structure of Scientific Revolutions.* Chicago: University of Chicago Press, 1962.

Kuran, Timur. *Freedoms Delayed: Political Legacies of Islamic Law in the Middle East.* Cambridge: Cambridge University Press, 2023.

Kuran, Timur. *Islam and Mammon: The Economic Predicaments of Islamism.* Princeton: Princeton University Press, 2004.

Kuran, Timur. *The Long Divergence: How Islamic Law Held Back the Middle East.* Princeton: Princeton University Press, 2011.

Kuran, Timur, and Jared Rubin. "The Financial Power of the Powerless: Socio-Economic Status and Interest Rates under Partial Rule of Law." *The Economic Journal* (London) 128, no. 609 (2018): 758–96.

Kuru, Ahmet T. *Secularism and State Policies Toward Religion: The United States, France, and Turkey*. New York: Cambridge University Press, 2009.

Kuru, Ahmet T. *Islam, Authoritarianism, and Underdevelopment: A Global and Historical Comparison.* Cambridge: Cambridge University Press, 2019.

LaFantasie, Glenn W., ed. *The Correspondence of Roger Williams in 2 Volumes: 1654–1682.* Providence: Brown University Press, 1988.

LaFantasie, Glenn W., ed. "From a letter to Major John Wilson and Connecticut Governor Thomas Prence." In *The Correspondence of Roger Williams* (Volume 2: 1654–82). Providence: Brown University Press (1988): 617–18.

Langfitt, Frank. "Hundreds of Scholars Say U.S is Swiftly Heading Toward Authoritarianism." Heard on "All Things Considered," National Public Radio, April 25, 2025. https://www.npr.org/2025/04/22/nx-s1-5340753/trump-democracy-authoritarianism-competive-survey-political-scientist.

Leingang, Rachel, and Stephanie Kirchgaessner. "Kevin Roberts, Architect of Project 2025, Has Close Ties to Radical Group Opus Dei." *The Guardian*, July 26, 2024. https://www.theguardian.com/us-news/article/2024/jul/26/kevin-roberts-project-2025-opus-dei.

Levin, Jeff. "Religion and Mental Health: Theory and Research." *International Journal of Applied Psychoanalytic Studies* 7, no. 2 (2010): 102–15.

Levy, Leonard. Virginia Declaration of Rights and Constitution of 1776 (June 12 and 29, 1776). *Encyclopedia of the American Constitution* 6 (2000): 2799–2800.

Li, Xiangping, and Fenggang Yang. 2006. "Protestant Ethics and the Construction of Social Trust: Christian Enterprises in Contemporary China." In *From the Armchair to the Field: Selected Articles of the Beijing Summit on Chinese Spirituality and Society* 2, edited by Shining Gao and Fenggang Yang. Beijing: China Social Sciences Press, 2010.

Lilla, Mark. *The Stillborn God: Religion, Politics, and the Modern West.* New York: Knopf, 2007.

Lipka, Michael. "Why People with No Religion Are Projected to Decline as a Share of the World's Population." Pew Research Center, April 17, 2017. http://www.pewresearch.org/fact-tank/2017/04/07/why-people-with-no-religion-are-projected-to-decline-as-a-share-of-the-worlds-population/.

Little Sisters of the Poor Saints Peter and Paul Home v. Pennsylvania et al. No. 19–431, 2020. https://www.supremecourt.gov/opinions/19pdf/19-431_5i36.pdf.

Locke, John. *A Letter Concerning Toleration*. Translated by William Popple, 1689. www.constitution.org/jl/tolerati.htm#01.

Madison, James. "Memorial and Remonstrance Against Religious Assessments," 1785. https://founders.archives.gov/documents/Madison/01-08-02-0163.

Mahmood, Saba. *Religious Difference in a Secular Age: A Minority Report.* Princeton, NJ: Princeton University Press, 2016.

Makridis, Christos Andreas. "Human Flourishing and Religious Liberty: Evidence from 150 Countries." *PLOS ONE* 15, no. 10 (October 1, 2020). https://journals.plos.org/plosone/article?id=10.1371/journal.pone.0239983

Maleki, Ammar, and Pooyan Tamimi Arab. "Iranians' Attitudes Toward Religion: A 2020 Survey Report." GAMAAN: The Group for Analyzing and Measuring Attitudes in Iran, August 2020. https://gamaan.org/wp-content/uploads/2020/09/GAMAAN-Iran-Religion-Survey-2020-English.pdf.

Marshall, Katherine. "Towards Enriching Understandings and Assessments of Freedom of Religion or Belief: Politics, Debates, Methodologies and Practices." *CREID Working Paper 6*, January 2021. Coalition for Religious Equality and Inclusive Development. Brighton, UK: Institute of Development Studies.

Marshall, Paul. "Patterns and Purposes of Contemporary Anti-Christian Persecution." In *Christianity and Freedom, Volume II: Contemporary Perspectives.* Edited by Allen D. Hertzke and Timothy Samuel Shah. New York: Cambridge University Press, 2016.

Marshall, Paul, and Nina Shea. *Silenced: How Apostasy and Blasphemy Codes Are Choking Freedom Worldwide.* New York: Oxford University Press, 2011.

Martin, Robert, and Roger Finke. "Defining and Redefining Religious Freedom: A Quantitative Assessment of Free Exercise Cases in the U.S. State Courts, 1981–2011." In *Religious Freedom in America: Constitutional Roots and Contemporary Challenges.* Edited by Allen Hertzke. Norman: University of Oklahoma Press, 2015.

"Mary Dyer." *Encyclopedia Britannica*, May 28, 2003. https://www.britannica.com/biography/Mary-Barrett-Dyer.

McCrummen, Stephanie. "The Army of God Comes Out of the Shadows." *The Atlantic*, February 2025. https://www.theatlantic.com/magazine/archive/2025/02/new-apostolic-reformation-christian-movement-trump/681092/.

Mefford, Brian. "Russian Orthodox Church Declares 'Holy War' Against Ukraine and West." Atlantic Council, April 9, 2024. https://www.atlanticcouncil.org/blogs/ukrainealert/russian-orthodox-church-declares-holy-war-against-ukraine-and-west/.

Meierrieks, Daniel, and Laura Renner. "Islamist Terrorism and the Status of Women." *European Journal of Political Economy* 78C, Article 102364 (June 2023). https://www.sciencedirect.com/journal/european-journal-of-political-economy/vol/78/suppl/C.

Miller, Robert T., and Ronald B. Flowers, editors. *Toward Benevolent Neutrality: Church, State, and the Supreme Court.* Waco, TX: Baylor University Press Imprint, 2020.

Monsma, Stephen V. "Faith-based NGOs and the Government Embrace." In *The Influence of Faith: Religious Groups and U.S. Foreign Policy.* Edited by Elliott Abrams. Lanham, MD: Rowman and Littlefield, 2001.

Munthe, Christian. "Conscience Refusal in Healthcare: The Swedish Solution." *Journal of Medical Ethics* 43, no. 4 (April 2017): 257–59. https://doi.org/10.1136/medethics-2016-103752.

My Mercy Encompasses All: The Koran's Teachings on Compassion, Peace & Love. Gathered & Introduced by Reza Shah-Kazemi. Emeryville, CA: Shoemaker & Hoard, 2007.

Narayan, Deepa. *Voices of the Poor: Can Anyone Hear Us?* Oxford: Oxford University Press, 2000.

Nelson, Sean, and Paul Teller. "The Bible Is Yet Again on Trial in Finland." *National Review*, May 24, 2024. https://www.nationalreview.com/2024/05/the-bible-is-yet-again-on-trial-in-finland/.

Newman, John Henry. "Letter to the Duke of Norfolk." In *Newman Reader,* 1874. https://www.newmanreader.org/works/anglicans/volume2/gladstone/index.html

Nichols, Hans. "Scoop: Activist Leonard Leo Pushes to 'Weaponize' Conservatives." *Axios*, September 12, 2024. https://www.axios.com/2024/09/12/leonard-leo-conservative-groups-funding.

Nussbaum, Martha C. *Creating Capabilities*. Cambridge, MA: Harvard University Press, 2011.

Oliver, Jill, and Quentin Wodon. "Faith-Inspired Health Care in Sub-Saharan Africa: An Introduction to the Spring 2014 Issue." *The Review of Faith & International Affairs* 12, Vol. 1 (Spring 2014): 1–7.

Open Doors. "Situation of Religious Freedom for Christians: Nigeria." *World Watch List 2025*. file:///C:/Users/14057/Downloads/Nigeria-Media_Advocacy_Dossier-ODI-2025%20(1).pdf.

Ott, Mack. "Religious Freedom and Economic Progress: A Philosophical and Empirical Exploration." *Journal of Private Enterprise* 20, no. 2 (Spring 2005): 68–96.

Owen, John. *The Clash of Ideas in World Politics: Transnational Networks, States and Regime Change, 1510–2010*. Princeton, NJ: Princeton University Press, 2010.

Owen, John. *Confronting Political Islam: Six Lessons from the West's Past*. Princeton, NJ: Princeton University Press, 2014.

Özdamar, Özgür, and Yasemin Akbaba. "Religious Discrimination and International Crises: International Effects of Domestic Inequality." *Foreign Policy Analysis* 10, no. 4 (2014): 413–30.

Patel, Eboo. *Acts of Faith: The Story of an American Muslim, the Struggle for the Soul of a Generation*. Boston: Beacon Press, 2010.

Penn, William. *The Great Case of Liberty of Conscience,* 1670. University of Michigan Library Digital Collections, Early English Books Online. https://quod.lib.umich.edu/e/eebo/A54146.0001.001?rgn=main;view=fulltext.

Peng, Liu. "The Achilles Heel of China's Rise: Belief." Beijing: Pu Shi Institute for Social Sciences, July 25, 2012. A summary is available at: https://www.asianews.it/news-en/The-Achilles%27-Heel-of-China%27s-Rise:-Belief-25379.html.

Pentin, Edward. "Interreligious Leaders to Sign Historic Declaration Against Human Trafficking." *National Catholic Register*, December 2, 2014. https://www.ncregister.com/blog/interreligious-leaders-to-sign-historic-joint-declaration-against-human-trafficking.

Pew Global Attitudes Project. "World Publics Welcome Global Trade—But Not Immigration." *Highlights from the 2007 Pew Global Attitudes 47-Nation Survey*. October 4, 2007. http://pewglobal.org/reports/pdf/258topline.pdf.

Pew Research Center. "A Closer Look at How Religious Restrictions Have Risen Around the World." July 15, 2019. https://www.pewresearch.org/wp-content/uploads/sites/20/2019/07/Restrictions_X_WEB_7-15_FULL-VERSION-1.pdf.

Pew Research Center. "The Future of World Religions: Population Growth Projections: 2010-2050." April 2, 2015. http://www.pewforum.org/2015/04/02/religious-projections-2010-2050/.

Pew Research Center. "The Gender Gap in Religion Around the World: Women are Generally More Religious than Men, Particularly Among Christians." March 2, 2016. https://www.pewresearch.org/religion/2016/03/22/the-gender-gap-in-religion-around-the-world/.

Pew Research Center. "The Global Religious Landscape." December 18, 2012. https://www.pewresearch.org/religion/2012/12/18/global-religious-landscape-exec/.

Pew Research Center. "Global Restrictions on Religion Rise Modestly in 2015, Reversing Downward Trend." April 11, 2017. http://www.pewforum.org/2017/04/11/global-restrictions-on-religion-rise-modestly-in-2015-reversing-downward-trend/.

Pew Research Center. "Government Restrictions on Religion Stayed at Peak Levels Globally in 2022." Pew Research Center, December 18, 2024. https://www

.pewresearch.org/wp-content/uploads/sites/20/2024/12/PR_2024.12.18_restrictions-on-religion-2022_report.pdf.

Pew Research Center. "Key Findings from the Global Religious Futures Project." December 21, 2022. https://www.pewresearch.org/religion/2022/12/21/key-findings-from-the-global-religious-futures-project/.

Philpott, Daniel. "The Catholic Wave." *Journal of Democracy* 15, no. 2 (2004): 32–46.

Philpott, Daniel. "Explaining the Political Ambivalence of Religion." *American Political Science Review* 101, no. 3 (2007): 505–25.

Philpott, Daniel. "Has the Study of Global Politics Found Religion?" *Annual Review of Political Science* 12 (2009): 183–202.

Philpott, Daniel. *Just and Unjust Peace: An Ethic of Political Reconciliation*. New York: Oxford University Press, 2012.

Philpott, Daniel, ed. *Politics of Past Evil: Religion, Reconciliation, and the Dilemmas of Transitional Justice*. Notre Dame, IN: University of Notre Dame Press, 2006.

Philpott, Daniel. *Religious Freedom in Islam: The Fate of a Universal Right in the Muslim World Today*. New York: Oxford University Press, 2019.

Philpott, Daniel. "Why Religious Freedom Is a Human Right." *The American Journal of Jurisprudence* 68, no. 3 (December 2023): 177–94.

Philpott, Daniel, and Timothy Samuel Shah. "In Defense of Religious Freedom: New Critics of a Beleaguered Human Right." *Journal of Law and Religion* 31, no. 3 (2016): 380–95. http://www.jstor.org/stable/26336712.

Philpott, Daniel, and Timothy Samuel Shah, eds. *Under Caesar's Sword: How Christians Respond to Persecution*. Cambridge: Cambridge University Press, 2018.

Pope Francis. *Fratelli Tutti: On Fraternity and Social Friendship*. Encyclical Letter issued October 3, 2020. Vatican City: Vatican Press, 2020.

Putnam, Robert D. *Bowling Alone: The Collapse and Revival of American Community*. New York: Simon & Schuster, 2000.

"Religion and State Project." Bar-Ilan University, May 14, 2018. https://ras.thearda.com/ras-downloads/.

Religious Freedom and Business Foundation, 2025. https://religiousfreedomandbusiness.org.

Religious Freedom Institute. Blog on Sexual Orientation and Gender Identity Policy, May 16, 2025. https://religiousfreedominstitute.org/category/topic-guides/sexual-orientation-and-gender-identity-policy/.

Renn, Aaron M. *Life in the Negative World: Confronting Challenges in an Anti-Christian Culture*. Grand Rapids, MI: Zondervan, 2024.

Rieffer-Flanagan, Barbara Ann. *Promoting Religious Freedom in an Age of Intolerance.* Cheltenham, UK: Edward Elgar, 2022.

Sacks, Jonathan. *The Dignity of Difference: How to Avoid the Clash of Civilizations.* London: Continuum, 2003. https://rabbisacks.org/.

Saiya, Nilay. "Christian Nationalism's Threat to Global Democracy." *The Review of Faith & International Affairs* 22, no. 1 (2024). https://www-tandfonline-com.ezproxy.lib.ou.edu/doi/full/10.1080/15570274.2023.2204679.

Saiya, Nilay. *The Global Politics of Jesus: A Christian Case for Church-State Separation.* New York: Oxford University Press, 2022.

Saiya, Nilay. *God's Warriors: Religious Violence and the Global Crisis of Secularism.* New York: Oxford University Press, 2025.

Saiya, Nilay. "Religion, State, and Terrorism: A Global Analysis." *Terrorism and Political Violence* 31, no. 2 (2016): 204–23.

Saiya, Nilay. "The Religious Freedom Peace." *The International Journal of Human Rights* 19 (2015): 369–82.

Saiya, Nilay. "The Rise of Theocratic Democracy." *Journal of Democracy* 4, no. 4 (October 2023): 66–79.

Saiya, Nilay. *Weapon of Peace: How Religious Liberty Combats Terrorism.* Cambridge: Cambridge University Press, 2018.

Saiya, Nilay, and Anthony Scime. "Explaining Religious Terrorism: A Data-Mined Analysis." *Conflict Management and Peace Science* 32, no. 5 (2015): 487–512.

Saiya, Nilay, and Stuti Manchanda. "Monks Behaving Badly: Explaining Buddhist Violence in Asia." *International Security* 49, no. 4 (Spring 2025): 119–59.

Saiya, Nilay, and Stuti Manchanda. "Paradoxes of Pluralism, Privilege, and Persecution: Explaining Christian Growth and Decline Worldwide." *Sociology of Religion* 83, no. 1 (Spring 2022): 60–78.

Saiya, Nilay, Tasneem Zaihra, and Joshua Fidler. "Testing the Hillary Doctrine: Women's Rights and Anti-American Terrorism." *Political Research Quarterly* 70, no. 2 (June 2017): 421–32.

Saperstein, Rabbi David. Event transcript: "Lobbying for the Faithful." Pew Research Center, November 21, 2011. https://www.pewresearch.org/religion/2011/11/21/lobbying-for-the-faithful-event-transcript/.

Sarkissian, Ani. "Religious Reestablishment in Post-Communist Polities." *Journal of Church and State* 51, no. 3 (Summer 2009): 472–501. https://www.jstor.org/stable/23921633.

Sarkissian, Ani. "Religious Regulation and the Muslim Democracy Gap." *Politics and Religion* 5, no. 3 (2012): 501–27. https://doi.org/10.1017/S1755048312000284.

Sarkissian, Ani. *The Varieties of Religious Repression: Why Governments Restrict Religion*. New York: Oxford University Press, 2015.

Scoville, Warren C. "The Huguenots and the Diffusion of Technology. I." *Journal of Political Economy* 60, no. 4 (1952): 294–311.

Scoville, Warren C. "The Huguenots and the Diffusion of Technology. II." *Journal of Political Economy* 60, no. 5 (1952): 392-411.

Seiple, Chris. "The Call of Covenantal Pluralism." Templeton Lecture on Religion and World Affairs. *Foreign Policy Research Institute*, October 30, 2018. https://www.fpri.org/article/2018/11/the-call-of-covenantal-pluralism-defeating-religious-nationalism-with-faithful-patriotism/.

Seiple, Chris, and Dennis Hoover, eds. *The Routledge Handbook of Religious Literacy, Pluralism, and Global Engagement*. New York: Routledge, 2022.

Sen, Amartya. *Development as Freedom*. New York: Knopf, 1993.

Senturk, Recep. "Human Rights in Islamic Jurisprudence: Why Should All Human Beings Be Inviolable." *The Future of Religious Freedom: Global Challenges*. Edited by Allen D. Hertzke. New York: Oxford University Press, 2013.

Shah, Rebecca S. "Christianity Among the Marginalized: Empowering Poor Women in India." In *Christianity and Freedom Volume II: Contemporary Perspectives*. Edited by Allen D. Hertzke and Timothy Samuel Shah, 107–32. Cambridge: Cambridge University Press, 2016.

Shah, Rebecca S. "Religion and Economic Empowerment Among the Enterprising Poor." *The Review of Faith & International Affairs* 11, no. 4 (2013): 41–45.

Shah, Rebecca Samuel, and Timothy Samuel Shah. "Chapter 10: Religious Freedom Among the Marginalized in Bangalore, India." In *Christianity in India: Conversion, Community Development, and Religious Freedom*. Edited by Rebecca Samuel Shah and Joel Carpenter. Minneapolis: Fortress Press, 2018.

Shah, Rebecca Supriya, and Timothy Samuel Shah. "The Other Invisible Hand: How Freedom of Religion or Belief Fosters Pro-Social and Pro-Development Outcomes for the Poor." In *What About Us? Global Perspectives on Redressing Religious Inequalities*. Edited by Mariz Tadros. Institute for Development Studies, University of Sussex, UK, 2022.

Shah, Rebecca S., and Timothy Samuel Shah. "Participatory Methods and the Freedom of Religion and Belief." In *Using Participatory Methods to Explore Freedom of Religion and Belief*. Edited by Jo Howard and Mariz Tadros. Bristol, UK: Bristol University Press, July 27, 2023.

Shah, Rebecca S., and Robert Woodberry. "Religion and Economic Empowerment: A Growing but Still Tentative Relationship." A literature review working paper, August 2015.

Shah, Timothy Samuel, and Allen D. Hertzke, eds. *Christianity and Freedom, Volume I: Historical Perspectives.* New York: Cambridge University Press, 2016.

Shah, Timothy Samuel, and Nathan Berkeley, eds. *Freedom of Religious Institutions in Society*, special issue of *Religions.* Basel, Switzerland: MDPI, 2022. https://www.mdpi.com/journal/religions/special_issues/free_reli.

Shah, Timothy Samuel, and Jack Friedman. *Homo Religiosus? Exploring the Roots of Religion and Religious Freedom in Human Experience.* Cambridge and New York: Cambridge University Press, 2018.

Shah, Timothy Samuel, Matthew J. Franck, and Thomas F. Farr. *Religious Freedom, Why Now? Defending an Embattled Human Right.* Princeton, NJ: Witherspoon Institute, 2012.

Shah, Timothy Samuel, Alfred Stepan, and Monica Duffy Toft, eds. *Rethinking Religion and World Affairs.* New York: Oxford University Press, 2012.

Shah, Timothy Samuel, Alfred Stepan, and Monica Duffy Toft. "Spiritual Capital and Economic Enterprise." Oxford Centre for Religion & Public Life, June 26, 2007. http://www.ocrpl.org/2007/spiritual-capital-and-economic-entrerprise/.

Shea, Nina. *In the Lion's Den: A Shocking Account of Persecution and Martyrdom of Christians Today and How We Should Respond.* Nashville: B&H Publishing Group, 1997.

Shea, Nina. "Religious Freedom in American Foreign Policy." In *Religious Freedom in the World: A Global Report on Freedom and Persecution.* Nashville, Tennessee: Broadman & Holman Publishers, 2000.

Shortle, Allyson, Eric L. McDaniel, and Irfan Nooruddin. *The Everyday Crusade: Christian Nationalism in American Politics.* New York: Cambridge University Press, 2022.

Singha, Sara. "The Challenge and Leaven of Christianity in Pakistan." In *Christianity and Freedom Volume II: Contemporary Perspectives.* Edited by Allen Hertzke and Timothy Samuel Shah. New York: Cambridge University Press, 2016.

Singh Jolly, Rajdeep. Interview by author with this former leader of the Sikh Coalition. Washington, DC, 2009.

Slade, Stephanie. "The Fight for Religious Liberty Is Never Going to End: We'd Better Get Used to It." *America Magazine*, February 15, 2017. https://www.americamagazine.org/politics-society/2017/02/15/fight-religious-liberty-never-going-end-wed-better-get-used-it.

Smith, Adam. *An Inquiry into the Nature and Causes of the Wealth of Nations—Volume 1.* First published in 1776. Republished in two volumes by The

Liberty Fund, 1976. https://oll.libertyfund.org/titles/smith-an-inquiry-into-the-nature-and-causes-of-the-wealth-of-nations-cannan-ed-vol-1.

Smith, Adam. "Of the Expense of the Institutions for the Instruction of People of all Ages." *The Founders Constitution*, Book 5, Ch. 1, Pt. 3, Article 3 (1776). https://press-pubs.uchicago.edu/founders/documents/amendI_religions31.html.

Smyth, John. "Propositions and Conclusions Concerning True Christian Religion, Containing a Confession of Faith of Certain English People, Living at Amsterdam." *Baptist Confessions of Faith*. rev. ed. 2. Edited by William L. Lumpkin and Bill J. Leonard. Valley Forge: Judson Press, 2011.

Soroush, Abdolkarim. *Reason, Freedom, and Democracy in Islam*. New York: Oxford University Press, 2000.

Soroush, Abdolkarim. "Religious Tyranny Is Crumbling: Rejoice!" Open Letter to Mr. Khamenei, September 13, 2009. https://drsoroush.com/en/religious-tyranny-is-crumbling-rejoice/.

Soroush, Abdolkarim. "You Have Turned Iran into a Grim Land." Open letter to Mr. Seyyed Ali Khamenei, leader of the Islamic Republic of Iran, December 22, 2011. https://drsoroush.com/en/you-have-turned-iran-into-a-grim-land/.

Stark, Rodney. *America's Blessings: How Religion Benefits Everyone, Including Atheists*. Templeton Foundation Press, 2012.

Stark, Rodney. *The Triumph of Christianity: How the Jesus Movement Became the World's Largest Religion*. New York: HarperOne, 2011.

Stark, Rodney. *The Triumph of Faith: Why the World Is More Religious Than Ever*. Wilmington, DE, ISI Books, 2015. Reprint, New York: Regnery Gateway, 2023.

Stepan, Alfred. "Religion, Democracy, and the 'Twin Tolerations.'" *Journal of Democracy* 11, no. 4 (October 2000): 37–57. https://doi.org/10.1353/jod.2000.0088.

Stepan, Alfred, and Graeme B. Robertson. "An 'Arab' More than 'Muslim' Electoral Gap." *Journal of Democracy* 14, no. 3 (July 2003): 30–44. https://doi.org/10.1353/jod.2003.0064.

Stevenson, Alexandra, and Zixu Wang. "China's Population Falls, Heralding a Demographic Crisis." *The New York Times*, January 16, 2023. https://www.nytimes.com/2023/01/16/business/china-birth-rate.html.

Stewart, W. Christopher, Chris Seiple, and Dennis R. Hoover. "Toward a Global Covenant of Peaceable Neighborhood: Introducing the Philosophy of Covenantal Pluralism." *The Review of Faith & International Affairs* 18, no. 4 (2020): 1–17.

Stoll, Davis. *Is Latin America Turning Protestant?* Berkeley: University of California Press, 1990.

Sudan Peace Act. Public Law 107-245. October 21, 2002.

Sullivan, Winnifred Fallers. *The Impossibility of Religious Freedom.* Princeton, NJ: Princeton University Press, 2005.

Sullivan, Winnifred Fallers, Elizabeth Shakman Hurd, Saba Mahmood, and Peter G. Danchin, eds. *Politics of Religious Freedom.* Chicago: University of Chicago Press, 2015.

Tadros, Mariz. "Conclusion." In *What About Us? Global Perspectives on Redressing Religious Inequalities.* Edited by Mariz Tadros. Sussex, UK: Institute of Development Studies, 2022.

Tadros, Mariz. "Copts of Egypt: Defiance, Compliance, and Continuity." In *Christianity and Freedom, Volume II: Contemporary Perspectives.* Edited by Allen D. Hertzke and Timothy Samuel Shah. New York: Cambridge University Press, 2016.

Tadros, Mariz, ed. *What About Us? Global Perspectives on Redressing Religious Inequalities.* Brighton, UK: University of Sussex Institute of Development Studies, 2022.

Talitha Kum, International Network of Consecrated Life Against Human Trafficking. International Union of Superiors General, 2025. https://www.talithakum.info/.

Taylor, Charles. *A Secular Age.* Cambridge, MA: Harvard University Press, 2007.

Taylor, Matthew D. *The Violent Take it by Force: The Christian Movement That Is Threatening Our Democracy.* Minneapolis, MN: Broadleaf Books, 2024.

Thames, H. Knox. *Ending Persecution: Charting the Path to Global Religious Freedom.* Notre Dame, IN: University of Notre Dame Press, 2024.

Thuswaldner, Gregor. "A Conversation with Peter L. Berger: 'How My Views Have Changed.'" *The Cresset* 77, no. 3 (Lent 2014): 16–20.

Tillich, Paul. *The Courage to Be.* New Haven: Yale University Press, 1970.

Tocqueville, Alexis de. *Democracy in America—Volume 1.* First published in French in 1835. Republished and translated by Harvey Mansfield. Chicago: University of Chicago Press, 2000.

Toft, Monica Duffy. "Religion, Terrorism, and Violence." In *Rethinking Religion and World Affairs.* Edited by Timothy Samuel Shah, Alfred Stepan, and Monica Duffy Toft. New York: Oxford University Press, 2012.

Toft, Monica Duffy, Daniel Philpott, and Timothy Samuel Shah. *God's Century: Resurgent Religion and Global Politics.* New York: W.W. Norton, 2011.

Tong, Joy K. C., and Fenggang Yang. "Trust at Work: A Study on Faith and Trust of Protestant Entrepreneurs in China." *MDPI Religions* 7, no. 12 (2016).

Trejo, Guillermo. *Popular Movements in Autocracies: Religion, Repression, and Indigenous Collective Action in Mexico.* New York: Cambridge University Press, 2012.

Trimble, David, and Nathaniel Hurd. "Why Does the Infrastructure Bill Include Sexual Orientation and Gender Identity Language?" Blog. Religious Freedom Institute, August 6, 2021. https://www.religiousfreedominstitute.org/blog/why-does-the-infrastructure-bill-include-sexual-orientation-and-gender-identity-language.

United Nations. "Academic Impact: Sustainability." United Nations, 2025. https://www.un.org/en/academic-impact/sustainability.

United Nations General Assembly. *Universal Declaration of Human Rights*, A/RES/217(III), 1948. https://www.un.org/en/about-us/universal-declaration-of-human-rights.

United Nations General Assembly. *International Covenant on Civil and Political Rights*. Resolution 2200A (XXI) (1966). https://www.un.org/en/development/desa/population/migration/generalassembly/docs/globalcompact/A_RES_2200A(XXI)_civil.pdf

United States Commission on International Religious Freedom. "2025 Annual Report." March 2025. https://www.uscirf.gov/sites/default/files/2025-03/2025%20USCIRF%20Annual%20Report.pdf.

United States Commission on International Religious Freedom. "USCIRF Warns that Forced Sterilization of Uyghur Muslims Is Evidence of Genocide." June 30, 2020. https://www.uscirf.gov/release-statements/uscirf-warns-forced-sterilization-uyghur-muslims-evidence-genocide.

VanderWeele, Tyler. "Association Between Religious Service Attendance and Lower Suicide Rates Among US Women." *JAMA Psychiatry* 8 (2016): 845–51.

VanderWeele, Tyler J. "Chapter 4: Spiritual Well-Being and Human Flourishing." In Adam Cohen, ed., *Religion and Human Flourishing.* Waco, TX: Baylor University Press, 2020.

Villa, Virginia. "Four-in-Ten Countries And Territories Worldwide Had Blasphemy Laws In 2019." Pew Research Center, January 25, 2022. https://www.pewresearch.org/short-reads/2022/01/25/four-in-ten-countries-and-territories-worldwide-had-blasphemy-laws-in-2019-2/.

Voltaire, François-Marie. *Letters on the English.* Originally published as *Letters Concerning the English Nation* in 1733. Republished in New York: Dover Publishing, 2011. http://public-library.uk/ebooks/58/98.pdf.

Wang, Qunyong, and Xinyu Lin. "Does Religious Beliefs Affect Economic Growth? Evidence From Provincial-Level Data in China." *China Economic Review* 31 (2014): 277–87. https://www.wsj.com/world/xi-china-economy-capital-investment-3439d31a.

Wei, Lingling. "Xi Jinping Chokes Off Crucial Engine of China's Economy." *The Wall Street Journal*, July 13, 2023. https://www.wsj.com/world/xi-china-economy-capital-investment-3439d31a.

Whitehead, Andrew L., and Samuel L. Perry, *Taking America Back for God: Christian Nationalism in the United States*. New York: Oxford University Press, 2020.

Williams, Roger. *The Bloudy Tenet of Persecution, for Cause of Conscience*. In *On Religious Liberty: Selections from the Works of Roger Williams*. Originally published as a book in 1644. Reprint. Edited by James Calvin Davis. Cambridge, MA: Harvard University Press, 2008.

Wodon, Quentin. "Faith-Inspired Schools in Sub-Saharan Africa: An Introduction to the Summer 2014 Issue." *The Review of Faith & International Affairs* 12, Vol 2 (Summer 2014): 1-4.

Woodberry, Robert. "The Missionary Roots of Liberal Democracy." *American Political Science Review* 106, no. 2 (2012): 244–74.

Woodruff, Paul. *Reverence: Renewing a Forgotten Virtue*. New York: Oxford University Press, 2001.

Woodward, Kenneth L. "How I Became a 'Christian Nationalist.'" *Washington Post,* May 16, 2023. https://www.washingtonpost.com/opinions/2023/05/16/white-christian-nationalism-definition/.

Wydick, Bruce, Robert Dowd, and Travis J. Lybbert. "Hope and Human Dignity: Exploring Religious Belief, Hope, and Transition Out of Poverty in Oaxaca, Mexico." In *The Practice of Human Development and Dignity*. Edited by Paolo G. Carozza and Clemens Sedmak, 139–62. Notre Dame, IN: University of Notre Dame Press, 2020.

Xie, Sella Yifan, and Jason Douglas. "China's Fading Recovery Reveals Deeper Economic Struggles." *The Wall Street Journal*, May 30, 2023. https://www.wsj.com/world/chinas-fading-recovery-reveals-deeper-economic-struggles-31f4097b.

Yang, Fenggang. "The Growth and Dynamism of Chinese Christianity." *Christianity and Freedom, Volume II: Contemporary Perspectives*. Edited by Allen D. Hertzke and Timothy Samuel Shah. Cambridge: Cambridge University Press, 2016.

Young, Cathy. "The Bizarre Right-Wing War on Empathy?" *The Bulwark*, April 21, 2025. https://www.thebulwark.com/p/bizarre-right-wing-war-empathy-misogynistic-abrego-garcia-suicidal-civilizational-musk-barrett-gad-saad.

Zhang, Lihui. "Are International Human Rights Organizations Effective in Protecting Religious Freedom?" *Religions* 12, no. 7 (2021): 479.

INDEX

ALLEN D. HERTZKE

is professor emeritus of political science at the University of Oklahoma. He is author or editor of ten books, including *Freeing God's Children* and *The Future of Religious Freedom*. He served a ten-year term on the prestigious Pontifical Academy of Social Sciences at the Vatican.

www.ingramcontent.com/pod-product-compliance
Lightning Source LLC
Chambersburg PA
CBHW050224270326
41914CB00003BA/557

* 9 7 8 0 2 6 8 2 1 1 0 6 6 *